DIS/AGREEING IRELAND

CONTEMPORARY IRISH STUDIES

Series Editor Peter Shirlow (The Queen's University of Belfast)

Paul Hainsworth (ed.)
Divided Society:
Ethnic Minorities and Racism in Northern Ireland

Denis O'Hearn
Inside the Celtic Tiger:
The Irish Economy and the Asian Model

Peter Shirlow and Mark McGovern (eds)
Who are 'the People'?:
Unionism, Protestantism and Loyalism in Northern Ireland

Gerry Smyth
Decolonisation and Criticism:
The Construction of Irish Literature

Gerry Smyth
The Novel and the Nation:
Studies in the New Irish Fiction

DIS/AGREEING IRELAND

IRELAND

Contexts, Obstacles, Hopes

Edited by
James Anderson
and James Goodman

Pluto Press

LONDON · STERLING, VIRGINIA

First published 1998 by Pluto Press
345 Archway Road, London N6 5AA
and 22883 Quicksilver Drive, Sterling, VA 20166-2012, USA

British Library Cataloguing in Publication Data
A catalogue record for this book is available from the British Library

ISBN 0 7453 1280 2 hbk

Library of Congress Cataloging-in-Publication Data
Dis/agreeing Ireland : contexts, obstacles, hopes / edited by James
    Anderson and James Goodman.
        p.   cm.   — (Contemporary Irish studies)
    Includes bibliographical references and index.
    ISBN 0–7453–1280–2
    1. Northern Ireland—Politics and government—1994 2. Conflict
management—Northern Ireland—History—20th century. 3. Peace
movements—Northern Ireland—History—20th century. 4. Ireland–
–Politics and government—20th century. I. Anderson, James 1941– .
II. Goodman, James, 1965– . III. Series.
DA990.U46D57 1988
941.60824—dc21   98–34974
                                                                 CIP

Designed and produced for Pluto Press by
Chase Production Services, Chadlington, OX7 3LN
Typset from disk by Gawcott Typesetting Service, Buckingham
Printed in the EC by Athenaeum Press, Gateshead

'To the memory of the anti-sectarian United Irishmen, defeated by the forces of reaction in 1798 with consequences which are still with us two hundred years later'

Contents

Preface and Acknowledgements

The idea of this book emerged from a conference which James Goodman organised in London after the first paramilitary 'cease-fires' of autumn 1994, and before publication of the British–Irish 'Framework Documents', the basis for the 'Belfast Agreement' of April 1998. The conference was financed by the Socialist Society, supported by the Troops Out Movement and hosted by the Camden Irish Centre, to all of whom we extend our thanks. And special thanks are due to the Centre and to a contributor for proceeding despite threats of violence from extreme British nationalists, one claiming to represent a fascist organisation. Much has happened in the intervening period and the changes are reflected in the chapters which follow, but the basic factors underlying the conflict are largely unchanged. Since at least the Framework Documents' publication in 1995, the rough outlines of a possible settlement have been fairly clear.

Since then most of the contributors have shared in the ongoing process of evaluation and re-evaluation, optimism tending to alternate with pessimism. The swings were reflected in the changing title of the projected book. As the idea began to take shape in 1995, the book was to be called 'Agreeing Ireland', but after the breakdown of the IRA ceasefire in 1996 it became 'Disagreeing Ireland'. Then, after the ceasefire was reinstated in July 1997 we renamed it 'Dis/Agreeing Ireland'; and despite the 'Agreement' of April 1998 we decided to stick with that title, conscious of the fact that many of the old disagreements have still to be resolved. At another, perhaps more profound level, we were also increasingly conscious of the paradox that 'agreement' will come only through 'disagreements'. As elaborated in our concluding chapter, an 'agreed Ireland' will only be achieved by creating more scope for island-wide *dis*agreements about a range of important *non*-national questions to do with social class, gender, human rights, the environment and so forth, questions which tend to be 'crowded out' or marginalised by the unresolved 'national problem'. Building island-wide politics around such questions has the potential to deliver emancipation from the religious and national divisions which the United Irishmen tried to remove from Ireland 200 years ago.

Our thanks to all who have made this book possible, from the initial conference onwards and particularly our contributing authors. We would also like to thank the Open University where we did much of our previous research on Ireland; and James Goodman thanks the UK Economic and Social Research Council for funding his doctoral research, and the Research Committee of the Open University for funding post-doctoral work, on Irish and European integration. Both of us would also like to thank our present institutions for supporting our ongoing work on these issues.

James Anderson,
Department of Geography
and Centre for Transnational Studies,
University of Newcastle-upon-Tyne

James Goodman,
Faculty of Humanities
and Social Sciences,
University of Technology,
Sydney

Notes on Contributors

James Anderson has published widely on nationalism, European integration and Ireland. He edited *The Rise of the Modern State*, and co-edited *A Global World? Re-ordering Political Space*, Oxford University Press, 1995. He teaches in the Department of Geography, University of Newcastle-upon-Tyne where he is Associate Director of the recently established Centre for Transnational Studies.

Christine Bell is a co-author of 'telling stories of women who kill', published in *Social and Legal Studies*, 1996. She works in the Faculty of Law, Queen's University, Belfast, where she is Director of the Centre for Human Rights.

Jerry Fitzpatrick is a founder member of the Labour Party Irish Society, a socialist society of the British Labour Party which campaigns for Irish unity and self-determination. He works for a Dublin-based trade union.

Conor Foley is author of *Legion of the Rearguard: The IRA and the Modern Irish state*, Pluto Press, 1992; and *Human Rights and Human Wrongs: The Alternative Report to the United Nations Human Rights Committee*, Rivers Oram Press, 1995. He has worked as a policy officer at Liberty, the National Council of Civil Liberties (Britain) and for the Connolly Association and War on Want in London.

James Goodman is author of *Nationalism and Transnationalism: The National Conflict in Ireland and European Union Integration*, Avebury Press, 1996; and *Single Europe, Single Ireland? Uneven Development in Process*, Irish Academic Press, 1999. He works as a researcher in the Faculty of Humanities and Social Sciences, University of Technology Sydney, Australia.

James White McAuley is author of *The Politics of Identity: A Loyalist Community in Belfast*, Avebury Press, 1994; and is active in the British Association of Irish Studies. He works in the Department of Sociology, University of Huddersfield.

Robbie McVeigh is author of *Harassment: It's Part of Life Here*, Committee for the Administration of Justice, Belfast, 1994. He worked at the Belfast-based Centre for Research and Documentation, which highlighted the importance of the colonial legacy for understanding contemporary Ireland. He writes as a member of the West Belfast Economic Forum.

Ronnie Munck is author of *The Irish Economy: Results and Prospects*, Pluto Press, 1993; co-editor of *Postmodern Insurgencies: Political Violence, Identity Formation and Peace-Making in Comparative Perspective*, Macmillan, 1998; and co-editor (with D. O'Hearn, below) of *Critical Development Theory: Contributions to a New Paradigm*, Zed (forthcoming). He works in the Department of Sociology, University of Liverpool.

Liam O'Dowd is co-editor of *Northern Ireland, Between Civil Rights and Civil War*, CSE Books, 1981, and of *Borders, Nations and States: Frontiers of Sovereignty in the New Europe*, Avebury Press, 1996. He has done extensive research on the Irish border and teaches in the Department of Sociology, Queen's University of Belfast.

Denis O'Hearn is an economist and sociologist in the Department of Sociology, Queen's University of Belfast. He edits the *Irish Journal of Sociology* and is a board member of the West Belfast Economic Forum. His publications include *Inside the Celtic Tiger: Irish Economic Change and the Asian Model*, Pluto Press, 1998; and (co-edited with R. Munck, above) *Critical Development Theory*, Zed (forthcoming).

Rosemary Sales has extensive research experience in Ireland and is author of *Women Divided: Religion and Politics in Northern Ireland*, Routledge, 1997. She teaches in the Department of Sociology and Social Policy, Middlesex University.

A Framework of Selected Dates

1695 Beginning of Penal Laws – mainly anti-Catholic, but also anti-Presbyterian.

1789 French Revolution and Republican ideals of 'liberty, equality and fraternity'.

1791 Founding of the Republican 'Society of United Irishmen' in Belfast.

1795 Founding of the sectarian Protestant 'Orange Order' in Co. Armagh.

1796 Large French invasion in support of the United Irishmen fails due to a storm.

1798 Defeat of the United Irishmen – in Antrim, Down and Wexford.

1800 Act of Union politically integrating Ireland with Great Britain.

1829 'Catholic Emancipation' – allowing Catholics to become British MPs.

1835 First serious anti-Catholic rioting in industrialising Belfast.

1843 British force O'Connell to end mass meetings for repeal of the Act of Union.

1845–8 The Great Famine kills over one million and leads to mass emigration.

1848 Young Ireland nationalist rising fails.

1864 First expulsion of Catholics from shipyards in Belfast.

1867 Rising of Irish Republican Brotherhood – the Fenians – is crushed.

1868 Disestablishment of the Protestant Church of Ireland.

1886 First Irish Home Rule Bill defeated by unelected House of Lords.

1892–3 Ulster Unionist Convention and Lords oppose Second Home Rule Bill.

1906 Ulster Unionist Council founded to oppose Home Rule for Ireland.

1907   Formation of Sinn Fein League.

1912   Over 400,000 Ulster Protestants sign Covenant against Third Home Rule Bill.

1913   Ulster Volunteer Force formed to militarily oppose Home Rule; followed by formation of rival National Volunteers to fight for Home Rule.

1914–18 First World War – with UVF and National Volunteers fighting for Britain.

1916   Easter Rising declaring an Irish Republic is crushed and its leaders executed.

1918   General Election: pro-republic Sinn Fein wins 73 of the Irish seats in the London Parliament; the Nationalist 'Home Rule' Party 6; Unionists 26.

1919   Sinn Fein MPs set up Republican parliament – Dáil Éireann – in Dublin.

1919–21 The War of Independence – Irish Republican Army versus British forces.

1920   Government of Ireland Act partitions Ireland and provides for a (still-born) Council of Ireland to link North and South and facilitate their reunification.

1921   Establishment of Northern Ireland with its own 'Home Rule' parliament.

1922   Irish Republicans, following Treaty with Britain, set up Irish Free State Dáil.

1922–3 The Civil War in the Irish Free State over the Treaty's terms; and anti-Catholic 'pogroms' in North.

1933   Anti-Treaty leader Eamon de Valera, founder of Fianna Fáil, becomes Taoiseach. Unemployed Catholics and Protestants, organised by left-wing Republicans, campaign jointly in Belfast, until divided again by sectarianism.

1935   Serious sectarian disturbances in Belfast.

1937   New Constitution passed by Dáil claims Northern Ireland in Articles 2 and 3.

1939–45 Second World War – the North a participant, the South officially neutral.

1949   South declares itself the Republic of Ireland and leaves the Commonwealth; Britain's response is the Ireland Act giving the Northern Ireland parliament at Stormont a formal veto over Ireland's reunification.

1956–62 IRA's 'border campaign' fails; Stormont operates internment without trial.

1965   Southern and Northern Prime Ministers Sean Lemass
        and Terence O'Neill hold first official meetings in
        Belfast and Dublin – vociferously opposed by Rev. Ian
        Paisley and by unionists in O'Neill's own party.

1966   Ulster Volunteer Force formed; first Catholic
        murdered in present 'Troubles'.

1967   Formation of the Northern Ireland Civil Rights
        Association.

1968   Police attack on civil rights march in Derry leads to two
        days of rioting.

1969   Marches, counter-demonstrations, civilian and police
        violence result in the British Army taking over control
        from the police, and in the Provisional IRA splitting off
        from the Official IRA. Unionists force O'Neill to resign
        as PM.

1970   Formation of the Social Democratic and Labour Party;
        and of the Alliance Party.

1971   Formation of Paisley's Democratic Unionist Party. The
        Unionist government's policy of mass internment
        without trial feeds IRA recruitment.

1972   'Bloody Sunday' – 13 unarmed civilians in Derry are
        killed by the British Army. Paramilitaries on both sides
        intensify actions. The British government imposes
        Direct Rule; publishes 'The Future of Northern
        Ireland' discussion document.

1973   The UK and the Republic of Ireland join the European
        Economic Community.
            The Northern Ireland Constitution Act gives a
        majority of the Northern Ireland electorate (rather than
        its dissolved parliament) a veto over Irish reunification.

1973–4 Sunningdale Agreement establishes the new Northern
        Ireland power-sharing Assembly and a cross-border
        Council of Ireland, but both destroyed by Unionist
        opposition, particularly the 'Ulster Workers' Strike'.
        Direct Rule is reimposed.
            In Dublin and Monaghan 33 people are killed by no
        warning car-bombs with allegations that British agents
        and Loyalists are responsible. Armed conflict – mainly
        IRA versus British, Loyalists versus Catholics –
        continues to 1990s.

1981   Republican prison hunger strikes, with deaths of
        Bobby Sands and nine other prisoners, restore political
        status for paramilitary prisoners, while related mass

mobilisations begin to establish Sinn Fein as an electoral force. The Anglo–Irish Intergovernmental Council is established.

1983   Referendum in the South on decriminalising abortion is defeated.

1984   New Ireland Forum in Dublin involves all of Ireland's nationalist parties except Sinn Fein and other Republicans.

1985   Anglo–Irish Agreement establishes Intergovernmental Conference and gives Southern government consultative role in the North despite unionist opposition.

1986   Referendum in the South on right to divorce is defeated.

1990   Secretary of State Peter Brooke says Britain has 'no selfish economic or strategic interest' in Northern Ireland and would accept Ireland's unification by consent.

1991–2   Inter-party talks (excluding Republicans and Loyalists) end inconclusively.
        Official completion of the Single European Market.

1993   Talks and joint statement by John Hume (SDLP) and Gerry Adams (SF) rules out an 'internal settlement' for Northern Ireland and asserts right to national self-determination of the Irish people as a whole. Revealed that British government had secret contacts with the IRA. 'Downing Street Declaration' by the British PM and the Irish Taoiseach to facilitate paramilitary ceasefires.

1994   IRA calls a ceasefire in August, Loyalist paramilitaries in October.

1995   In February the two governments publish their joint 'Framework Documents' – the basis for 'peace talks' and a political settlement.
        First of the 'Drumcree' Orange march confrontations occurs in July. In September David Trimble is elected as leader of the Ulster Unionist Party.

1996   In January the 'Mitchell Report' on decommissioning is rejected by British Prime Minister, John Major, and in February the IRA ends its ceasefire with a bomb in London's Canary Wharf.
        Northern Ireland Forum elections to all-party talks.
        Sinn Fein polls a record vote but it is excluded from the talks while the IRA bombing campaign continues, most notably in central Manchester.

1997 In the May General Election, Tony Blair's Labour Party wins a huge majority at Westminster, and Mo Mowlam starts implementing the policy devised by the previous government.

   In July the IRA restores its ceasefire. In September Sinn Fein agrees the non-violent principles of the 'Mitchell Report' and joins the 'peace talks' which culminate in the 'Belfast Agreement' of April 1998.

1998 The 'Belfast Agreement' encompasses all the unionist/Loyalist and nationalist/Republican political parties in Northern Ireland, with the exception of some fringe Republican and Loyalist groupings connected with paramilitaries not on ceasefire, and the Democratic Unionist and UK Unionist parties which remained outside the 'talks' and oppose the 'Agreement'.

List of Abbreviations

AIA	Anglo–Irish Agreement
AIB	Allied Irish Bank
CAJ	Committee on the Administration of Justice
CLMC	Combined Loyalist Military Command
DUP	Democratic Unionist Party
EC	European Community
ECHR	European Convention on Human Rights
EEC	European Economic Community
EMU	European Monetary Union
EOI	Export-orientated industrialisation
EPA	Northern Ireland (Emergency Provisions) Act
EU	European Union
FPR	Forum for Peace and Reconciliation
GDP	Gross Domestic Product
GNP	Gross National Product
IDB	Industrial Development Board
IDI	Industrial Development Authority
INLA	Irish National Liberation Army
IRA	Irish Republican Army
IRSP	Irish Republican Socialist Party
ISI	Import-substitution industrialisation
LRC	Labour Representation Committee
LVF	Loyalist Volunteer Force
NIF	New Ireland Forum
PTA	Prevention of Terrorism (Temporary Provisions) Act
PUP	Progressive Unionist Party
RUC	Royal Ulster Constabualry
SAS	Special Air Services
SDLP	Social Democratic and Labour Party
SEM	Single European Market
SNP	Scottish National Party
TD	Teachta Dála (Member of the Dáil)
UDA	Ulster Defence Association

UDP	Ulster Democratic Party
UDR	Ulster Defence Regiment
UFF	Ulster Freedom Fighters
UUP	Ulster Unionist Party
UVF	Ulster Volunteer Force
WSN	Women's Support Network

Introduction

James Anderson and James Goodman

The rebellion of the United Irishmen against British rule in Ireland was defeated in 1798. We've dedicated this book to their memory and inspiration, not because they founded Irish nationalism and republicanism two hundred years ago, but because the Society of United Irishmen continues to stand for replacing the politically and socially divisive sectarian labels of 'Catholic, Protestant and Dissenter' with 'the common name of Irishman' (Dickson *et al.*, 1993). In these less overtly sexist times we should add 'Irishwomen' and indeed there were many women among the rebels of '98. For a time they succeeded in creating a mass movement which brought together people from all three of Ireland's main religious-political groupings – the dissenting Presbyterians, some of whose Belfast members were the key initiators of Irish republicanism; the episcopalian Protestants of the state 'Church of Ireland', many of whom opposed their co-religionists among the landlords and the Orange Order; and the economically and politically dispossessed Roman Catholics who formed the majority of the country's population.

These rebels make a nonsense of today's common assumption that there are two immutable religious-political 'traditions' fixed in Ireland since the Reformation and seventeenth-century colonisations by Britain – 'Catholic/nationalist' and 'Protestant/ Loyalist-unionist'. The rebels united across the supposedly fixed divides of religion and ancestry, from north to south, in a struggle to remove the 'external' link with England which, like good nationalists, they saw as 'the never failing source' of all their troubles. Unfortunately for them, however, there were also 'internal' Irish sources. The United Irishmen were defeated by the English or British state, but local sectarianism was mobilised against them, most notably in the landlord-sponsored Orange Order which was instituted just four years after the United Irishmen; and many who butchered them were their fellow countrymen, including some Irish Catholics as well as Irish

Protestants. Sectarianism won the day and on many occasions since with dire results.

Despite the 'Belfast Agreement' of April 1998 and its foundations in the British/Irish 'Framework Documents' of 1995, the anti-sectarian dream of the United Irishmen still seems very far from fulfilment. But it remains as valid two centuries later and is essential to any genuine resolution to the present conflict over Northern Ireland. However, the strategies appropriate to achieving the dream at the end of the eighteenth century are not necessarily appropriate at the end of the twentieth. The whole structure of society has changed; our world is much more interdependent and transnational. Moreover, the flaws in nationalism – Irish nationalism, British nationalism, nationalism in general – have become much more apparent.

Unfortunately the 'Agreement' – even if implemented properly, which is a big 'if' – looks likely to reproduce these flaws, albeit in modified and perhaps less virulent form. It signifies important progress – though not as much as promised in the Framework Documents. But rather than constituting a genuine resolution or settlement, it really marks a new phase in the conflict over Northern Ireland's internal government, over its relations with the Irish Republic and Britain, and indeed over its very existence as a separate statelet.

This book addresses the question of what strategies are needed to resolve these national problems in today's context; what are the obstacles and what are the hopes of overcoming them? The authors come from a wide variety of backgrounds – Northern and Southern Irish, British, Australian, North and South American; activist and academic; Protestant and Catholic and neither; nationalist and unionist and neither – and they provide a variety of perspectives on the conflict and its resolution. But all would agree that there are no purely 'external' or 'internal' solutions – indeed it will be argued that 'internal/external' distinctions are part of the problem.

The chapters cover the wider contexts of the conflict; the conditions underlying it, particularly questions of economy, class and gender; the politics of the main protagonists, including the two states; ideas about what an 'agreed Ireland' might look like and proposals for achieving it. Chapter 1 outlines the nature of these problems in terms of the theory and practice of nationalism and transnationalism, the general flaws in nationalist doctrine and its particular failures in Ireland. It introduces the possibilities, and the limitations, of transnational cross-border developments as a

route towards a solution. The next three chapters focus on
'contexts'. Chapter 2 looks at Ireland's partly colonial development in relation to Britain, arguing that Ireland is 'between two
worlds – coloniser/colonised, First World/Third World'. It
stresses the importance of the British state; and the need for
demilitarisation, democratisation, economic integration and
reconciliation, both cross-community in Northern Ireland and
between North and South. It urges breaking with the ingrained
structures of the colonial nexus, mental and material. Chapter 3
focuses on the economics of Partition, the North's dependency on
Britain, and the South's reliance on North American investment.
It compares the South's advantage in depending on a 'winner'
with the North's dependency on a 'loser', but argues that both
dependencies are undesirable and that a joint or integrated
approach offers the only hope of overcoming them. The
European Union, and particularly its Single Market, has introduced major new and *non*-nationalist socio-economic dynamics
for the reintegration of North and South. Their character and
potential are assessed in Chapter 4 on the basis of interview
surveys in Belfast and Dublin. The national conflict has been a
major obstacle to the creation of a 'single island economy', but
conversely the non-nationalist dynamics could help resolve the
conflict.

Then the following chapters focus on nationalisms as facilitator
and obstacle to conflict resolution. Chapter 5 discusses nationalism in Southern Ireland and how it has diverged from
traditional Irish nationalism following Partition in 1920, the
attainment of statehood, the declaration of an Irish Republic in
1949 and, especially, the onset of the present Northern 'Troubles'
30 years ago. It analyses the contrasting dynamics of 'irredentist',
'partitionist' and 'cosmopolitan' nationalisms, concentrating
particularly on 'cosmopolitan' visions of national unity which
have been frustrated in the past by British and unionist conceptions of state sovereignty as an indivisible absolute. With
increased North–South integration in the EU, and modifications
to British and unionist positions, the cosmopolitan form of official
Irish nationalism is gaining ground. The other, contrasting,
nationalism to merit special attention – in Chapter 6 – is British
nationalism in Britain, a generally neglected but constitutive
ingredient of the conflict, closely linked with unionism and an
obstacle to a settlement. This is a nationalism which particularly
in its 'strong' version defines itself 'against Europe' and also
'against Ireland', but often it is simply unacknowledged or

escapes scrutiny, or it hides behind Ulster unionism which apparently can always be blamed when things go wrong. It is obscured too by the peculiarly British notion that the ruling power in Northern Ireland, the British state, is a mere disinterested seeker after peace between two 'warring Irish tribes', rather than an active participant in the conflict – part of the problem as well as, by necessity, part of a solution. For the immediate future this largely means the British Labour government, and Chapter 7 looks at the prospects and record of Labour Party policy, traditionally more sympathetic to Irish reunification than the Conservatives, but now apparently less so under Tony Blair's leadership and not immune from British nationalism either.

Social and human rights problems in Northern Ireland are also central to the conflict, and the highly charged issue of job discrimination is discussed in Chapter 8. It illustrates how gender discrimination combines with sectarianism to the detriment of working-class interests in general, and of Catholic women workers in particular. Addressing sectarianism means addressing sexism, and vice versa. A similar distortion of the political agenda is reflected in a 'human rights deficit' which goes hand-in-hand with Northern Ireland's democratic deficit. As Chapter 9 shows, the North has been used as a 'testing ground' for repressive legislation, which in some cases has later been applied in Britain. It suggests that there needs to be a fundamental, 'root and branch' reappraisal of human rights with legally entrenched guarantees.

The final four chapters focus on different political forces involved or potentially implicated in the conflict and its resolution: the Republican movement, Loyalist unionist organisations, women's groups, the working class and other non-nationalist entities. Chapter 10 looks at Sinn Fein's strategy and at alleged or potential splits between 'realists' and 'fundamentalists' in contemporary republicanism. It illustrates the dominance of 'realists' for most of the period since the late 1980s, and emphasises the emergence of a more explicitly democratic discourse which, despite some set-backs, is opening up new political possibilities. Chapter 11 likewise argues that some strands of unionism have also been involved in a 'rethink'. It focuses on urban working-class loyalism in communities economically marginalised and politically alienated both from middle-class unionism and the British state, and it shows that different socio-economic interests and conceptions of the 'union' produce different and sometimes conflicting unionisms, fracturing the traditional unionist class alliance and upsetting assumptions or assertions of an unchanging unionist identity. The more accommodating negotiating stance of the new parties linked to Loyalist paramilitaries highlights the divisions in unionism and the possibility of working-class unionists developing alternatives to the evangelical loyalism of Paisley's Democratic Unionist Party.

In contrast, Chapters 12 and 13 explore the potential for conflict resolution by looking at issues and forces which 'bridge' the national and sectarianised divide in Northern Ireland and the jurisdictional divide between North and South. Chapter 12 focuses on women's groups which have recently taken on a much more public role in the politics of reconciliation, particularly with the participation of the cross-community and explicitly anti-sectarian Women's Coalition in the 'peace talks'. But territorial state sovereignty – and particularly Britain's legacy of a peculiarly archaic and absolute conception of sovereignty – remains the basic issue or underlying source of the national conflict in Ireland. In the concluding Chapter 13 we argue that it can only be confronted and weakened through the establishment of various North–South institutions and the development of cross-border political communities which define themselves in non-nationalist terms.

Northern unionists and nationalists have been locked into what is widely seen as a 'zero-sum' conflict – one gains, the other loses, and vice versa. But actually it is a self-defeating '*negative*-sum game' in which a majority on all sides lose, not least workers and women. To escape this fate and achieve a genuine political settlement, the sorts of cross-border arrangements envisaged in the 1998 'Agreement' would be a significant start. They are, however, even less adequate than those promised in the Framework Documents, most obviously where the Unionist Party managed to have important areas of economic, industrial and trade policy excluded from the remit of North–South bodies. On the other hand North–South integration has its own dynamics which could push developments beyond the Framework Documents scenario. It may indeed be a matter of 'when' rather than 'if' – the unionists continuing to delay but not able to stop the logic of transnational cross-border integration. But in any event, the territorial framework and the forms of democratic participation need to be radically extended if we are to escape the confines of national conflict. Border-crossing transnationalism and the *non*-nationalist politics of class, gender and other concerns are, paradoxically enough, just what is needed to end the conflict, and finally achieve the anti-sectarian United Irish dream.

1 Nationalisms and Transnationalism: Failures and Emancipation

James Anderson and James Goodman

Depending on your viewpoint, Northern Ireland may or may not be a 'failed political entity' as was once memorably claimed by the now disgraced ex-Taoiseach of the Irish Republic, Charles Haughey. But as was said of Haughey by a more respected ex-Taoiseach, Garret Fitzgerald, it certainly has a 'flawed pedigree'. Three decades of armed nationalist conflict over Northern Ireland's very existence, and the longer-running and continuing poison of sectarianism, are ample testimony to the costs of 'built-in' political disagreement. The 'flaws', however, go deeper than the particulars of the conflict between Irish and British nationalism in Ireland or the nature of the United Kingdom of Great Britain and Northern Ireland. They include the very nature of nationalism itself – a doctrine which has always promised to deceive. The results can be tragic as testified in the case of Ireland and a host of other situations, from Yugoslavia to Sri Lanka, Chechnya to Rwanda, the Middle East to East Timor.

Not surprisingly, people look to 'internationalism' or 'transnationalism' as a means of superseding the conflicts of nation states and national communities – of getting above and beyond what is seen as the petty parochialism of narrow nationalisms, to achieve emancipation from their mutually destructive animosities. Once the talk was of 'world government'. Now it is of 'globalisation' and 'European integration', harbingers of transnational communities which supersede the borders of states and of nations. 'World government' never got further than an often ineffectual United Nations, but 'transnationalism' in its various forms has grown hugely in the last three decades – more or less since the onset of the current 'Troubles'. As we shall see, this could help to facilitate a genuine political settlement in Ireland. However, as the Irish case also clearly demonstrates, nation states and national conflicts are not so easily 'superseded' – particularly as the very processes of 'globalisation' and 'European integration' can generate their own 'opposites', reviving nationalisms and region-alisms and reinvigorating loyalties to nation states and national sovereignty. Furthermore, while some talk of transnational eman-cipation from flawed nationalisms, others see nationalism as itself emancipatory, and sometimes with good reason.

Contemporary transnational developments offer some hopes of eventually finding a settlement to a conflict which goes back to the invention of Irish nationalism, the era of the French Revolution and earlier. The obstacles are still formidable, but there is just a chance that Ireland, famous world-wide for its supposedly insoluble national conflict, might pioneer a transna-tional settlement process which could have similarly wide significance or general applicability. The contemporary impor-tance of the international context means it is no longer appropriate to talk of the conflict in terms of 'the dreary steeples of Fermanagh and Tyrone' which according to Winston Churchill emerged from the mists completely unchanged after the upheavals of the First World War. There's even the chance we might be spared yet more dreary repetition of Churchill's dreary phrase. But either way, the Irish case can offer some general lessons which are applicable in other situations – just as the Irish situation is itself constituted and illuminated by prac-tices and theories which were first developed elsewhere, most notably nationalism, territorial sovereignty and transnational alternatives.

Nationalism's Tragic Ideals

Remembering J.M. Keynes's quip about anti-theoretical 'prac-tical' people actually being under the spell of some long-dead theorist, we can note that the doctrine of absolute territorial sovereignty beloved by unionists, including the fundamentalist Protestant Ian Paisley, was invented by a sixteenth-century Catholic Frenchman. And, ironically enough, he wanted to solve the problem of religious civil wars by asserting the 'divine right' of a Catholic king. No one suggests that particular 'solution' for Northern Ireland, but long-established theories of sovereign and national territory are at the nub of the conflict, important for the participants as for observers.

Nationalism links historically and culturally defined territorial communities, called 'nations', to political statehood, either as a reality or as an aspiration. Nations and states are specifically *territorial* entities – they explicitly claim and are based on particular geographical territories, as distinct from merely occupying geographical space, which is true of all social activity (Anderson, 1986, p. 117). The nationalist ideal is that they should coincide geographically in *nation states*: the nation's territory and the state's territory should be one and the same, each nation having its own state, and each state expressing the 'general will' of a single, culturally unified nation.

This has a very powerful democratic appeal, especially where democracy is denied by imperialistic neighbours or colonial powers, and – its positive aspect – the history of nationalism is closely bound up with the history of democratization. But nationalist theory promises more than it can ever deliver. In practice, nations and states often fail to coincide, frequently leaving sizeable 'national minorities' on the 'wrong side' of state borders. The happy spatial coincidence of a single cultural community with a single political sovereignty is rarely achieved in reality, and attempts to make reality fit the ideal have often had unhappy, indeed tragic, consequences. Nationalism has been directly implicated in some of the twentieth century's worst atrocities such as so-called 'ethnic cleansing'.

Furthermore, even where the ideal of geographical coincidence is approximated, nationalism has other serious flaws. Democracy is often sadly lacking in practice, and nationalism is in several respects inherently 'two-faced': forward-looking but also backward-looking to an often mythical or invented past; and divisive at the same time as it is unifying. It brings together different groups and classes in a political-cultural community defined as 'the people' or 'nation' with a strong shared and mutually supportive sense of belonging. Simultaneously, however, it separates out different 'peoples', emphasising *non*-belonging and fuelling conflicts between nations and between states, or at the very least impeding transnational cooperation. And the limited unity it offers around 'the national interest' often serves the interests of dominant social groups and classes, rather than 'the whole nation'. Like the heroic figures of Shakespearian tragedy, nationalism is brought down by fatal flaws of its own making.

Nationalism's Failures in Ireland

The first 'general lesson' from Ireland is that Northern Ireland, far from approximating nationalism's flawed ideal, is the result of a succession of failures in nation- and state-building. These were failures both from a British nationalist and from an Irish nationalist viewpoint (see O'Leary and McGarry, 1993), though the formal symmetry masks great inequalities and qualitative differences.

British nationalism developed out of the state-building of England's monarchs. This met its most serious obstacles in an Ireland which, unlike Britain, remained largely Roman Catholic – a potential ally for England's main Catholic rivals, Spain and France, to which Irish opponents of British rule periodically looked for help. By the eighteenth century, land ownership in Ireland was monopolised by the so-called 'Protestant Ascendancy', an episcopalian elite which was largely an extension of England's landed class. This 'Ascendancy' instituted the 'Penal Laws' discriminating against Catholics, and also against non-episcopalian Protestant 'Dissenters', mainly Presbyterians. But it was only when influenced by the French Revolution that the resulting Irish discontents came to be expressed in nationalism and republicanism.

Ireland's first nationalist, Republican movement, 'The Society of United Irishmen', uniting 'Catholic, Protestant and Dissenter', was mainly initiated by Belfast Presbyterians and established in 1791. But it was defeated militarily and politically by the British state and the 'Protestant Ascendancy', partly through their sponsorship of the explicitly sectarian Orange Order, instituted in 1795. Ever since then, Irish unionists, in a sense the 'shock troops' of British nationalism, have relied on anti-Catholicism for popular mobilization (see 'A Framework of Selected Dates').

The development of British nationalism was, according to its leading historian Linda Colley, 'heavily dependent ... on a broadly Protestant culture, a massive overseas empire, and recurrent war with France' (Colley, 1992, p. 6). But Ireland, more Catholic than Protestant,

> ... was never able or willing to play a satisfactory part in this Britishness ... cut off from Great Britain by the sea ... it was cut off still more effectively by the prejudices of the English, Welsh and Scots, and by the self-image of the bulk of the Irish themselves, both Protestants and Catholics. (Colley, 1992, pp. 8 and 322–3)

Whereas British nationalism has state-sponsored, imperialist and sectarian origins, Irish nationalism, by contrast, developed as an anti-colonialist movement and is anti-sectarian in principle as well as origin, although in practice it has often been imbued with Catholicism. Ireland, unusually for Western Europe, shares some of the characteristics of so-called 'Third World' countries and 'peripheral' economies (see Chapters 2 and 3), and for most of its life Irish nationalism has been an oppositional and 'sub-state' movement in a British-dominated context. It still is in Northern Ireland, the present apex of state-building and nation-building failures, where British and Irish nationalisms now meet 'head-on', in tragic testimony to the flawed ideal of the 'nation state'.

Irish unionists, their main concentration in the nine-county province of Ulster, campaigned from the 1880s under the slogan of 'Home Rule is Rome rule', to block the limited form of polit-ical autonomy on offer for the whole country in a UK and Empire framework. Their anti-Catholicism sometimes had a racist edge and they were encouraged by British Tories such as Lord Salisbury who first proposed the 'divide and rule' strategy of Partition and tried, without much local success, to sell the idea that there were 'two Irish nations' (see Anderson, 1980 and 1989). Most Ulster unionists did not want Partition, preferring to resist Home Rule on an island basis.

Yet Partition had a powerful purchase on British 'establish-ment' mindset. It was both consistent with racist notions of 'ethnic' hierarchy which privileged 'Anglo-Saxon Protestantism' over 'Celtic Catholicism', and it cast Westminster as 'holding the ring' between the contending aspirations of its warring subjects – a fantasy in which Britain was not only blameless but also eminently reasonable. In reality, it was to establish the 'zero-sum' politics of 'minority' and 'majority'. It largely ignored the substantial territor-ial intermingling of the different political groups. It squandered the opportunity for a more 'positive-sum' joint endeavour in a single redefined political entity, in favour of a prescription more in line with British imperial interests and racist conceptions.

The Westminster House of Commons had voted for Irish 'Home Rule' in 1886, only to have it vetoed by the unelected House of Lords. But when this right of veto was removed and it became clear in the decade before 1920 that this tactic could not succeed, the Ulster unionists, with the backing of the British state, opted for Partition and a six-county Northern Ireland. There were no democratic plebiscites, either Ireland-wide or on the basis of the six northern counties, although – or rather because – large parts of Northern Ireland had Irish nationalist majorities. But overall, this new territorial entity gave unionists a 'safe', roughly 'two to one', majority of Protestants, assumed to be unionist, over Catholics, assumed to be nationalist, compared to a much narrower majority – about 55 to 45 per cent – if the three Ulster counties with large Catholic majorities, Donegal, Cavan and Monaghan, had not been excluded. For the roughly 900,000 unionists in what is now Northern Ireland, the 'price of their own salvation ... was the abandonment of their fellow unionists, around 300,000, outside the north-east' (Kennedy, 1988, p. 1). Unionists in Donegal, Cavan and Monaghan had been an integral part of Ulster opposition to Irish 'Home Rule' – signatories of the 'Ulster Covenant' in 1912 – but now, in their own view, they were 'thrown overboard from the lifeboat' so that the 'safe majority' in the six counties could be secured.

A Protestant-dominated Northern Ireland in 1921 was thus the outcome of a largely failed unionist attempt to prevent Irish nationalists achieving 'Home Rule'. However, while Ireland's Partition represented a retreat for British nationalism and state-building, by the same token, Ireland's separatist nationalism failed to secure the allegiance of a majority of the predominantly Protestant population of north-east Ireland (ironically the main area of its founders). Partition meant that part of the claimed national territory, together with a disaffected Irish nationalist minority, remained inside the British state. The preservation of Northern Ireland's built-in Protestant majority became unionism's 'territorial imperative', and one whose sectarian implications have recently been sharpened by the increasing size of the Catholic minority (from about 35 per cent of the Northern Ireland population in 1971, to around 42 per cent in 1991; see Anderson and Shuttleworth, 1994 and 1998).

The conflict has sometimes been termed a 'double minority problem': a large Irish nationalist minority in Northern Ireland's one and half million population, and a Northern unionist minority out-numbered by over four-to-one in Ireland's total population of some five million. It might be better though to see it now as a 'triple minority problem'. If we take the UK as the territorial unit, the Northern unionists constitute less than 3 per cent of the state's population, potentially vulnerable to a majority of the other 97 per cent which is not committed to Northern Ireland remaining in the UK. So the North's unionists might be seen as vulnerable on two fronts – or as the 'tail' which has so far succeeded in 'wagging' the Irish and the British 'dogs'.

Emancipation from Failures?

The present conflict is not solvable within the nationalistic, territorial terms of reference traditionally shared by Irish nationalists and unionists both in Ireland and Britain. While Northern Irish unionism is increasingly distanced from an overarching British identity – declining in Britain with the weakening of its formative influences such as the empire and Protestantism (Colley, 1992, p. 8) – the Northern unionists do still get support from an influential right-wing rump of British nationalists (including Viscount Cranbourne, grandson of Lord Salisbury, who was one of John Major's main advisers on Northern Ireland), and from a more diffuse nationalist 'Britishness' present in all the main political parties and the media in Britain (as discussed in Chapter 6). But in situations such as Northern Ireland, where people with conflicting national allegiances are intermingled in the same territory, national conflicts are likely to lead to problems of political deadlock, or violence, or both. The nation state ideal is either unattainable or not worth the cost in human lives and human misery. Hence the attractions of redefining sovereignty and territoriality – but also the dangers of wishful thinking.

Contrary to fashionable notions about 'the death of the nation state', conflicts of sovereignty and nationalism are not about to disappear. However, the 'globalisation' and transnational integration of recent decades (see McGrew, 1995) do mean that many of the assumptions underlying nationalism and the nation state are becoming increasingly problematic (see Anderson, 1995a and 1996). Exclusive forms of sovereignty, and notions of politics and democracy as tied to 'national' territory, are in some respects being transcended, particularly within the European Union (see Goodman, 1997). In consequence the prospects for a significant recasting of exclusive territorialities in Ireland, through North–South institutions, seem better than in the 1920s, or even the 1970s, which saw the failure of previous attempts to 'bridge' the border with a 'Council of Ireland'. Such 'bridging' would puncture the pretensions of exclusive sovereignty which sustain the conflict. Accepting 'national sovereignty' as unproblematic was always a block to imagining a solution, but there is now a growing awareness that if a solution is to be found a rethinking of territorial sovereignty is essential.

To the extent that it 'dismantles' the ideological and material structures which reproduce the conflict, this approach could be 'emancipatory' in the sense defined by Ruane and Todd (1996).

They provide the best available account of the overlapping dimensions of difference – religious, ethnic, colonial, national – and the binary oppositions – Catholic/Protestant, settler/native, progressive/backward, Irish/British – which constitute the conflict. They analyse how it is reproduced by the structures of dominance, dependence and inequality, involving the British state and Protestants and Catholics in Ireland, though with a dynamic for change in the recovery of power by Catholics. This recovery led to political independence for the South and it has continued since the 1960s as the Catholic community in the North has gained greater leverage. They show the limits of the two main types of 'solution' generally considered: Northern Ireland's full integration into either an exclusively Irish state, the traditional Irish nationalist goal, or an exclusively British state, the unionist demand. In contrast, they argue for 'emancipation' defined as 'dismantling a system which constitutes two communities in mutually antagonistic and destructive relationships', moderating the differences and deconstructing their mutually reinforcing conflations, and undoing the structures of dominance, dependence and inequality. They rightly focus on 'emancipation' in the general sense of people transforming a system which 'distorts and limits their potentialities', in the process transforming themselves, rather than the more limited sense of a particular group struggling to emancipate itself from domination by another group (which of course is how nationalist struggles are normally conceived). As they establish very clearly, the objective should be to resolve the conflict, not simply to manage or contain it (see Ruane and Todd, 1996, pp. 290–306).

However, the 'recovery of Catholic power' is not the only dynamic for change. There are other dynamics, several of which are discussed in the chapters that follow. But the greater problem is that Ruane and Todd do not really answer 'the fundamental question' – which they so clearly established as the main priority – of how to dismantle the relationships which reproduce the conflict. Instead, they give a schematic answer which does little more than restate the question. What should 'emancipation' involve? How have government policies and party politicians measured up to the challenge? What role can be played by other institutions and groupings in civil society? In Senator George Mitchell's oft-quoted phrase, what does it take to 'decommission the mindsets' of the Northern conflict? This book is an attempt to answer these questions.

Conflict Mismanagement

As is clear from numerous accounts, from different perspectives, official British government policy over the years has been one of not-very-benign neglect, combined with excuses that 'the problem is that there is no solution'. Policy has been characterised by inconsistencies and about-turns, by 'balancing acts' which make few friends and many enemies, by the non-implementation of policies which might improve things if vigorously pursued, or by 'too little, too late' (e.g. O'Leary and McGarry, 1993; Keogh and Haltzel, 1993; McKittrick, 1994; Coogan, 1995; and see 'Selected Dates'). Since the late 1960s, government strategy has been predominantly one of conflict management and containment, though after three decades without a solution, *mis*management might be more accurate.

From the 1920s, when Northern unionists succeeded in stopping the half-hearted attempts of government to institute a compromise on territorial partition through a cross-border Council of Ireland, the British government generally abdicated its responsibilities and left Northern Ireland to its own unionist devices. When in 1969 it had to intervene directly in what was effectively a one-party sectarian statelet run by Protestants for Protestants – in the words of its first Prime Minister, James Craig, 'a Protestant parliament for a Protestant people' – its intervention was conceived in terms purely internal to Northern Ireland as part of the United Kingdom (see Whyte, 1990).

In 1949 there had been a significant, and as it turned out disastrous, constitutional policy shift from the attempted compromise of the 1920s. A minority Dublin government (whether unconcerned or unaware of the Partitionist implications) declared the South to be an independent Republic outside the British Commonwealth. The British responded with the 1949 Ireland Act giving the unionist-dominated Stormont parliament in Belfast a formal veto over Irish reunification, a veto which would be updated in a 1973 Act which gave the same power to a majority in a Northern Ireland referendum (to allow for the absence of a Belfast parliament under 'direct rule' from London). This may appear reasonable and 'democratic' – until Northern Ireland's origins and built-in unionist majority are remembered. In fact it skewed developments away from peaceful conflict resolution and towards war. For unionists it meant that Northern Ireland's place in the union was explicitly less secure than that of all other parts of the UK where 'Westminster' sovereignty remained 'non-negotiable'. Unionism's sectarian 'territorial imperative' was thus reinforced, with Northern nationalists to be kept in permanent minority status and treated as 'the alien threat within'. Effectively, unionists were given a further *dis*incentive to negotiating with their nationalist neighbours. The possibility of a negotiated peaceful settlement was structurally blocked and, with everything seeming to hinge on whether or not unionists retained their majority, sectarianism was actively encouraged. The door was closed on a 1920s-style territorial compromise, and it is possible to see the 1973 'Sunningdale Agreement', the 1985 Anglo–Irish Agreement and the 1998 'Belfast Agreement' as attempts to reopen that door.

Structures of Intransigence

With structural relationships which 'stacked the cards' against Northern nationalists *and* against a negotiated settlement, the logic of policy should be to change the structure so that unionists are encouraged rather than discouraged from negotiating. But at times the reverse has happened, and perhaps this should be no surprise given the fact that the 'territorial integrity' of the British state is at stake and its leadership, like Ulster unionism, is imbued with British nationalism (see Chapters 6 and 13). Previous British governments, led by self-proclaimed British believers in 'the Union', have strengthened the Northern unionists' 'powers of veto', while at the same time increasingly posing as 'neutral' in partnership with the Dublin government. For Britain, the 1949 and 1973 Acts put the immediate constitutional responsibility on Northern Ireland's electorate and allowed British governments to adopt a 'neutral' stance, safe in the knowledge that the union was in fact secure in the hands of the North's unionist majority.

In the 1992 'Brooke talks' and the 1993 Downing Street Declaration, Britain stated it had 'no selfish strategic or economic interest in Northern Ireland'; and the 1995 'Framework Document' asserted that its 'primary interest ... [was] to see peace, stability and reconciliation established by agreement among all the people who inhabit the island of Ireland' (HMSO, 1995). But these fine words were 'balanced' by a strengthening of the 'majority consent' provisions. Whereas in the language of the 1949 and 1973 Acts the unionist majority could only block a proposal for Northern Ireland to 'cease to be part of' the UK, under the 1985 Anglo–Irish Agreement 'consent' was required for 'any [unspecified] change in the status of Northern Ireland'. By 1995 the British government was asserting that Northern 'consent' was required for any measures having constitutional implications, which could cover a host of things. Not surprisingly, some unionists, encouraged in their intransigence, were happy to give it the widest possible interpretation as a veto over any changes which favoured nationalists.

In fact most unionists now wanted the purely 'internal' Northern Ireland power-sharing 'solution' which they themselves had resolutely opposed in the 1960s and 1970s, and which the British authorities knew was no longer an option. The 1960s civil rights campaign, mainly but not exclusively by the systematically disadvantaged Northern Catholics, resulted in mass demonstrations, police and Loyalist counter-attacks and, in turn, a revival of the IRA. It had been a largely spent military force whose failed campaign against border installations in the 1950s had been widely seen as an irrelevance, even by erstwhile supporters. The British government's response was to bring in the British Army in 1969 and to institute a series of purely internal reforms of the state apparatus, including the local police and military forces, and local government. Designed to curb local unionist power and its worst excesses, this culminated in the imposition of Direct Rule from London in 1972.

However, there was also a parallel, if gradual and inconsistent, shift in policy towards more recognition of the island-wide as well as UK context of the conflict, its 'double minority' aspect, and acceptance of the Dublin government as a 'junior partner' in conflict management. It was first clearly signalled in a key government document in 1972, *The Future of Northern Ireland*. But the cross-border dimension followed behind and remained subordinate to the goal of internal power-sharing, and to the constitutional guarantee – the 1973 Act, actually demonstrated in a 'border poll' – that Northern Ireland could only leave the UK with the 'consent' of a majority of its electorate. Only then was the 'Sunningdale' Council of Ireland proposal mooted; and when it was destroyed by the Ulster Workers' 'Strike' in 1974, the 1973 Act continued in place, though the power-sharing executive did not. With their 'consent' guaranteed by their built-in majority in Northern Ireland, there was little incentive for unionists to negotiate a settlement with nationalism. As we have seen, the asymmetrical structuring of relationships constituted an incentive for unionists *not* to negotiate.

To some extent this was offset by the 1985 Anglo–Irish Agreement which gave the Southern government a role, albeit a consultative one, as an advocate for Northern nationalists. This was to be diminished if and when unionists agreed to the nationalists representing themselves directly in a power-sharing Northern assembly. But although the British government now officially recognised that its partitioning of Ireland had created 'two minorities', the politically important one to be accommodated was always the unionist one. Its 'consent' clause was already enshrined in law, but this was not matched by any similar guarantees for Irish nationalist 'consent': their cross-border 'Irish dimension' remained a vague promise yet to be delivered. And even if delivered as proposed in the 1998 'Agreement', the continuing reluctance to centrally address the problem of territorial sovereignty means there will still be asymmetry of treatment, not the 'equality' and 'parity of esteem' supposedly on offer.

It might be objected that the views of the unionists, expressed through a democratic majority within Northern Ireland, should take precedence. But that simply brings us back to the fact that the dispute is about what the proper framework for democracy should be. It immediately raises the nationalist objection that Northern Ireland itself is a gerrymandered framework in which they, the nationalists, are predetermined losers – the major reason why some of them have felt justified in resorting to armed struggle. Yet the official search for solutions is still based mainly on accepting the disputed framework as the basis for a 'democratic' settlement. So far, none of the governments involved has faced up to this dilemma, not least as they themselves remain wedded to theories that see sovereignty and democracy only in terms of state territory. It is not only Northern 'mindsets' which need 'decommissioning'.

Tory Policy and Ineptitude

This was clearly seen in the political mismanagement following the first 1994 ceasefires – the failure to seize and build on the new if wary optimism, the squandering of political opportunities which led to the breakdown of the IRA ceasefire, the political vacuum which encouraged a vicious spiralling of sectarianism in the North. The governments of John Major and John Bruton, whether by (British) design or (Irish) ineptitude in the face of unionist objections, allowed their 'Framework Document' to be virtually forgotten almost as soon as it was published in February 1995. Instead, the political agenda was dominated by fruitless semantics about whether the ceasefire was 'permanent', and by public posturing about the unattainable objective of prior 'decommissioning' by the paramilitaries. The failure to actually

engage the paramilitaries' representatives in meaningful negotiations was further compounded in January 1996 when John Major
summarily rejected Senator Mitchell's proposals that 'decommissioning' should proceed in parallel with substantive negotiations.
The ending of the IRA ceasefire followed almost immediately;
and it was only when the IRA blew up London's Canary Wharf in
early February, killing two people, that the British government –
moving with uncharacteristic speed and contradicting its own
'mantra' about 'never giving in to terrorism' – acceded to
demands that a date be set for inclusive all-party negotiations,
and on the basis suggested by Mitchell.

John Major was widely believed to be a remarkable British
Prime Minister for 'caring' about Ireland and devoting a lot of
time to it. But he was mainly remarkable in being the first Prime
Minister in 20 years to be handed a 'ceasefire' on a plate – by the
Irish government of Albert Reynolds, and by John Hume and
Gerry Adams – and in then frittering away the possibility of a
political settlement. Major's intelligence services had not believed
a ceasefire would happen; and when it did, he persisted in casting
doubts on its 'permanence' which turned out to be self-fulfilling.
The foot-dragging, non-implementation of his administration was
explained, even excused, in some British circles by his reliance on
Ulster unionist votes at Westminster, but it may also have been
due to internal opposition from right-wing British nationalists in
the administration and state apparatus (see Chapters 6 and 13).
In any event, it was left to the new Labour Secretary of State, Dr
Mo Mowlam, to implement British policy with a vigour and
imagination inconceivable in her unlamented predecessor, Sir
Patrick Mayhew, and for that she deservedly has the gratitude of
the great majority of people in Ireland. On the other hand, the
substance of what she implements is actually Tory policy, and it
is clearly biased towards the British and unionist *status quo*,
keeping constitutional change to a minimum.

Practical and Theoretical Deficiencies
Contrary to official 'common sense' which still prioritises the
'internal' Northern aspects of accommodation, the main hope for
a genuine democratic settlement lies in developing North–South
institutions. They would give some practical expression to 'parity
of esteem' for Irish nationalists in Northern Ireland; and they are
also necessitated by the quite separate 'economic dynamic' of the
Single Market which points to the creation of a single, unified
Irish economy, and to a related but wider 'socio-cultural

dynamic' which requires an 'all-Ireland' civil society (see Chapter 4). Here the official strategy is seriously deficient.

As Ruane and Todd pointed out with respect to the 'Framework Document', while the 1998 'Agreement' contains the 'germ of an emancipatory approach', the actual proposals constitute such an elaborate system of constitutional and institutional checks and balances designed to reassure each 'national minority', that it is difficult to see how they could produce anything like the radical changes that are required. Even worse, there is a real danger of reinforcing rather than transcending sectarian divisions and political differences. However well intentioned in terms of achieving a 'fair balance' between 'the two conflicting communities', the dualism of taking the two communities as given, and institutionalising power-sharing within Northern Ireland, with the cross-border dimension given a decidedly secondary role, continues to be more in line with 'conflict management' than 'emancipation' (Ruane and Todd, 1996, pp. 315–16).

The strategy reflects a theory of nationalism which sees national identity essentially in terms of fixed ethnic categories, and as being necessarily the only or most important basis of political identity. Even if those responsible deny that they follow this theory, the practical tendency of their policies is to make reality fit the theory, in a sense forcing people into one or other national 'camp'. Likewise, the cross-border dimension of official policy is also based on inadequate theory. While policy has moved beyond a purely 'internal settlement' and the traditional view of sovereignty as a territorial absolute, it has not moved very far. An 'internal' solution, still fashionable in the policy debate of the 1980s (see Whyte, 1990), is a contradiction in terms given that the conflict is at root about the existence of Northern Ireland and about relationships between North and South, between the North and Britain, and indeed between all three. The fundamental dispute is about territorial sovereignty, and where lines should be drawn on the map, not primarily about what happens inside the lines, though that too is important. Yet most efforts to resolve – or should that be 'manage and contain'? – the conflict still give priority to 'internal power-sharing' and rest on an acceptance of the existing territorial framework, albeit tempered by comparatively weak forms of North–South cooperation and intergovernmentalism. On the other hand, while official North–South transnationalism is relatively impoverished, it is a significant advance on previous reality and it may well be amenable to further development.

Nationalist Theory and Power-Sharing

The dominant international relations theories of 'realism' and 'functionalism' inform this policy debate, and it is in their inter-connections with nationalist theory that a solution is being sought. Thus, rather than charting all the twists of policy, which in any case will probably take new and unpredictable turns, it is more useful to map out the various theoretical assumptions which underpin official strategies and party-political positions, and then highlight the theoretical basis for 'emancipatory' alternatives.

Unionist special pleading about Irish nationalism being narrowly 'ethnic' and exclusive, contrasted with British nation-alism as founded on an inclusive 'civic' nationalism, or the equally spurious distinction between an Irish state dominated by nation-alism and a multi-national UK state need not detain us here (but see Chapters 5 and 6). We have already seen that *all* nationalisms are flawed, and Irish and British nationalisms inevitably share many of the same flaws, as they mirror-image each other. Rather, what concerns us is the particular 'ethno-nationalist' interpreta-tion of political identity which is generally embodied in official policy, the 'conflict management' strategies which result, and the possibility of more open-ended interpretations.

One influential, perhaps dominant, understanding of nation-alism – and one generally shared by nationalists themselves – is to see group identity as a universal human need, and a particular identity as an inherent, inherited characteristic internal to each nation or ethnic group. It may be activated or stimulated by external factors, such as industrialisation or the rise of capitalism, but basically it is always there, largely unchanged and unchange-able (e.g. Smith, 1981).

This is the view which, at least implicitly, underpins proposed power-sharing within Northern Ireland. Whatever its intellectual flaws – and they are substantial – it seems to fit neatly with 'reality on the ground', with the ideas of unionists and nationalists them-selves and their centuries-old conflict, and with the needs of British policy. Better for instance to see the national animosities as internal to 'the two Irish tribes' rather than at least partly a product of the British state, which by establishing and main-taining Northern Ireland has given sectarianism a continuing institutionalised reality. In accepting the 'reality' of ethnic groups and national identities as essentially fixed, official policy colludes in perpetuating the divisions, and the conflict.

There can of course be a fine line between either recognising current reality and working to change it, or simply assuming that it is inevitable and accommodating to it. 'Benign', liberal policies which encourage 'parity of esteem' and power-sharing between the so-called 'two traditions' do recognise that there is more than one valid cultural and political identity in Northern Ireland (a significant advance on unionist majoritarianism); and in some respects they can replace conflict with accommodation (another significant advance). However, because this entire strategy is premised on a pragmatic acceptance of sectarian divisions within a Northern Ireland framework, it cannot supersede them, and in the last analysis the overall effect is to further entrench sectarianism.

Underlying such policies is the 'consociationalism' model formulated by a Dutch political scientist, Arend Lijphart (e.g. 1983, pp. 166–7). In contrast to the basic Westminster model of 'winner-takes-all' within territorially-defined electoral entities, consociationalism offers a set of *non*-majoritarian devices for diffusing and sharing power within the given territory. A power-sharing government is drawn from the different groups and segments in the society, a high degree of autonomy is delegated to each group, and minorities are given a veto to protect their particular interests. There can be separate voting systems for each 'ethnic group', with the implication that political parties and perhaps also individual voters would be classified, or would have to classify themselves, into one or other 'ethnic' category. Thus ethnic differences are recognised officially and ethnic conflict is consensually managed.

Understandably, this model has its attractions in conflict-ridden Northern Ireland, and it can indeed have some limited positive effects in certain circumstances (see Douglas, 1998). But overall it has very limited possibilities, even in its own terms, and especially if it is the centre-piece of a mainly 'internal' strategy. As Taylor (1994) has shown, in a withering if perhaps over-stated critique, the 'consociational model' has very serious defects. It is empiricist in failing to address the complex social dynamics of ethnic or national identity, uncritically accepting the primacy and the permanency of ethnic divisions, and further reifying them. It simply assumes that ethnicity is the independent, pre-existing cause and 'motor' of conflict, rather than questioning why and how ethnic divisions arose, why they are sustained, and how they might be superseded. It actively excludes other perhaps more fruitful social categories, other bases of political mobilisation such as gender and class which cross-cut ethnic divisions. Where it defines just two main 'ethnic groups', people who do not want to belong to either are forced to 'take sides', and the 'middle ground' of compromise or alternative politics is thereby actively eroded and ethnic polarisation is further reinforced.

As Wilford (1992) points out, consociationalism endorses a bleak view of humanity, with distrust seen as endemic. Rather than promoting social contact and cooperation, it effectively argues the virtues of segregation. In short, while its advocacy of 'power-sharing' appears factual, fair and liberal, the model is weakly based and reactionary in its assumptions and effects. However, from the viewpoint of governments trying to manage the conflict, it has the advantages of dealing with symptoms rather than causes, and not requiring a fundamental restructuring of state and society. It also helps to deflect blame from Britain, and facilitates its self-presentation as a 'neutral' facilitator of reconciliation. But this is bought at the price of further entrenching conflict.

If ethnic or national identity were a self-evident 'given' – implying 'natural', biological or racial categories, British 'settlers' and Irish 'natives', Protestants and Catholics, existing in separate unbroken bloodlines since the Reformation – how could we account for the Presbyterian United Irish men and women, or indeed the subsequent political realignment of most Presbyterians to the unionist cause. Rather than being 'set in stone', ethnicity and political identities are historically changing and changeable creations. Paradoxically, it is the very weakness and general 'invisibility' of 'ethnic' differentiation in the North of Ireland (e.g. same language, same skin colour), combined with local patterns of geographically intermingled territories, which gives sectarianism in the North its particular virulence. Rather than being simply the expression of difference, its function is precisely to maintain the differentiations, and this can be hard work in a situation where the marks of class are generally much more obvious than those of nation or religion. So, for instance, there is the long-established 'supremacist' heritage of Orange marches through Catholic areas which asserts that Northern Ireland is 'Protestant territory'. Territoriality as a symbol of political control, linking local and national spatial scales, is central to the sectarian politics of Northern Ireland, seen most dramatically in recent years in the conflicts surrounding 'Drumcree' (see Anderson and Shuttleworth, 1998).

There are in fact other theories besides 'ethno-nationalism' which give better, more contextual understandings (e.g. Nairn,

1977; Blaut, 1987). In their different ways they stress the importance of the wider international setting in creating and reshaping
nationalisms, and hence they are potentially much more useful for
dealing with conflicts such as the one in Ireland. Indeed, as
nationalisms change, they can become more compatible with
transnational developments, as Chapter 5 suggests for the
'cosmopolitan' nationalism of Southern Ireland.

Transnationalist Theory and Emancipation

While official policy still gives most emphasis to 'internal power-
sharing' in Northern Ireland, transnationalism holds the key to
'emancipation'. But, to 'emancipate', it will need to go well
beyond the weak North–South 'neo-functionalism' of the 1998
Agreement. While conservative 'realism' and liberal 'functionalism' dominate government policy and party politics, there is
also a third category of critical and Marxist-influenced
approaches to cross-border developments. The three perspectives
(see, e.g. Brown, 1992) provide a useful conceptual framework
for understanding the conflict and how it might be solved.

When unionists and Tories oppose cross-border institutions as
a threat to British sovereignty and an unstable 'halfway house' to
full Irish sovereignty over the North, they argue on 'realist'
grounds (whether or not they are always aware of the fact). In the
'realist' perspective, interstate integration must lead to the dominance of one or other state, one nationalism at the expense of the
other, as reflected in the 'zero-sum' terms of unionist political
rhetoric. Either Northern Ireland is absorbed into a Dublin-run
all-Ireland republic, as traditionally nationalists have hoped and
unionists have feared; or, alternatively, as unionists have uncon-
vincingly speculated, the Irish Republic is reabsorbed into the
British-dominated ambit from which it tried to escape in 1921.
'Realism' rests on a traditional reading of state sovereignty as
absolute. It sees civil society as primarily 'state-contained' society,
and relations between societies as subordinate to, and dependent
on, intergovernmental relations.

The liberal 'functionalist' perspective, on the other hand,
developed largely in 'mirror-image' opposition to the dominant
'realism' and generally sees states as the product of civil society,
rather than the other way around. Transnational functional integration is seen as primarily a matter for civil society, avoiding the
contentious 'high politics' of state sovereignty in favour of the

'low politics' of matters such as cross-border trade, tourism and transport infrastructure. It is seen as gradually shifting governance towards 'world regions' such as the EU and relegating states to a limited role, as just one of many sites of political life. Hence 'functionalists' avoid the 'territorial trap' of assuming that 'state' and 'civil society' are necessarily co-terminous (Agnew, 1994), but tend to exaggerate 'globalisation' and see it as a harmonious process, implying that anachronistic state structures are the only obstacle to transnational integration.

When Irish nationalists see EU integration as necessarily leading to Ireland's integration and reunification they reflect 'functionalist' influences. The 'apolitical' notion that North–South integration was mainly an economic matter which could largely be left to civil society was a central element in the mainly Southern 'technocratic anti-partitionism' (Lyne, 1990) which developed from the 1950s (see Chapters 4 and 5). Its professed hope that joint membership of the 'European community' would solve the national problem has a 'post-nationalist' equivalent in the hope that regional identities in the EU might replace nationalist ones. The 'functionalist' suggestion that globalisation and international interdependency are making the nation state redundant has been echoed by some 'constitutional' Irish nationalists, most notably John Hume, leader of the North's Social Democratic and Labour Party (Kearney, 1988), though many Irish still retain their traditional 'realist' attachment to Ireland's sovereignty and an all-Ireland republic.

These very sketchy depictions of 'realism' and 'functionalism' must be qualified by explicit recognition of their 'neo' versions. With the rise of multinational corporations and transnational organisations like the EU, 'realists' came to accept that states are not the only important international actors, but now argue that states remain the most important actors and are actually strengthened rather than undermined by the supporting web of transnational institutions. Similarly, 'neo-functionalists' came to acknowledge, not only that states cannot easily be side-stepped, but also that they can be positive agents of international integration, though with a practical role confined to 'low politics' as in the cross-border institutions outlined in the Agreement.

In Ireland the failure to develop North–South institutions has reflected collusion between 'realist' and 'functionalist' perspectives; the former wish to separate 'politics' from 'economics' in the hope of preserving political sovereignty as sacrosanct, while the latter think that integration would be facilitated if the contentious 'high politics' of sovereignty could be avoided or down-played. But both perspectives can be contested from a Marxist-influenced 'critical' standpoint which emphasises the causal forces and emancipatory potential of exploited and oppressed groups within society, and the need to confront the pretensions of states and sovereignty. Far from being sacrosanct, sovereignty has already been substantially altered by EU integration; and far from being avoidable, it remains the nub of the conflict in Ireland. As Rosenberg (1994) has demonstrated, 'realism's' fixation with state sovereignty, and its sharp dichotomy between 'internal' and 'external' affairs, is based on the specifically capitalist separation of the supposedly 'non-political' economics of civil society from the 'political' realm of states and sovereignty. In reality, civil societies and states are all interconnected sites of political struggle. In class-divided societies, subordinate social classes and other groupings resist exploitation or oppression, and to do so effectively they have to challenge existing political arrangements and present their own alternative agendas for social organisation and state action. In principle and sometimes in practice, such developments can question the separations of 'national' and 'foreign' and challenge the legitimacy of the state's system, highlighting its authoritarian character in maintaining the capitalist order (Gill and Law, 1989; Hirsch, 1995). There is thus no smooth transition from nation states to transnationalism as envisaged by 'functionalists', and nor is the state the prime mover as in 'realism'.

Conclusions

The political stalemate in Ireland is directly related to nationalistic 'realist' perspectives. Attempted solutions to the conflict have mainly rested on introducing elements of 'neo-functionalism', but a successful resolution requires a more thoroughgoing, critical or Marxist-influenced approach to cross-border development.

The 'realist' and peculiarly archaic British conception of sovereignty as a territorial absolute, the exclusive and indivisible preserve of the 'Crown in Parliament' at Westminster, encourages the 'zero-sum' approach which has precluded any solution in Ireland short of the all-out but unattainable victories both 'sides' have traditionally sought. The unionist assertion of exclusively British territoriality has been a pyrrhic victory, the financial costs of which are mainly borne by the increasingly alienated taxpayers

of Britain. In theory the unionists had a 'winner takes all' form of
sovereignty, but most of the supposed 'winners' have actually
been losers, with working-class Protestants as well as Catholics
bearing the brunt of the conflict.

The more irredentist modes of Irish nationalism 'mirror-
image' the British and unionist claims to exclusive territoriality.
But, Irish nationalism, unlike the British and unionist varieties,
has developed less exclusivist forms which aspire to reconciliation
across the island and beyond, fuelled by a functional integration
between North and South. These more accommodating forms of
'cosmopolitan nationalism' (discussed in Chapter 5) waver
between relying on more-or-less 'automatic' processes of cross-
border integration, and a more guided, state-centred process of
North–South 'neo-functional' integration.

But, as already suggested, even this approach is inadequate.
Transnational integration is highly conflictual as dominant social
groupings vie with each other and with subordinate social forces
for control of the process. Emancipation from the stalemated
national conflict obviously requires some political accommodation between Republicans and Loyalists (see Chapters 10 and
11). But, more fundamentally, it also requires the active growth
and participation of *non*-national forces, such as women's and
working-class movements (as is argued in Chapters 8, 12 and 13).
Challenging domination and oppression North and South on a
mutually supportive or island-wide basis would develop new
cross-border political communities and undercut the fixation with
territorial sovereignty. Cross-border mobilisation around
common agendas would directly impact on political consciousness and redefine political identities at the same time as it furthers
social interests.

That said, it is also the case that such developments in civil
society, including the cross-border cooperation of business interests, would be greatly facilitated by comparable developments in
the transnational institutions of state. Indeed the two types of
transnational development should be seen as mutually reinforcing
rather than alternatives. Together they would open up new border-
crossing fault-lines in Irish society, redefining the social order in
the South as in the North. Nothing less will do if there is to be
emancipation from the dead end of counterposed nationalisms.

2   The British/Irish 'Peace Process' and the Colonial Legacy

Robbie McVeigh

The British/Irish conflict is one of the oldest and most complex of colonial conflicts. Colonial involvement in Ireland by the English polity began formally with the military conquest of part of the country ('the Pale') by the Anglo-Norman King Henry II in 1171 AD. Every subsequent development in Irish society was structured by the colonial process, including the transition from feudalism to capitalism, urbanisation and industrialisation. Each of these huge processes was given the colonial imprimatur. The British state arrived in Ireland as an openly colonising power and at different times used almost every type of institutionalised violence – genocide, slavery, forced migration, starvation and war – to try and subdue resistance. The colonial plantation of parts of Ireland in the sixteenth and seventeenth centuries – notably most of the province of Ulster – added a further defining dimension to the British/Irish nexus. Contemporary Ireland still carries the hallmarks of this colonial history – from the attrition of the Irish language and the corruption of indigenous family and place names, to the systemic emigration, underdevelopment and division characteristic of colonial formations. In consequence, 'decolonising' Ireland and healing the wounds associated with the colonial process is no easy task. Every party to the conflict – British and Irish, settler and native, coloniser and colonised – has had its identity forged at the colonial interface. The colonial legacy continues to structure British and Irish lives in just as profound a way as sexuality or gender or race or class.

It is difficult to overestimate the importance of the colonial legacy for understanding contemporary Ireland and its relationship with Britain and the wider world. We can find crucially important perspectives on Ireland by focusing on the parallels between Irish and 'Majority World' experience. We must learn from places like South Africa, Latin America and the Middle East with experience of similar peace processes and similar legacies of colonialism. It is especially important that we learn from their successes and failures at this historic moment in Irish history. Ignoring this colonial legacy does no service to the prospects for peace, reconciliation and political settlement of the Irish/British conflict. This is not to argue that colonialism explains every contradiction and nuance in Irish society; it is to argue, however, that without an analysis of colonialism and its effects on Ireland, the analysis of most aspects of division and conflict is both limited and flawed (Caherty et al., 1992).

My argument begins by looking at the colonial legacy in British/Irish relations – particularly the way in which this has structured British state policy in Ireland. It then examines the implications of this legacy for the ongoing 'peace process'. I suggest that attention to the colonial legacy reveals four key projects, each of which is a necessary but not sufficient condition for a successful peace settlement between Ireland and Britain: demilitarisation, democratisation, economic development and reconciliation.

The Colonial Legacy

Notwithstanding the transparency of the legacy of colonialism, the British/Irish conflict has been popularly 'decolonised'. While the island itself has palpably not been 'decolonised', most explanations of the conflict have been. One of the most successful strategies of British rule has been to redefine colonial conflict as something else – an atavistic sectarian war, an internal dispute, a terrorist problem. In the process, the British state has successfully reinvented itself as a neutral peacekeeper. It has also reworked opposition to colonialism – particularly, of course, armed resistance to the colonial state – as 'terrorism'. This means that even to name the conflict as a 'colonial' one can be represented as colluding with and endorsing every tactic, every mistake, every atrocity committed in the name of anti-colonialism. This is a remarkable piece of revisionism that leaves most outside observers and many oppositional voices in Ireland without a paradigm to explain inequality, injustice and repression within the North of Ireland.

Despite the success of this project, there is only one possible response from anyone interested in an emancipatory analysis of the Irish situation. This to reiterate that the British/Irish conflict *is* a colonial conflict. The key question for those who want to argue otherwise, is when did it stop being a colonial conflict? They must either argue that it never was a colonial conflict or that – at some point – Ireland made the remarkable transition from colonised to decolonised without anyone noticing. Those who have gone with the 'never colonised' argument have the significant problem of dealing with the fact that for hundreds of years the British state insisted that the conflict was a colonial one. Government and settler ideology often made this colonial context explicit. It is instructive, for instance, that Poynings Law – the classical legislation that marked Ireland as colonial political formation – remains a British statute in force.

Denial of Ireland's colonial history is a relatively new phenomenon. Take the example of Lecky – the feted nineteenth-century unionist historian:

In the history of Ireland ... we may trace with singular clearness the perverting and degrading influence of great legislative injustices, and the manner in which they affect in turn every element of national well-being. This portion of the history of the Empire has usually been treated by English historians in a very superficial and perfunctory manner, and it has been obscured by many contradictions, by much prejudice and misrepresentation.

Lecky goes on to suggest:

The edicts of more than one Plantagenet king show traces of a wisdom and a humanity beyond their age; and the Irish modes of life long continued to exercise an irresistible attraction over many of the colonists; but it was inevitable, in such a situation and at such a time, that those who resisted that attraction, and who formed the nucleus of the English power, should look upon the Irish as later colonists looked upon the Red Indians – as being, like wild beasts, beyond the pale of moral law. Intermarriage with them was forbidden by stringent penalties, and many savage laws were made to maintain the distinction. (1892, p. 4)

Later historians – whatever their thoughts on revisionism and contemporary Irish politics – have usually supported the notion that: 'the natives and newcomers, for all their deep disagreements, came to share the common assumption that though a kingdom in theory, Ireland was a colony in fact' (Brady and Gillespie, 1986, p. 21).

Despite the weight of this evidence, the 'never-colonised' argument has been tried. Take, for example, Brian Walker's, 'Ireland: European or Colonised'. This argument at least has the attraction of simplicity:

> [I]t is incorrect to describe Ireland's situation in the nineteenth and twentieth centuries, and earlier, as 'colonial' or 'post-colonial' pure and simple. Obviously there were and are problematic connections between Ireland and Britain, but Ireland's development, north and south, cannot be seen simply in a colonial context ... . Setting Irish history, not in a 'British' or 'colonial' but in a European setting, can bring special insights into the development of people and society in Ireland. (1990, pp. 38, 39)

The limitations of such an approach are palpable, however. We could of course try to broaden the dichotomies: India: Asian or colonised?; Zimbabwe: African or colonised? Brazil: American or colonised? The recognition of local or regional specificity to 'problematic connections' in any of these cases does nothing to negate the overarching stamp of the colonial imprimatur.

So there is little depth in the Ireland was 'never colonised' argument. People who want to deny the colonial present are forced to come up with a date for the arrival of the decolonised or post-colonial situation. They rarely do this but we might suggest a couple. The first is 1800 and the Act of Union. At this point – it might be argued – the colonial era closed and Ireland became part of the British state. But the union was imposed against the expressed will of the vast majority of the Irish people and it instituted a form of government for Ireland that tolerated the starvation and emigration of half its population over the course of the next century. Moreover, many colonial powers never made any formal political distinction between colony and imperial heartland. For example, Portugal simply defined its colonial acquisitions as provinces of the Portuguese state. The French state continues to do this: justifying its nuclear testing on the peoples and islands of the Pacific by insisting that these remain 'part of France'. There is thus nothing implicitly decolonising about incorporation into the imperial heartland.

The other obvious date for the end of the colonial nexus is 1922 with the withdrawal (more or less) of Britain's formal claim to sovereignty over most of Ireland. The trouble with this line of argument is that in 1922 the British state maintained its jurisdiction over the Six Counties in the north of Ireland where the continuing effects of its colonial policy were most transparent. Indeed the 1920–22 period saw the *creation* of Northern Ireland – a state formation characterised by social, economic, political and cultural divisions imposed by the colonial process. There is nothing 'uncolonial' about the fact that a majority of people in the newly created statelet supported the continued link with Britain, any more than the white settler majorities in the USA or Australia proves that these countries were not colonised. In fact the Northern Ireland statelet was created deliberately to perpetuate a settler bloc majority – in this sense it was a specifically colonial formation.

'Revising' Irish history in order to 'decolonise' and depoliticise it is factually incorrect and intellectually dishonest. Furthermore, this revision does no service to the pursuit of peace and justice on the island. We have to address the colonial legacy directly in order to transcend its negative and corrupting consequences. The colonial legacy is complex. It structures Irish society and British–Irish relations in ways which remind us that the 'problem' is not just internal to the Northern Ireland statelet. There are different colonial dimensions to the situation. First, there is the sense in which many of the leading protagonists of the conflict in Ireland still see themselves as 'settlers' and 'natives', despite over three hundred years of coexistence since the 'Plantation' of Ulster. The mentalities associated with 'settler' and 'native' are still rooted in many ways of articulating division and conflict. Take as one small example of this the questions of identity which are raised by the continuing debate on the very name of the city of Doire/Derry/Londonderry (Moore, 1996, pp. 8–21). This is a contemporary debate but one rooted explicitly in the process of colonisation, expropriation and plantation and in the sense of being a 'settler' or a 'native'.

'Settler–native' conflicts have proved to be the most bloody and intractable dimensions of colonialism in many parts of the world like South Africa, Israel and Algeria. Ireland's experience of colonialism is unique – it cannot be simplistically equated with any of these other settler–native conflicts but this does nothing to reduce the extent to which 'settler' and 'native' mentalities contribute to the intensity of the conflict and the divisions which ensue. It is clear that there is no point in 'forgetting' the colonial past in order to reconcile a conflict which is a legacy of present-day colonialism (O'Dowd, 1990).

Ireland, North and South, is also structured by the 'new circuits of imperialism' which have supplemented and replaced direct political colonial involvement. The Irish economy is particularly vulnerable to the economic colonialism of transnationals with their headquarters elsewhere. Ireland is also vulnerable to cultural colonialism. For example, much of the media in the North is directly controlled from Britain – including BBC Northern Ireland and the *Belfast Telegraph*; in the South, British newspapers dominate the print media and television is largely composed of British- and US-made programmes.

This example hints at the broader colonial matrix within which Ireland finds itself. While much was made of the importance of the American Irish lobby in terms of its ability to force the hand of the US government on Ireland, the reality was that this influence paled into insignificance when compared to the symbiotic relationship between the British and the US. In the 'new world order' the dependability of the British state is much more important to the US government than the cause of peace and justice in Ireland – Irish Americans hold little sway in the UN Security Council. In short, geopolitics became much more significant than internal politics in determining how far the US was prepared to push the British towards peace. In assuming that the US would play a key role as peacemaker, most observers underestimated the importance of the intimacy of the British/US relations.

The North of Ireland also continues to be a colonial formation in a more specific sense. 'Direct Rule' is a form of administrative colonialism by which the Northern Ireland statelet is ruled by British ministers and a civil service with little local political accountability. Northern Ireland is characterised by a 'dependency culture', managed by a highly centralised administration, almost in the manner of a Crown colony. This administration is not democratically accountable to the people of Northern Ireland in any sense. Such a situation encourages the privileging of some groups at the expense of others – economically, politically, culturally and militarily – in the interests of managing conflict and generating acquiescence, if not active consent, to the existing regime. The result is the institutionalisation of divisions within and between both communities in the North and between both communities and their counterparts in the South.

Finally there is the sense in which Ireland, North and South, has itself become a neo-colonial power through membership of the European Union. This development in turn transforms Ireland's relationship with the Majority World as it clearly separates Ireland and the Irish people from most of the rest of the colonised world. The Southern Irish economy has become increasingly identified as a 'Celtic Tiger' and other European countries with colonial histories like Scotland have begun to see it as a model of success in economic development. While simplistic notions of spectacular Irish economic growth ignore continuing legacies of unemployment and emigration, the opposing notion of an Irish economy rooted in colonial underdevelopment seems equally simplistic. This supports the notion that Ireland is 'between two worlds' with structural linkages in each. Ireland belongs completely in neither the First World nor Majority World; it is neither completely coloniser nor colonised (Caherty *et al.*, 1992; O'Hearn, 1994).

The British State and Decolonisation

One of the most significant consequences of situating contemporary Ireland in terms of these different colonial dimensions is that it 'deneutralises' the British state in Ireland. Attention to the colonial legacy makes it clear that the British state is not a disinterested observer. Britain has a selfish, strategic and economic interest in Northern Ireland – that is why it claims sovereignty. Moreover, a party that has had a multitude of selfish strategic and economic interests in Ireland for the past 800 years is singularly ill-qualified to play the part of 'honest broker' or 'neutral peacekeeper'. The question of who should play this role – indeed whether it is necessary at all – remains moot. The most obvious candidates are international bodies like the United Nations, the Council of Europe or the Organisation for Security Co-operation in Europe. The model of the UN monitoring role in El Salvador might be a useful one to follow. It bears emphasis, however, that Britain can never fulfil this role in Ireland. The British state is a major part of the problem; it is a key party to the conflict; it will be a key party in peace negotiations; it cannot but be partisan. This deneutralising of the British state clears the decks for proper analysis of its role in the conflict. It also demands further analysis of the real role of the British state if it is neither peacekeeper nor disinterested observer.

If the British state remains selfishly interested in the North of Ireland, what light does this throw on its role in the peace process? Does the British state really want peace? The simple answer to this lies in the definition of peace used. Martin Luther King said that, 'Peace is not the absence of conflict but rather the presence of justice'. His definition implies two very different notions of what peace is about. If peace is simply the absence of sustained violent conflict, then most elements within the British state – including the British 'establishment' and both the Conservative and Labour parties – *do* want peace.

There is no doubt that the war in Ireland was costing Britain in a whole series of ways (Tomlinson, 1994 and 1995). First, it was costing in terms of British lives. The slow attrition of 'last night another soldier' never produced a reaction approaching the popular American rejection of US involvement in Vietnam. Nevertheless, it remained unpopular with a British populace that has consistently voiced its own lack of commitment to involvement in the North of Ireland. Second, it was costing a huge amount of money in terms of the subvention to Northern Ireland and the billions of pounds that it has spent fighting the war. Not least, is the substantial cost of bankrolling the 40,000 people involved directly in the security industry. Third, it was costing in terms of bad publicity around the world. Exposure of human rights abuses committed by the state was minimised by media manipulation and censorship but there is no doubt that regular criticisms by internationally respected groups like Amnesty International, Helsinki Watch and the United Nations Human Rights Committee were unwanted and embarrassing. Finally, it was costing the British in terms of the spread of the conflict to Britain. Bombs and bomb-scares in the City of London did untold damage to the security of the City as a centre for international finance capital. These cost millions of pounds in terms of physical damage and potentially billions in terms of lost confidence. The symbolic watershed was the point at which insurance companies began to refuse to cover for bomb damage in Britain – it had become a war which British capitalism was unable or unwilling to bankroll.

Against all these factors, there are continuing benefits of British involvement in the North of Ireland. Not least of these is the continuing power of unionism as a conservative ideology and a key part of British nationalism. While the importance of victory in Ireland is clearly less central than it was to imperialist forces in Britain in 1912 when the Conservative Party was prepared to endorse mutiny by the British Army in support of the Union, it is still a cornerstone of right-wing British nationalism. The British Labour Party may be less convinced of the importance of the Union to its own vision of its national project but it remains locked into 'bipartisanship' in its approach to Ireland and the British left has shown little ability to free itself of the accumulated weight of traditional British unionist attitudes towards Ireland. Indeed, there are aspects of Blairism which hint at a 'new unionism'.

Aside from ideological factors, there are the undoubted advantages of the Six Counties as a training ground for the British Army. There are also, as we saw in the final year of the last Tory government, smaller short-term benefits when unionist political support can be mobilised in the interests of British parliamentary party politics. Very few people in the British establishment, however, are committed in the longer term to the idea that these advantages significantly outweigh all the other costs of the war.

Britain's continuing involvement in Ireland is best explained as a form of *colonial entropy*. It is caught up in a colonial present because of its colonial past. Across centuries of colonial history, Britain had selfish economic and strategic interests in Ireland and was prepared to defend these interests – whatever the majority of the Irish people wanted. This entropy means that the cost–benefit analysis of the situation is increasingly finely balanced for the British state. The costs of remaining in Ireland – military, financial and ideological – are not sufficient to force a formal withdrawal. Neither are the benefits so great that the British state is prepared to make enormous sacrifices in order to stay in Ireland. The British state is unsure of how to withdraw from Ireland in its interests – as it has done from most of its other former colonies – but neither can it see how its long-term interests will be served by remaining in Ireland. Put bluntly, Northern Ireland is no longer 'as British as Finchley' as Margaret Thatcher once famously proclaimed, but it remains slightly more British than Hong Kong.

This reading of the contemporary role of the British state in Ireland suggests that under the narrow definition of peace – the absence of conflict – it does want peace. The problem for everyone who supports the peace process is that it appears increasingly clear that this is *all* that the British state wants. It is not committed to the presence of justice. It wanted paramilitary violence – particularly the Republican military campaign – to stop. When it stopped, the British state argued that the whole situation had been effectively resolved.

The narrowness of the British vision has surprised many people. Many actors in Ireland that had argued forcibly against the use of political violence – notably the Irish government, Southern Irish political parties and the SDLP – believed that the benefits of ending the campaign would be experienced fairly quickly after the ceasefires. This has not been the case. The British government has appeared dishonest, disingenuous and prepared to undermine the whole process in the interests of its own survival. It seemed shocking that – as the Tory government majority reduced in Westminster – the peace process was sacrificed on the altar of government survival. The government was prepared to compromise the whole process in order to guarantee the support of the Ulster Unionist Party in parliamentary divisions. In the aftermath of the brutalisation of residents on the Garvaghy Road in Portadown in July 1997, there was little evidence to support the notion of a sea-change in British state policy under the Blair administration (see also Chapters 6, 7 and 9).

So, where does that leave us? First, the importance of Martin Luther King's broader definition of peace is confirmed rather than denied. If peace is about the presence of justice, then we are nowhere near securing peace in the North of Ireland. In 1998 we are at the start of a process rather than at the end of it. There is an absence of justice in terms of the continuing state of emergency. For example, the United Nations Human Rights Committee recently called for the British state to end its derogation from the International Covenant on Civil and Political Rights and criticised the apparatus of laws infringing civil liberties. It also called for the closure of Castlereagh Detention Centre. These are only the most visible injustices: there is an absence of justice in terms of the security forces and policing practice; an absence of justice in terms of continuing economic discrimination and inequality; and an absence of justice in terms of the lack of parity of esteem between unionists and nationalists.

It needs to be said that until these underlying injustices are tackled there will always be a predilection towards violence in the North – this will be the case whatever the political leadership of either the Loyalist or Republican movements decides to do. This tendency towards violence may take the shape of the all-out military conflict we saw until the 1994 ceasefires. Alternatively, it may take the shape of the lower-level violence we have seen since – attacks on churches and Orange halls by sectarian elements in the two communities, attacks on peaceful protesters by the RUC, attacks on Catholics living in Protestant areas and so on (Pat Finucane Centre, 1995).

The widespread violence of the summers of 1996 and 1997 following the events at Drumcree merely underlined the fact that Northern Ireland is far from being a society at peace (CAJ, 1996).

It bears emphasis, of course, that most of this violence took place without any organised involvement by 'paramilitary' organisations at all. In the main, Republican and Loyalist paramilitary groups stood aside from the Drumcree stand-off in 1996. They were not central to either the widespread intimidation by people associated with the Orange Order which brought the whole society to a standstill or the unrest which followed it in both Republican and Loyalist areas. Neither were they associated with the state violence which accompanied the forcing of Orange parades through Catholic areas and the uprisings which followed this. Of course Republican and Loyalist organisations have been associated with continuing violence after the two ceasefires of 1994 – notably involvement in sectarian killings on the Loyalist side and killings by Direct Action Against Drugs on the Republican side. Nevertheless, their incomplete ceasefires have exposed the myth that they are somehow responsible for the totality of violence in the North. In short, with or without the paramilitary organisations, the Northern Ireland statelet is still characterised by violence and an absence of peace.

To reiterate, unless there is justice, there will be no peace. If the British Labour government is serious about peace, it has to be convinced of the centrality of justice issues. If it continues to prevaricate, then other actors in the equation will have to encourage it. This includes, crucially, the Irish government as well as other external actors like the US government and the European Union. The British state is a core part of the problem and, until this is recognised by the British government, it cannot be part of the solution. Deneutralising the British role helps to clarify the challenges facing the peace process. Instead of a neutral arbiter, we find a British state still claiming jurisdiction over the North based on its colonial acquisition of Ireland. We find the British ruling political party committed to maintaining the Union and the opposition Tory party still organising and canvassing support in the Six Counties. We find the political instincts of the British establishment remaining steadfastly unionist and tempered only by a pragmatism based on war weariness and external pressure. In short we find a party with a selfish interest in the Northern Ireland statelet. There were three key military blocs involved in the war – British state, Loyalists and Republicans. There are now two larger blocs or loose alliances involved in political negotiations – British state/unionists/ Loyalists and Irish state/nationalists/Republicans. None of these actors is neutral, none of them disinterested and each of them is pursuing its own agendas. *If* there is to be a 'peacekeeper' or an 'honest broker', it cannot be the British state – it clearly must come from outside these blocs.

The 'Peace Process'

The relative absence of violence in the North should be seen as the beginning of a process much more than the ending of one. We are at the beginning of a negotiations process which offers the possibility of lasting peace and democracy in Ireland. It is useful to dichotomise the peace process and suggest that there are really two distinct *processes*. These are organically linked but they involve distinct objectives and problems. One is essentially *military* in character; the other is essentially *political*. There is nothing particularly unique about these processes – they have characterised most colonial situations as they have moved towards decolonisation.

In Ireland the military process involves, primarily, the combatants to the war over the past 30 years. On the British state side, the British Army, the Royal Irish Regiment, the Royal Ulster Constabulary; on the Republican side the Irish Republican Army, the Irish National Liberation Army and the Continuity Army Council; and on the Loyalist side, the Ulster Defence Association and the Ulster Volunteer Force (formerly the 'Combined Loyalist Military Command') and the Loyalist Volunteer Force. The objective of any peace process must be to demobilise every one of these combatants – to end their function in terms of the use and threat of violence.

The task is to remove each of these military or paramilitary elements from the Northern Irish polity. This is clearly a huge problem, not just because there are militarists on all sides of the struggle – as there were in say, South Africa or Nicaragua – but also that these actors play a leading and often predominant role. The one advantage in terms of the peace process is that while each of these is strongly militarist there is no possibility of them achieving their expressed aims through military struggle (McVeigh, 1994a). The political context of the conflict has, in very different ways, inched the military actors towards a recognition of the need for a political process which can achieve their aims. It is no accident that former combatants on the Republican and Loyalist side have played a key role in shifting the focus away from military towards political solutions.

Put simply, the truth that no party is likely to secure its goals through the exclusive use of violence is hard to ignore, even for the most convinced of militarists (McVeigh, 1994). The British state has operated a policy of military repression and political reform since at least the 1970s (O'Dowd *et al.*, 1981). The Republican movement moved in this direction in the wake of the 1981 hunger strikes and the famous 'ballot box in one hand, armalite in the other' strategy. Loyalists have been more limited and tentative in this process – but a space has developed (Price, 1995; Shankill Think Tank, 1995). While the militarist dimension is yet to be repudiated in an absolutist way by any side, all parties are prepared to accept at least the *primacy* of politics. This acceptance opened up the current 'peace process' as a predominantly *political* process.

The political process, however, involves a much wider set of players: centrally, the unionist and nationalist populations in the North; more broadly the British and Southern Irish people and their governments; and, more peripherally, other interested parties like the US government and the European Union. To be successful the process has to reconcile the conflicting aims of each of these parties: first, the basic contradiction between unionism and nationalism in the North; second, the broader contradiction between two competing nationalisms – British and Irish – manifested in a British government committed to the union and partition and an Irish government committed to ending both. This process is being facilitated by outside actors that are less overtly unionist or nationalist and more concerned with a solution which ensures that the Northern Ireland conflict intrudes less in their internal politics.

At one level this stand-off is a zero-sum game: there is a basic contradiction between the state formations aspired to by nationalism and unionism, which means that whatever one achieves, the other loses. There are, however, areas of broad agreement which allow for meaningful negotiations. The most tangible of these is peace itself. Very few people in the Six Counties enjoy the consequences of the war – the insidious, pervasive threat of violence, the restrictions on civil liberties, the war mentalities, the brutalising effects of the militarism, the randomness of sectarian harassment – which affected all parties to the conflict. Despite the much-vaunted prospect of new investment, employment, increased tourism and agreed political structures, the main peace dividend for most ordinary people in the North of Ireland will be peace itself. There is also broad agreement that current arrangements for government in Northern Ireland are unacceptable. Parties of all complexions want to get back to the process of government. There is also agreement around some specific issues like the need for a Bill of Rights to protect basic rights and liberties. There is a case for negotiation and compromise around these common-alties; for example, it might be the case that Unionists wanting a return to local autonomy would be convinced that such a move is only possible if it is accompanied by a commitment to power-sharing.

This said, the aspirations remain formally contradictory. In the zero-sum aspects of the equation, it is the case that *unionists will lose* in any peace settlement – in the same way that white South Africans 'lost' with the ending of apartheid. If the ideal unionist solution is the Northern Ireland statelet pre-1972, then the compromise will fall well short of this. Similarly, it may be possible to guarantee unionist political identity, but it is no longer possible to deny nationalist political identity. It may be possible to guarantee a unionist right to march but it is no longer possible to simultaneously deny a nationalist right to march. It may be possible to promote separate and specific economic and social development in unionist areas but it is no longer possible to simultaneously prevent similar developments in nationalist areas. These issues are at the core of the much discussed notion of 'parity of esteem'.

There needs to be a basic acceptance that the Northern Ireland statelet has been at war for the last 25 years – and in a state of emergency for its entire existence – because there is something deeply wrong with it. There is no point reiterating the old myths about pathological communities. These platitudes suggested that if only the 'terrorists' or 'the men of violence' had disappeared, the conflict would be resolved. This is utter rubbish; Republican and Loyalist political violence was a symptom rather than a cause of *state pathology*. There was something profoundly wrong with the Northern Ireland state 1921–72 – that is why it collapsed. There has been something profoundly wrong with the Northern Ireland statelet under 'Direct Rule' since 1972, this is why it produced such a bitter divisive war. If peace is to be secured, the settlement must seek a state formation that recognises this history and transcends it. If we are to have a Northern Irish polity that encourages peace, it will not look like Stormont and will not look like the current 'Direct Rule' state. These state formations failed to provide any of the necessary conditions for peace – neither justice, nor democracy, nor reconciliation, nor cooperation, nor equality. If this is recognised by all parties, there would be enough common ground and common commitment to bring unionists and nationalists into a process of meaningful negotiation.

It also needs to be said that this political process should not only end the marginalisation of Northern unionists and nationalists. It also offers a unique opportunity to bring different disempowered groups in Ireland from the margins to the centre (Clár na mBan, 1995). It is crucial that civil society in Ireland, North and South, is mobilised to secure the peace. The community and voluntary sectors have a key role to play in this process: to make sure that the 'peace dividend' reaches the grass roots and empowers the most marginalised communities; to make sure that negotiations are genuinely inclusive of all sectors of Irish society; and to ensure that human rights and civil liberties remain central to the agenda and do not end up as a bargaining tool. This is a perfect opportunity for the governments to include all the sectors which have been excluded from the polity.

Indeed, the peace process does not only have implications for the North. The implications of the process for Southern Irish society need to be discussed and celebrated just as much. If there is to be 'peace and reconciliation' in Ireland, this process cannot be restricted to relations between unionists and nationalists in the North or relations between North and South; it must involve everyone on the island. Peace and reconciliation must look at the situations of the marginalised and disempowered in the South as much as the North. It is not enough that Republicans be brought in from the margins of Irish politics: women, working-class communities, Irish speakers, minority ethnic groups including Travellers, lesbians and gays, disabled people and other minorities have to be brought to the centre as well. We need to enter a new phase of *reconstruction*, bringing about profound changes in the nature of the culture, and polity and economy in Ireland, North and South and in Britain. There are four key elements in this reconstruction process, each of which is crucially structured by the colonial legacy.

Demilitarisation

Demilitarisation is the first major task of any decolonisation process. One of the most destructive legacies of the colonial state formation in Ireland was the acceptance of the primacy of violence for almost its entire duration. The British state never attempted to govern Ireland through the expressed will of the people but rather through military conquest and paramilitary repression. The Stormont regime merely replicated this approach in a localised and more overtly sectarian way – although it did at least carry the legitimacy of a formal democratic mandate. Since the collapse of Stormont and the advent of 'Direct Rule', Northern Ireland has been at war. This 'normalisation' of war needs to be reversed, as a precondition of the demilitarisation process (Tomlinson, 1994). The infrastructure of coercion built up by the British state in Northern Ireland has to be dismantled; harassment and intimidation by the state has never been an appropriate response to political disaffection. Repression did not address the causes of Republican or Loyalist violence and it will not secure the peace process. As long as the police and army remain organically linked to 'one side' of the conflict the propensity towards political violence will remain – whatever strategy the political leadership of the nationalist and Loyalist communities choose to follow.

The coercive legacy of colonialism all over the world has proved to be a hostile climate for the promotion and protection of human rights. Much of the struggle over human rights revolves around terms such as security and repression – what is one group's security is often repression for someone else. In Northern Ireland, the level of militarisation is striking: the sheer scale of security measures, the visibility of weaponry, the scope of powers available to the state security apparatus and the normalisation of state harassment (McVeigh, 1994b). These circumstances and the long history of 'special powers' legislation make claims of 'returning to normality' meaningless, if not downright disingenuous. Respect for human rights and the repeal of repressive emergency legislation are central to any proposals for a settlement of the conflict (CAJ, 1995).

In the short term there is an urgent need to remove the British military from the equation. There cannot be any real 'peace' so long as the army remains central to 'policing'. As Murphy (1997) has convincingly argued, the British Army can never play a 'peacekeeping' role in Ireland. Around 12,000 regular British Army soldiers and 7,000 locally recruited Royal Irish Regiment troops remain integral to security policy in the North, 'in support of the civil power'. Removing this continuing role in security policy is a precondition of lasting settlement. No one can accept the desirability of a state so centrally policed by a standing army trained to fight wars, rather than to police a democratic society in a non-violent manner. Alongside this aspect of demilitarisation, there is a clear need for the transformation of the Royal Ulster Constabulary (RUC) – the local paramilitary police force. The RUC is clearly unacceptable in many areas of the North of Ireland (Fisher, 1995). Whether one talks of disbandment or restructuring the RUC, it is clear that a peacetime police service will look nothing like the present force. A plethora of research and documentation has confirmed the serious questions around policing and the criminal justice system. The creation of a police service that is representative, accountable and responsive to communities is one of the fundamental challenges for the peace process. An independent effective complaints system with the law applied equally to officers and civilians is also needed; the legal system should comply with international human rights mechanisms and standards, and human rights training is essential for any new police service. Beyond this, there is also a need to resource aspects of community policing which have developed as a consequence of the failure of the law and order model of policing which obtains north and south of the border (Connolly, 1997). Movement away from violent sanctions like punishment beatings and towards other more appropriate and effective sanctions is an obvious part of this process.

The other major immediate task of demilitarisation is the release of political prisoners. The very notion of there being 'political prisoners' in Ireland is highly contested. One of the key parts of British government criminalisation strategy since the 1970s has been to insist that prisoners convicted for 'terrorist' offences are not political. Many of the most important political leaders in Irish history, however, have spent time in prison – including Wolfe Tone, Daniel O'Connell, Charles Stuart Parnell, William Johnston, Constance Markievicz and Eamon de Valera. Of current party leaders, Ian Paisley, Gerry Adams and Proinsias de Rossa have been interned or imprisoned for 'political offences'. This history of imprisonment means that prisons issues in Ireland have never been reducible to simplistic arguments about crime and punishment. Moreover, both Republican and Loyalist prisoners regard themselves as political prisoners; and there is *de facto* recognition in the criminal justice system that they are different from 'ordinary decent criminals' or ODCs, the term used by the state for 'ordinaries'. The most commonly used method of identifying a political prisoner is whether or not they have been convicted of a 'scheduled offence'. While some prisoners are recognised as politicals for non-scheduled offences (for example

the non-payment of fines by unionists after the Anglo–Irish
Agreement), and some are non-politicals for scheduled offences
(every murder and crime involving the use of firearms is automatically scheduled and has to be de-scheduled if it is to be
recognised as 'non-political'), conviction under scheduled
offences remains the most objective benchmark of political status.
Thus defined, there are approximately 300 Republican prisoners
and 300 Loyalist prisoners in Northern Ireland. There are also
around 100 Republican prisoners in the Republic of Ireland, in
England, and elsewhere in the world.

The ongoing peace process in Ireland has focused attention on
the question of some kind of amnesty or early release for these
prisoners. The key role played by former prisoners in the peace
process makes clear that released prisoners are much more likely
to contribute to the process than undermine it. As Gormally and
McEvoy argue:

> ... the issue of early release for politically motivated prisoners is
> crucial to any peace process which follows a violent political conflict.
> Whatever the particular positions taken up by negotiating parties at
> any given time, we would argue that, until the question of the prisoner
> is agreed then nothing, that will create a final solution, is agreed.
> (1995, p. 43)

There are already a number of precedents for early release.
Official IRA prisoners were released after the Official IRA
declared a ceasefire. Private Thain and Private Clegg (both
British soldiers convicted of murder while on duty in Northern
Ireland) were released back to their regiments after serving only
two and a half years. Loyalist and Republican prisoners have
served far longer sentences for much less serious offences; there
are also numerous miscarriage of justice cases. Despite this, in the
case of Private Clegg, the British government was happy to
release a convicted murderer, not just back into society, but back
into his regiment where he was rewarded with a promotion. In
this context, the early release of other political prisoners seems
only too reasonable.

At the same time, the process of demilitarisation needs to be
monitored; it has to provide mechanisms for a parallel demobil-
ising of Republican and Loyalist paramilitary arsenals. However,
it needs to be recognised that neither Loyalist nor Republican
paramilitary groups are prepared to disarm unilaterally. Whatever
questions this raises about their own commitment to non-violent

strategies, this is the reality of the situation. Loyalist and Republican commitment to peace has to be measured in terms of the discipline both groups have displayed during the ceasefires rather than the continued existence of substantial arsenals. Further decommissioning is necessary but it is only possible in the context of the wider process of demilitarisation. While the existence of huge paramilitary arsenals is a problem, this is far less important than the question of whether they are being used or not. Demilitarisation will be a multilateral process requiring discipline and concessions on all sides – paramilitary demilitarisation will not occur without a concomitant demilitarisation on behalf of the British state.

Democratisation

The process of democratisation is also vital to any settlement of colonial conflicts. Again, the colonial legacy in Ireland militates against this since the process of British colonialism was characterised by the absence of democracy. There is a pressing need for structures which facilitate dialogue between nationalists and unionists, and between North and South. There are particular problems in terms of the democratic deficit in Northern Ireland. Nobody should be satisfied with the current situation of 'administrative colonialism' under direct rule, which means that no one from the North of Ireland – nationalist or unionist – plays a meaningful role in their own government. It is ironic that 'Direct Rule' – imposed as it was against the wishes of unionists – made the Northern Ireland statelet even less democratic than it had been under the Stormont regime. Local councils have been left with the job of 'collecting the rubbish and burying the dead'; all other public sector functions are controlled by British government ministers. None of these is elected in Northern Ireland, and often they have not been elected at all, since they come from the British House of Lords. It is striking that there was – rightly – much discussion of a 'constitutional crisis' in Scotland when popular support there for the ruling British Conservative Party had fallen to around 25 per cent. It was rarely pointed out, however, that the Conservatives had next to zero support in Northern Ireland – in the Forum election of 1997 the Conservative Party received 0.48 per cent of the vote. This only hints at the scale of the 'democratic deficit'. There clearly needs to be more democratic control over the management of the Northern Irish polity; we also need to find ways

of decentralising power in Ireland, North and South and introducing the principle of local democracy into every level of
government and public service.

It bears emphasis that this process cannot simply involve
democratisation of the Northern Ireland state, as an 'internal
solution'. The Stormont government used formal democracy to
underpin an overtly and unapologetically sectarian state. In 1920
Northern Ireland was simply the largest land mass that could be
created with a safe unionist majority. Democratisation must
deconstruct the Northern Ireland state, and this involves
acknowledgement that the state boundaries themselves had no
democratic legitimacy. Democratisation is not simply about
making structures in the Six Counties more democratic, but also
about recognising the anti-democratic nature of the Northern
Ireland statelet.

We have recently seen South Africa leapfrog Western democracies as it develops sophisticated mechanisms to protect
minority rights and maximise access to power for the marginalised. This has transformed the country from a racist colonial
formation to an advanced democracy over a relatively short
period of time. There is now at least the possibility of the North
of Ireland developing in a similar fashion. We might see a
sectarian colonial formation transformed into an example of
twenty-first century democracy. Such a settlement could provide
a model of good practice for Britain and the rest of the European
Union. This could redefine difference in Ireland as a creative and
positive force rather than a cause of perpetual conflict and
violence. We might also see the development of a constitutional
infrastructure for peace, involving a constructive, inclusive
dialectic between a decentralised formal democracy and an
entrenched Bill of Rights, capable of protecting the rights and
identity of every minority and majority group in Ireland.

Economic Integration and Development

There will be limited peace and reconciliation without serious
attention to economic justice. If peace is to be organically rooted,
the settlement must begin to dismantle the colonial distortions
inherent in the Irish economy. At base this requires analysis of the
location and role of Ireland within the world economy with the
aim of what Denis O'Hearn has called 'breaking the cycle of
dependence':

> A basic logic of the world economy, and a basic aim of its leading states and institutions, is to remove options from the non-industrial and semi-industrial regions, just as a basic logic of capitalism is to remove options from working people. For countries, the only alternative *at this time* to participating in the world trading system is widespread poverty and isolation. Some small and poor countries, Ireland among them, have even found it impossible to remain outside of emerging trade blocs like the European Union or the North American Free Trade Agreement. ... Breaking the cycle of dependence will be difficult. Strategically placed countries like Ireland and the rest of the EU periphery must take the lead. (O'Hearn, 1994, pp. 60 and 61, original emphasis)

The immediate economic challenge for the peace process, however, is the transformation of the Northern Ireland statelet from a war economy. The conflict has become an integral part of the economy of the North and is responsible for employing, directly and indirectly, as much as one-quarter of the full-time workforce. Productive employment has to be found for workers in the security industry – RUC, RIR, prison officers and so on. Equally, Republican and Loyalist volunteers, prisoners and ex-prisoners have to be reintegrated into the peacetime economy. Alongside this, more vigorous action has to be taken to address institutionalised sectarian discrimination in the North. Of course, existing nationalist disadvantage should not be corrected by 'equality of misery' with proportionate levels of unemployment and disadvantage on either side of the sectarian divide. If peace is to be entrenched there is a need for sustained economic growth and an end to mass unemployment for both unionists and nationalists.

There are, however, profound structural problems for the Irish economy and these need to be addressed as part of the peace process. Current optimism about the prospects of the Northern and Southern economies should not obscure the potentially devastating effects of Ireland's integration into the Single European Market. While these effects may be partially offset by short-term transfers from the EU, the long-term prospects for further transfers are poor, especially with the proposed enlargement of the EU to the East. Among the negative effects of economic integration may be a further reduction in the coherence of the Northern and Southern economies, a widening gap between the multinational sector and the indigenous sector and the relative diminution of links between North and South, and between various localities now linked separately to the European system and the international economic system. To counteract these impacts, moves have been already made, with the support of business organisations, to create an integrated all-Ireland economy. This integration, however, should be much more thoroughgoing and strategically oriented than is currently envisaged. It must also be recognised that integrating businesses and business elites is not the same as integrating the mass of the population in a common economy. In particular, it is necessary to involve those who have been excluded from beneficial participation in the economy, the unemployed, the low-paid, women and those living in particularly disadvantaged areas (see Chapter 4).

One of the greatest barriers to economic integration is the existence of two state structures on the island, each with its own economic, administrative and political agendas (Mansergh, 1995). These agendas often conflict without regard to the interests of Northern Ireland and the border counties of the Irish Republic. European integration as such will not cause the border to disappear – indeed the practice of the EU in channelling money through both centralised state institutions often exacerbates the problems of cross-border coordination and integration. Perhaps even more important is the state dependency of both economies. Both states are major economic actors in their own right, North and South, hence much of the onus of economic integration must rest on them. The Northern economy in particular is heavily dependent on the subvention from Westminster. While this underpins the standard of living in the short run, in the long run it has distorted the economy and has not prevented the collapse of the productive base in the North.

There is a clear need for specific economic intervention in the Irish border region. Liam O'Dowd has argued that new arrangements for the border area must be part of any overall settlement of the conflict in Ireland (1994). The Irish 'border' was never intended as an international boundary. Over a period of 70 years it has developed many of the characteristics of such, in ways which have compounded its historical legacy of coercion and exclusion. It is clear that European economic integration and intergovernmental cooperation as such will not cause the border to wither away. Instead, the tensions around the Irish border region demonstrate the problematic relationships which exist between state sovereignty, democracy and economic integration. These relationships need to be addressed and revised as part of any democratic negotiation and compromise. A Border

Development Commission, for instance, could be a step in this direction while helping to transform the region from a buffer zone to a bridge between both parts of Ireland.

A new look must be taken at the way in which politics and economics intersect. To pretend that the economy in Ireland has an existence of its own distinct from the administrative and political institutions of both states is sheer nonsense. This being the case, much more attention needs to be paid to the institutional framework for economic development. This is in line with wider thinking in economics generally, where it is increasingly recognised that governance structures impact significantly on economic performance.

Reconciliation

One of the most repugnant legacies of colonialism has been the survival of divisions and hatreds born out of the colonial process, and sustained under neo-colonialism. The longevity of racism rooted in colonialism – whether in South Africa, North America or Australia – illustrates the intractability of hatred created at the colonial nexus. Ireland is no different – we find racism, sectarianism and bigotry rooted in dispossession and expropriation, triumphalism and inequality, fear and anger produced by colonial history. The need for genuine reconciliation is transparent. The process of reconciliation is less dependent upon apportioning blame for different 'atrocities' than facilitating some kind of 'healing' on all sides which allows people to come to terms with the consequences of violence over the past 25 years. There needs to be a debate around the question of a general amnesty for all participants to the military conflict – state and non-state alike. Discussion and dialogue between different communities needs to be facilitated, and it is imperative that the North/South dimension of the process is not forgotten.

However, the 'right to truth' remains paramount; this is a fundamental requirement of reconciliation. To this end some method must be found to allow public discussion of human rights and humanitarian rights abuses by all sides to the conflict over the past 25 years. Support has emerged for the creation of a Truth Commission along the lines of South Africa's Truth and Reconciliation Commission or the Truth Commission in El Salvador. This would seek to establish the truth about deaths and incidents of violence perpetrated by all parties to the conflict –

Republicans, Loyalists and state forces. For example, if survivors and relatives wished, such a commission could address the 'Kingsmills massacre' (Republican), 'Bloody Sunday' (British Army) and the Dublin/Monaghan bombings (Loyalist/British intelligence).

Alongside this, there should be a formal apology to the Irish people from the British state. We have already seen expressions of remorse and apology from both Republicans and Loyalists. While building the future is more important than allocating blame for the past, it would be symbolically important if Britain were to acknowledge its own culpability for past conflicts and present divisions. This is not just about accepting that the state committed different atrocities over the past 26 years but also recognising the longer-term damage that was committed over the duration of the British colonial project in Ireland. This should also involve recognition of the damaging legacy of anti-Irish racism associated with British involvement in Ireland (Curtis, 1991). Indeed, if there were to be an epigrammatic explanation of why the peace process went into crisis, the most appropriate answer would be anti-Irish racism. The Conservative British government found it difficult to work on an equal basis with its Irish counterparts, and at some key stages resisted 'Irish interference' in 'British affairs'. This appeal to British nationalism carried a thinly disguised racist contempt; perhaps it is too much to ask that the English establishment transcend 800 years of anti-Irish propaganda, but at least it should aspire to a situation in which this no longer drives its policy towards Ireland.

Reconciliation will also involve a much more active approach to anti-sectarianism. Within this, there is the crucial importance of recognising inequality and disadvantage as part of sectarianism. This confirms the necessity of anti-sectarianism addressing structural as well as individual dysfunction. In particular, it confirms the central role of the state in producing and reproducing sectarian division. In the past, state-led anti-sectarianism has focused on the notion that 'one side is as bad as the other', and has quite deliberately failed to address the role of the Northern Ireland state in reproducing sectarianism. Anti-sectarianism has to get beyond blaming individual Protestants and Catholics. People who are disadvantaged by sectarianism do not need the 'non-sectarian' holidays which have become the defining feature of anti-sectarian intervention. Rather, they need equal and fair institutions and equality in every aspect of their lives – before the law, in the policing service, in employment, in housing, in education and in access to other goods and services. The project of addressing sectarianism needs to move away from endless agonising about 'community relations' and 'cultural traditions' and get down to the harder job of engaging with a state formation which is *the* key problem in terms of the reproduction of sectarianism in Northern Ireland (McVeigh, 1997).

There is also a specifically North/South dimension to the process of reconciliation. One of the most damaging legacies of partition is the diminution of links between communities in the North and South of Ireland. This has led to mutual antipathy, distrust and ignorance; not only between unionist and nationalist politicians, but also between ordinary people in both parts of the country. There is a need to raise consciousness in the North and South about the realities of life in the 'other' part of Ireland. Groups working on issues such as unemployment, human rights and 'Majority World' solidarity have a lot to learn from their counterparts across the border. Closer involvement North and South is central to healthy cultural, economic and political development over the whole island. Many of the problems are very similar and learning from each other can only be helpful; indeed, many of the problems are linked and cannot be tackled in isolation.

Resources should be made available for North/South work – especially cross-border networking between grassroots organisations such as community groups, local development initiatives and women's groups. There needs to be resourcing of skills training, the provision of information and the sustaining of cross-border linkages. These 'people to people' linkages are far less costly than huge flagship or infrastructure projects and may show much greater returns in generating new ideas, promoting reconciliation and encouraging genuine participative development.

This point links to a broader principle in terms of community reconstruction and development. The conflict in the North has produced organised and politicised working-class communities – especially in Republican areas. In reality these communities are far removed from the popular external stereotypes of urban blight and hopelessness and despair. The *Clár Nua* initiative in West Belfast was one example of the enormous potential of grassroots community organisations to contribute towards reconstruction (Clár Nua, 1995). *Clár Nua* was a community-based blueprint for change which developed detailed strategies for reconstruction across a range of issues: human rights, the natural environment, economic regeneration, education, housing, mental heath, women's policy, Irish language, cultural policy and child and youth policy. Most marginalised communities in Ireland, North and South, are capable of developing similar plans. They do not need the imposition of 'community development' or 'enterprise' cultures. Often these communities do not even require outside experts – whether in community development or reconciliation or mediation or business – they need the power and resources to transform their situations using a commitment and ability which is already in place.

Coda

Creating a genuine and lasting peace in Ireland will be a long and difficult process. Given that British/Irish relations have been defined at the colonial nexus for over 800 years, decolonisation will not be achieved overnight. As in South Africa and Palestine, the legacy of colonialism will not be eradicated by the end of war, or even with a political agreement. The legacies of British colonialism in Ireland – the acceptance of violence and militarism as appropriate political strategies, the pervasiveness of sectarianism and anti-Irish racism, the dependency of the Irish economy – will characterise all the parties to the British/Irish conflict for years to come.

It has to be said that the current process looks very little like a decolonisation process. Even if the political negotiations succeed, it is already clear that the most radical settlement they will come up with is some less overtly sectarian version of the Six County statelet, with the addition of some North/South executive powers. To draw on the international analogies, the post-settlement Six Counties will look much more like the present Palestinian Authority than post-apartheid South Africa. In other words *it will continue to be a colonial rather than a post-colonial social formation.* Whatever people might wish to the contrary, the remorseless logic of such a settlement is that it carries with it the seeds of future conflict and division.

This assessment is both pessimistic and realistic – it repudiates some of the false hope that was generated around the 'wouldn't it be great if it was like this all the time' idea of 'peace', which was completely abstracted from any sense of structure or agreement. In this context it is more important than ever to point to certain necessary conditions for lasting peace, emphasising that these are different from the necessary conditions for decolonisation. Without these conditions, even the limited goal of peace will be impossible.

First, there has to be a firm break with the past. It needs to be accepted that the settlement of 1921 and the 'temporary solution' of 'Direct Rule' were one-sided, anti-democratic and coercive. If there is to be a settlement, it will be a new form of inclusive democracy, not a return to the coercive formal democracy of 'majority rule' – for either Ulster unionists or Irish nationalists.

Second, there cannot be an 'internal' British settlement. North–South institutions, dialogue and exchange in Ireland are vital. While there *may* be a need for a continuing British dimension to the process, there cannot but be an increasing Irish dimension.

Third, there must be a transformation of the apparatus of repression. If the security forces in Northern Ireland continue to be constituted and act in a way that is both anti-democratic and nakedly partisan, a return to political violence is inevitable.

Fourth, there has to be a swift ending to the 'administrative colonialism' of Direct Rule. There is an urgent need to move the management of the Northern Irish polity towards democratic control involving all sections of the community. The democratic deficit in the Six Counties is just as critical as it was before the ceasefires and the reasons for the absence of democracy are even less plausible.

Finally, there is a need for urgency. The British government has dragged its heels through most of the peace process, content to repeat the mantra that, 'the peace process continues as long as no one returns to violence'. That was a dangerous nonsense. The peace process will continue as long as it appears to be leading somewhere. This is precisely because it is a *process* not an end-state – Northern Ireland is not yet 'at peace', but has been moving – agonisingly slowly – towards peace. It is crucial that that sense of movement be maintained.

If these conditions are met, there is a genuine prospect of lasting peace. It bears emphasis, however, that this will not lay to rest the importance of Ireland's colonial inheritance. Lasting peace would create the proper context within which to *begin* to excise the violent and debilitating legacy of British colonialism in Ireland. Until the rhetoric of 'peace' is turned into meaningful structures and agreements, however, there is always the threat of a return to the primacy of violence and repression on all sides of the British/Irish conflict. If present opportunities are tragically missed, it will be a direct consequence of the inability of the British state to come to terms with its own destructive colonial inheritance.

3   The Two Irish Economies: Dependencies Compared

Denis O'Hearn

Critical approaches to economic change usually consider dependence to be a bad thing, denoting the absence of self-sustained and articulated development. Yet there are clearly different forms of dependency. Semiperipheral zones that depend on investments from leading industrial corporations, for instance, are likely to be materially better off than peripheral regions that depend on incomes from tropical monoculture exports. This distinction is behind the half-true adage that the problem of 'Third World' countries is not that imperialists exploit them, but that imperialists do not exploit them *enough*.

The question also arises as to whether different kinds of dependency among semiperipheral regions that host foreign *industrial* investments also make a difference. Two such regional economies, in the North and South of Ireland, are likely to remain dependent on foreign capital and investments for some time to come. Thus, it is useful to ask whether there are significant differences in their respective forms of dependency and, if so, whether these differences give one region significant developmental advantages over the other.

Among regions that depend on inward industrial investments it may matter whether a region depends mainly on leading-sector capitals from economically ascendant or hegemonic regions, or whether its investments are primarily by firms from descending former hegemons. Cumings (1987) and others, for instance, have argued that the East Asian 'tigers' drew advantages from their specific form of dependence on capitals from an ascending hegemonic competitor, Japan. Unlike, for example, dependent countries in Latin America, South Korean and Taiwanese industrial sectors benefited from Japanese firms which established subcontracting rather than direct investment arrangements abroad. Such subcontracting arrangements allowed the South

Korean and Taiwanese states to induce greater indigenous capital investment, including participation in more capital-intensive and technology-intensive sectors for export, than was the case in regions dominated by US direct investments.

A similar comparison can be made between regions that depend on industrial investments by firms from ascendant or hegemonic powers, on the one hand, and declining former hegemons, on the other. In this century, especially after the Second World War, this distinction applied to regions that depended on investments from the United States as opposed to Britain. After Partition, and especially since the 1960s, the two parts of Ireland were distinguished economically by the degree to which the South came to depend on industrial investments from the United States while the North continued its dependence on Britain. Thus, a comparative question about the two Irish economies, which has obvious relevance for the question of whether a single all-Ireland economy is preferable to a partitioned one, is whether it is better to be dependent on a 'winner' like the US or a 'loser' like Britain. I will address this question in two parts: first, a comparative historical analysis of Southern and Northern Irish dependent development and, second, an analysis of the relationship between Northern economic decline and the 'union' with Britain.[1]

Historical Development, South and North

Although historians have focused on the rural consequences of seventeenth-century British land confiscations and the penal laws, Ireland's indigenous merchant class was as much a casualty. The failure of several early attempts at leading-sector industrialisation mainly by new English settlers, for reasons that are historically disputed, ensured that most of the island would remain a peripheral agrarian economy. This economy was highly dependent on food exports to England, produced under agrarian productive relations which were increasingly incompatible with the island's relatively high population density on the land. Depopulation and concentration of land tenure were major themes of nineteenth-century rural Ireland.

Yet, although Britain peripheralised most of Ireland as it achieved global hegemony, it appeared to give the north-east region an economic lift relative to the rest of the island. Following on from the Act of Union in 1800, the concentration of industry around Belfast was the other side of deindustrialisation elsewhere on the island. While deindustrialisation and famine left most of the island, including much of Ulster, depopulated, impoverished,[2] dependent on pastoral agriculture, and largely without a proletariat, the Belfast region developed a relatively concentrated industrial economy based on linen and shipbuilding.

A similar situation has been discussed by Wallerstein (1980), in a debate with Smout (1980) over Scottish development. Wallerstein concedes that some 'development by invitation' occurred in the Scottish lowlands despite its dependence on England, but he adds that such development was unstable and tenuous in the long term because it lacked internal momentum. Moreover, this development was regionally limited, so that the Scottish Highlands remained relatively impoverished.

The economy of north-eastern Ireland before Partition was never developed to the extent of Scotland's. Its industry remained highly concentrated in a few relatively stagnant sectors led by linen, and its settler elite was not as capitalistically advanced as Scotland's native elite, much less British capital. In general, its rates of technical change, wages, profit and economic expansion lagged far behind the industrial regions of Scotland or England. Its leading industries depended on imports of older technologies from the English industrial core, rather than developing their own linked capital goods sectors; and these leading sectors had low rates of innovation in their organisation of production and distribution (see O'Hearn, 1997).

Essentially, then, the conventional view that north-eastern Ireland was simply an outlying industrial region of Britain is mistaken. It was not a 'core' economy in any sense, but rather a semiperipheral region within a larger peripheral zone, with a very narrow industrial base that was strongly dependent on a single core market which also supplied many of its necessary productive inputs. This left it especially vulnerable to short-term and long-term downswings in the British economy. Much of Ulster, like the rest of Ireland, was a peripheral hinterland that depended entirely on exports to Britain, and on subsistence agriculture. As in many peripheral zones (e.g. Sao Paulo and rural Brazil, Kingston and rural Jamaica), Irish rural and urban regions were integrated by transport networks which facilitated foreign trade through coastal entrepôts, by shared labour markets, and by rural supply of urban demand.[3]

After Partition in 1921, the South of Ireland became politically independent but was still economically dependent on cattle exports to England. Its successive governments tried to overcome this dependence, first through import-substitution industrialisation (ISI) and then through export-oriented industrialisation (EOI). By the time the South embarked on EOI in the 1950s, it had already partially delinked its industrial economy from Britain's, although its agrarian exports were still highly dependent on the English market. EOI shifted its economic dependence from England to US capital, on which it depended for inward investments, exports and economic growth. The South of Ireland, then, essentially transferred its dependence from the prior nineteenth-century hegemon and now rapidly declining Britain, to the new postwar hegemon, the United States.

Although the North was more industrialised and materially better off than the South at Partition, it remained both politically and economically dependent on Britain under the 1920 Government of Ireland Act, as under the Act of Union. The Northern economy remained subservient to British economic interests and highly concentrated in agriculture, linen and shipbuilding. Its industry was semiperipheral: generally lower-wage and 'lower-tech' than the industries of England or even Scotland, with severely constrained markets for its products and fewer linkages among its industrial sectors, which created less impulse to reinvest profits in a self-expanding regional economy. Although linen is usually considered the region's 'leading sector', it was hardly in the same league as core leading sectors like cotton, engineering or cars. Ireland produced less linen in physical terms in 1900 than in 1830, even though the later period is considered to be the North's industrial 'heyday'. Belfast grew mainly because rural industry concentrated in the north-east, rather than because of any general expansion of the Ulster regional economy (O'Hearn, 1998). The narrowly-based Northern economy was thus precipitously vulnerable to collapse. Unlike the South, its independent policy making powers were far too limited for it to embark on alternative economic strategies in the face of crisis.

The North's long-term decline began with the end of British hegemony and its associated loss of commercial and industrial dominance in the early twentieth century. As England lost its competitive edge to later industrialisers like the United States and Germany, it also lost naval and trade supremacy, which was practically wiped out in two world wars. The demise of the British maritime economy was particularly disastrous for the narrowly-based economy of north-eastern Ireland. The linen industry, which had already stagnated (even though it concentrated) in the nineteenth century, declined rapidly with the introduction of synthetic fibres and the consequent collapse in demand for natural fibres in the 1950s. These events are analysed elsewhere (Isles and Cuthbert, 1957; Rowthorn and Wayne, 1988), so there is little need to restate them here except in broad outline.

The 1930s depression had hit the North extremely hard. Whereas British unemployment was 7.5 per cent in 1940, the North's unemployment stood at 20 per cent. Northern social services were far below British standards, infant mortality was 150 per cent higher than in Britain, per capita income was half the British average, and overcrowding was several times higher (Rowthorn and Wayne, 1988). A short wartime boom provided only temporary relief to the region's structural economic disadvantages.

By the 1950s and 1960s, a new set of differences between the Southern and Northern economies was emerging, in terms both of economic policy and performance. The Southern economy, responding to global pressures, had introduced an advanced package of policies to attract foreign capital by 1956 (O'Hearn, 1990). US investors were already beginning to dominate the industrial economy by the 1960s. They concentrated in the metals/engineering and chemical sectors, a pattern which intensified in the 1970s with the entry of a new wave of electronics, computer and pharmaceuticals firms. Although the Southern economy was severely weakened when free trade nearly decimated its indigenous manufacturing industries after Ireland joined the European Community (EC) in 1973, job losses in manufacturing were moderated because employment lost in failed Irish firms was partly replaced by new employment in transnational subsidiaries.

Economic change in the North was very different. Following the Southern example, Northern governments regularly asked Westminster to give them the power to introduce similar programmes to attract foreign capital, particularly tax breaks and grants. The British government refused many of these requests. The programmes that were allowed were introduced more slowly and less completely than in the South. Although the 1945 Industries Development Act (Northern Ireland) preceded Southern measures, the latter were far more comprehensive once they were introduced in the 1950s. The North's 1954 Capital Grants for Industry Act and subsequent measures provided lower rates of grant assistance to incoming investors than were available under Southern legislation. In addition, Northern policy makers periodically feared that the British government might let the grants programmes lapse, whereas Southern grants programmes were more clearly stable because they were sponsored by a committed Irish state rather than by a lukewarm distant government in London. This stability was reinforced by the creation of special semi-state bodies in the South to attract industries and administer grants: the Industrial Development Authority (IDA) was established in 1949 and An Foras Tionscail (the grants board) in 1959. In the North, on the other hand, no such specialised bodies were set up until the Industrial Development Board (IDB) in 1982. Until then, responsibilities for attracting and administering foreign investments were shared between the Department of Commerce and various agencies such as the Northern Ireland Finance Corporation (established in 1972) and the Northern Ireland Development Agency (established in 1976).

Moreover, British governments from the 1950s preferred to bring the largest investments to underdeveloped 'grey spots' in England or Wales, rather than to the North of Ireland. They bluntly informed Northern politicians and bureaucrats that England had its own deindustrialised regions and that it could not allow the North special status beyond these regions. The Northern Ministry (later Department) of Commerce was up against British ministers and bureaucrats, in departments such as the Board of Trade, who felt that while 'there is political kudos to be gained for getting a new industry into a "grey" spot on their list; there is none if it goes to Northern Ireland'.[4] For these reasons, Northern bodies were never able to compete fully with the Southern IDA in attracting inward investments, especially from the United States, nor could they compete with English regions for the largest and most important inward investment projects, even before the 'Troubles' restarted in the 1960s.

Once its degree of deindustrialisation became intolerable in the 1970s, the North was allowed to extend larger grants to foreign investors with fewer strings attached than in British regions.[5] Yet this was not sufficient to overcome its earlier disadvantages relative to the South. This was partly because other inducements besides grants were necessary to attract investors. In the 1990s, for example, Northern policy makers, business people and politicians still complained with some force that sharing Britain's 40 per cent corporate tax rate put the region at an insurmountable disadvantage to the South (which maintains a 10 per cent tax rate). On the other hand, foreign investors are attracted to the South not just by economic incentives but by a whole package of

economic and political support which has been consistently forthcoming from the 1950s. Once investors began to agglomerate in
the South, as in other regions of the semiperiphery such as
Singapore, more followed in their wake.

Instead of attracting US companies concentrated in leading
sectors such as computers and pharmaceuticals, the North in the
1950s and 1960s attracted mainly English companies in synthetic
textiles and other basic industrial products. The synthetic textiles
industry in the North was dominated by three English firms:
Cortaulds, ICI and British Enkalon. Employment in the sector
grew rapidly, from under 1,500 throughout most of the 1950s to
more than 9,000 in 1973, or 7 per cent of the Northern manufacturing workforce (NIEC, 1983, p. 38). Producing in the North
of Ireland was an adaptive response of wage-saving and grant-
seeking for these declining firms from a faded hegemonic
economy. It allowed some of them to maintain competitiveness
and profitability for a few years, against the general trend in
textiles and other basic sectors of moving production to the
periphery (the so-called 'new international division of labour'
described by Frobel et al., 1980). Once the oil crises raised the
cost of producing synthetic fibres, however, British firms in the
North were unable to compete and either moved to lower-cost
regions such as East and South-east Asia or failed altogether.
Between 1974 and 1982, when electronics investments were
booming in the South, nearly 8,000 jobs were lost in the Northern
synthetic textiles sector.[6]

As war made the North an unattractive site for non-British
foreign investments (not just a less competitive site), English
investments dried up, existing English subsidiaries failed, and
competition for non-British investments increased from the South
of Ireland, Scotland, Wales and England. At the state level,
government legitimacy depended on economic growth and job
creation, which in turn came to depend more and more on the
attraction of transnational corporate investments. Within states,
specific industrial development agencies amassed power and
resources according to their respective abilities to attract foreign
projects. Thus, competition over foreign investments was not
simply between the North and South of Ireland and other states,
but also between the specific agencies or departments in each
state that were responsible for attracting investments.

After the oil crises, the formerly hegemonic British industrial
economy declined so thoroughly that British governments
stepped up their efforts to attract offshore investments to the

English core. Such competition intensified throughout the European periphery in the 1980s, and even in parts of the European core, such as France. By the 1990s, Britain attracted 40 per cent of inward manufacturing investments into the European Union. But these projects were located predominantly in England, where Japanese companies in particular combined their preference for English-speaking workers with access to pan-EU markets and highly developed infrastructures that facilitated greater flexibility, subcontracting relations and 'just-in-time' production methods. Scotland and Wales received a share of foreign investments, but mainly competed with the South of Ireland and other parts of the European periphery for the export-platform type of investment.

Although many analysts and Northern politicians have blamed the war for deindustrialisation, other factors were primarily responsible. Even before the outbreak of war, there was a clear difference between the Northern and Southern patterns of investment attraction, which was related to their different patterns of dependence. During 1966–71, for instance, 51 foreign manufacturers opened plants in the North: 41 were British while only 10 were from elsewhere, employing 2,700 (Rowthorn, 1981, p. 9). During the same period, 94 non-British foreign firms opened in the South, employing 10,878 in 1971.

The degree to which factors other than the 'Troubles' were responsible for the downturn in new foreign investments in the North (even as they were booming in the South) is demonstrated by the timing of the downturn, which had already begun in the mid-1960s. The statistical technique of a running median, which identifies turning points in variables, shows that jobs 'promoted' in new foreign investments in the North began falling in 1963 (job 'promotions' are the numbers of jobs that are promised by incoming firms; they actually create only a fraction of these promised jobs). The most successful single year for attracting new foreign investments was 1961, when 5,811 jobs were promised in new foreign projects, though only about one-third of these jobs actually materialised (NIEC, 1983). Thus, less than 2,000 real jobs were brought to the North by non-British foreign companies in 1961, and after that time the numbers fell rapidly, to less than 150 jobs per year in the mid-1970s. While these numbers probably would not have fallen as far in the absence of conflict, it is also clearly true that factors other than war were primarily responsible for the North's inability to attract new foreign investments. The most important of these were its structural dependence on British investments and its political subservience to British policy makers, which tied the Northern economy to a source of manufacturing investments that was in rapid decline, while preventing it from attracting more expansive non-British firms.

The different experiences of the two Irish economies in attracting new investments are summarised in Figure 3.1. The North either attracted, or already had, a few relatively large foreign investments in the 1950s and 1960s, and actually had more employees in such firms than the South until 1970. Yet these investments were concentrated in a few basic textile and chemical projects, rather than in high-tech leading sectors. Furthermore, employment in non-British foreign subsidiaries in the South increased at twice the rate of the North during the 1960s. In the 1970s, foreign investments in the North practically stopped and disinvestments began to rise. At the same time, US companies began entering the South in large numbers in order to gain duty-free access to the European Common Market. The combination of British disinvestments (due to postwar decline and the 1970s oil crises) and insufficient new foreign investments (due to the lack of independent attraction policies and the disincentive of war) produced the opposite result, rapid industrial decline, in the North.

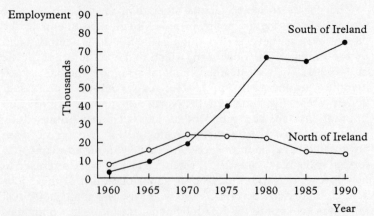

Figure 3.1 Employment in non-British TNC subsidiaries in Ireland, 1960–90

Source: Author's calculations from O'Hearn (1998), IDA employment surveys, NIEC (1983), Hamilton (1992).

Moreover, the North never attracted as *many* new foreign investment projects (in absolute *or* per capita terms) as the South, even in the 1950s and 1960s – just a few large investments. Although the North still reportedly had more jobs in US-owned subsidiaries than the South in 1973, it had attracted only a third as many subsidiaries. Ninety US subsidiaries employed an average of 145 people each in the South, while just 31 US subsidiaries in the North employed 559 people apiece. Thus, a culture of inward investment was never established that could attract greater numbers of 'followers'. In the South, such a culture of large numbers of incoming foreign firms, even if they were smaller firms on average, was partly the result of very effective public relations work by the Southern IDA, which quickly became one of the most successful agencies of its kind in the world.

This was especially important during the 1970s, when foreign investments into the South surged ahead of the North, and in the 1990s, when US firms attempted to rationalise their foreign operations by agglomerating them in fewer regions. During both of these periods, large numbers of firms agglomerated in the South of Ireland instead of in competing regions, including the North. US computer and pharmaceutical firms flooded into the South, where low taxes and a 'hands-off' state enabled them to amass huge profits through transfer pricing and other forms of creative accounting.

Meanwhile, the North's share of inward manufacturing investments into the 'United Kingdom', which was only 4 per cent in the early 1970s, fell below 2 per cent by the 1990s.[7] This combination of British economic withdrawal and few new investments created full-scale deindustrialisation in the North. As Figure 3.2 shows, manufacturing employment just about halved between 1955 and 1985, falling yet further in the 1990s. Its rapid decline from the 1970s cannot simply be attributed to the war because it so closely follows the British pattern, although more severely and from a lower employment base. While Southern Irish manufacturing employment became less stable and then declined in the 1980s and 1990s, the decline was less severe than in the North because US electronics and chemicals firms still had the potential to make periodic bursts of new investments, even if they were insufficient to maintain Southern employment levels.

As a result of these different experiences of inward investment, the Northern and Southern industrial economies were distinctively different by 1990. In that year, in the South, 629 non-British transnational companies employed 73,800 people. In the North, only 86 such subsidiaries employed just 17,826 people

(Hamilton, 1992, pp. 39–40). The structure of these investments reveals a further disadvantage for the North, as foreign activities are concentrated in traditional rather than leading sectors. In the South, just 27 per cent of foreign employment was in the more traditional food, clothing and textiles sectors, while 58 per cent (and rising) was in metals, engineering and chemicals. The Northern structure was the opposite: 51 per cent in food, clothing or textiles and only 34 per cent in metals, engineering or chemicals. Both economies, however, shared certain characteristic features of semiperipheral regions, including an increasing concentration of female employment and, along with this, increasing part-time and contract labour.

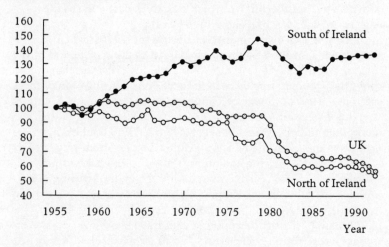

Figure 3.2   Index of manufacturing employment, Ireland and Britain, 1955–93 (1955=100)

Sources: Statistical Abstract of Ireland (various years), Employment Gazette (October 1994), ILO.

In the 1990s, as Southern Irish industrial activity became more and more concentrated in US leading sector projects, the differences between the North and South increased. The North competed for investments by extending larger grant packages than other regions. But without other structural features that would attract high-quality foreign investors, grants had little impact and in fact had negative consequences as they attracted the dregs of international capital that could only compete as large grantees. Many of these fled the North once their grants were used up or, in other cases, continue bleeding the IDB dry in an ongoing reverse-dependency relationship where the firm is more dependent on the state than vice versa. One example of such questionable investments was the DeLorean car fiasco of the early 1980s. In the mid-1990s, the IDB attempted to characterise a few East Asian projects as an 'influx' of 'high-tech' foreign investments in the wake of the short-lived IRA ceasefire. But these investments were neither an influx nor very high tech. The largest project, was to be by the Taiwanese Hualon textiles conglomerate. This had reportedly been rejected by the Southern IDA after their delegation to Taiwan failed to meet the company's executive director because he was in jail under suspicion of fraud.[8] Another investment, announced with fanfare as a 'high-tech electronics' project in the wake of the 1994 IRA ceasefire, actually made plastic cases for compact disks – it closed in 1996. A final 'high-tech' East Asian project makes plastic nozzles for water hoses.

Meanwhile, exports by Southern-based US computer and pharmaceutical subsidiaries boomed in the 1990s, creating relatively rapid rates of growth in gross domestic product that led some to exaggeratedly label the South as a 'Celtic tiger'.[9] Despite large British subsidies of Northern state spending, which kept economic activity artificially high, Southern output surpassed the North in the late 1980s. In late 1996, research by the British House of Commons predicted that Southern Irish per capita GDP would exceed British per capita GDP by the year 2000.[10]

Economic Decline and the Union

Even more than the South of Ireland, dependency has increased certain similarities between the Northern Irish economy and semiperipheral regions of the southern hemisphere. Manufacturing has fallen to 18 per cent of Northern employment, while services have swelled to 74 per cent. There is chronic unemployment and underemployment – the first partly disguised by a sectarian segmented labour market where Catholic men are consistently unemployed at two and a half times the rates of Protestant men; the second disguised by the rising proportion of women employees who, in the 1990s, made up nearly 60 per cent of the employed labour force but half of whom worked part time. Like the South, the North has a huge informal sector and, also like the South, large outflows of emigrants.

Unlike people in most non-European semiperipheral regions, however, the Northern Irish have been protected from the worst effects of economic decline by social welfare and employment programmes which are subsidised by the British exchequer. Since British social welfare programmes were extended to the North in 1945, London has subsidised a large and increasing proportion of state expenditures there. This fiscal subvention stood at more than four billion pounds (excluding most military costs) in the mid-1990s, funding half of Northern state expenditure and enabling the state to keep the standard of living relatively close to British levels. Under Thatcher, however, these British levels crumbled so rapidly that the Southern standard of living began to catch up with the North, and by the 1990s to exceed it in many respects (Goodman, 1996, pp. 162–5).

The North's dependence on the British subvention, on government sponsored jobs and on welfare, led Bob Rowthorn to refer to the region as a 'vast workhouse in which most of the inmates are engaged in servicing and controlling each other' (1987, pp. 117–18). Like a workhouse or prison, the gap between revenues and costs is paid by taxing an external population.

Ironically, this workhouse characteristic has recently become the main basis of the economic case for maintaining the union with Britain. Historically, unionist economic analyses were based on the degree to which the industrial north-east of Ireland was more like a region of Britain than the agrarian South. As late as the 1940s, average income per head in the North was about 75 per cent higher than in the South. Relatively prosperous Northern unionists pointed to the impoverished South as a warning of what could happen to them in a united Ireland. Differentials were particularly large in terms of social welfare and benefits, such as healthcare, at least until Thatcherism began to dismantle parts of the welfare state in the 1980s. During this time, many pundits surmised that unemployed Northern Catholics really did not want a united Ireland because they would lose their benefits.

However, once Southern standards of living and rates of economic growth approached and surpassed the North, unionist economists changed their tack. They now combine a rather fanciful ignorance of the true relative positions of North and South with the argument that the South cannot afford a united Ireland because it cannot meet the costs of subsidising Northern state expenditures. The first analysis is exemplified by rather absurd characterisations of the North as 'the most dynamic economic region of Britain' (Gudgin, 1995) or half-baked assertions that the

South is an economic failure, unbalanced by the far gloomier picture in the North (Hazelkorn and Patterson, 1994; Bew, 1996). But the second analysis, which is found in the unionist writings of economists like Roche and Birnie (1995), requires more of an answer because it contains a larger element of truth.

Briefly, these economists argue the following: first, that the Southern Irish state has, since Partition, shown itself unable to sustain economic development and achieve prosperity, as is indicated by its dependence on foreign investments, its slow growth rates and, especially, its public debt and high unemployment. Second, for various reasons, the Northern economy has also been sluggish, especially since the 1960s and 1970s, leading it to require a massive subvention from the British exchequer, equivalent to one-third of its GDP. Third, the subvention has maintained a Northern standard of living that is higher than that of the South, in terms of average quality of housing, spending power and so on; with wages (especially after taxes) remaining higher in the North than in the South. Fourth, because of Southern debt, sluggish economic growth and the high rate of income tax (partly necessary because foreign corporations hardly pay any taxes), the South is incapable of taking over this subvention and keeping Northerners living in the style to which they are accustomed. Therefore, fifth, the only adequate solution is the continuation of the 'union' along with the subvention.

This new economic unionism, however, rests on a static analysis which assumes that everything will remain the same except constitutional change. A united Ireland, it assumes, would simply sum its two constituent economies, neither of which would change in any crucial way. On the other hand, it also assumes that the existing differences between North and South would remain under a continued 'union'. In the first case, this unionist analysis ignores the potential economic benefits of a united Ireland, outlined by a number of social scientists, journalists, business people and others who have articulated arguments against the unionist case. They focus on the savings an all-Ireland economy could gain in lower transfer costs, cheaper unified infrastructure, gains from internal trade, larger markets enabling exploitation of new economies of scale, and so on (Rowthorn and Wayne, 1988; Quigley, 1992; Munck, 1993; Anderson and Hamilton, 1995; Bradley, 1996).

The second case simply assumes that under continued 'union', Britain would maintain its subsidy at the current level (or, more accurately, that it would continue to raise the subsidy to the extent necessary to keep Northern living standards within shouting distance of British ones). This ignores the considerable pressure that economic decline puts on Britain to reduce its fiscal leakages to the North. Moreover, economic decline induces austerity, so that even if the North maintains its standard of living relative to Britain it may become poorer relative to the South of Ireland. In broad economic terms, the unionist analysis fails to recognise the substantial *relative* economic advantages that the South has built up over the North by becoming dependent on US capital while the North remained dependent on investments by firms from a decadent former hegemon, which dried up in the 1970s.

In a dynamic context, continued 'union' limits Ireland's long-term potential to shake off economic peripherality. An all-Ireland political economy, especially in solidarity with other European peripheral countries, might make demands on the EU and coordinate policies for dealing with transnational corporations that could help it escape its dependency and peripherality. Unionist arguments, in their acceptance of the *status quo*, condemn both parts of the island to continue as dependent peripheries. This scenario is worse for the North because of its severe economic decline since the 1940s.

However, important as economic arguments are, the debate between unionism and republicanism in Ireland does not hinge primarily on economics. As Clayton (1996) and others argue, unionist ideologies are still strongly influenced by their colonial and settler self-identity. They strongly identify with supposed ethnic and 'mother-country' superiority, even where it defies economic rationality. This has been apparent, for example, in the ambivalence of many middle-class unionists towards the 'peace process' of the 1990s, and especially in their willingness to support violent activities such as those surrounding Orange marches, despite their clear negative impact on unionist commercial interests.

Conclusions

While the recent experience of the two Irish economies has relevance for the question of 'the union versus a united Ireland', it also raises an important and wider comparative historical question. Put simply, is it preferable to be dependent on an ascendant economic power or on a descendent one?

For over 30 years now, the South of Ireland has been dependent primarily on investments by corporate subsidiaries from the most powerful, indeed hegemonic, world power: the United States. This has severely constrained its economy, creating alternate periods of deep recession and illusory growth, chronically high unemployment, and other economic and social problems (O'Hearn, 1989; Munck, 1993). Foreign economic activities are disarticulated from domestic manufacturers, adding less to the Irish economy because they import most of their material inputs, export their output, and remove large proportions of their value added in the form of repatriated profits. Unlike core capitalist accumulation, one thing does *not* lead to another. As Mjoset (1992) puts it, the South experiences 'vicious cycles' of dependency rather than 'virtuous cycles' of innovation and expansion. Nonetheless, dependence on US investments has induced economic activity in leading sectors and created spurts of economic growth, however short-lived and however disconnected from the general well-being. The problems of dependence on US capital for the southern Irish economy mainly arise from the failure of foreign sectors to induce enough economic activity and to spread this activity to other economic sectors and to the population in general.

The North's problems of depending on Britain are much more severe. British decline led to the actual deindustrialisation of the North *without* replacement by any other viable economic activities. British-owned factories left the North primarily because of economic factors unconnected to the 'Troubles', while British restrictions on Northern policies limited the region's capacity to attract new industrial projects in their place. Conflict was an *additional* cause of the North's incapacity to attract foreign investments; it was already falling behind the South of Ireland in this respect by the early 1960s because of factors associated with its subordination to Britain. Only subsidies from London keep the North from collapsing into a level of poverty and underdevelopment usually associated with the Third World. Few of its existing manufacturers could survive without grants or direct subsidies. Many of its service jobs depend entirely on state sponsorship. Thus, while the economic position of the South is not attractive by core European standards, its dependence on a powerful expanding economy leaves it better off than the North, which has suffered from dependence on Western Europe's greatest economic failure this century.

In the medium term, the North could internalise many of the South's relative advantages within a united Ireland. If it were part of a single economy, on an island which US firms have clearly found attractive in the past, it could attract the same levels of investment as the South. The North's attractiveness could be increased by the creation of new infrastructures such as a Dublin–Belfast economic corridor. An all-Ireland economy, however, would not be sufficient, as foreign capital is attracted by political regimes as much as by economic conditions; it is the Southern *political* economy that has been constructed as an attractive base for US leading sector investments.

Of course, in world-systemic terms, these conclusions are limited. The North could become economically better off in a united Ireland. Perhaps other semiperipheral regions could improve their relative positions by changing their forms of dependence or their primary economic alliances. But one would hope that semiperipheral regions would aspire to something more than just becoming better off while leaving other regions behind, just as working-class movements aspire to something other than the elevation of their members above other workers. Even within Ireland, for instance, the creation of an all-island economy with a Dublin–Belfast economic corridor would probably reduce North–South inequality partly by increasing East–West inequality. Moreover, even periods of high growth in the South failed to reduce inequality among Irish classes – if anything, foreign-led economic growth has exacerbated class inequality.

Yet, given their crucial labour and material resources, and substantial market power, semiperipheral regions like the so-called European periphery may have the potential to change the entire system. But they will never achieve this in competition with each other. There is potential for alliances between *democratised* semiperipheral economies,[11] who between them (especially in alliance with core working classes) might have the potential to shift the balance of forces against core-domination in the global political economy. A unified and democratic Ireland could be the first step in such an alliance. Scotland and Wales certainly have a role to play in this regard, along with other semiperipheral states within the EU which might together push for social well-being rather than core competitiveness as a Union-wide goal. Ironically, if England could stop acting like the imperial world power that it no longer is, and reconcile itself to being an equal partner in such a semiperipheral alliance, it too could play a crucial role in changing the world-system.

Notes

1. I would like to thank Douglas Hamilton and the editors of this volume (the 'two Jameses') for their helpful comments on earlier versions of this chapter. I am also grateful for comments made by members of the Department of Sociology at Oxford, especially Roberto Franzosi and Gavin Williams.

2. Some records indicate that Ireland was not as impoverished as one might have expected by the start of the twentieth century (Bairoch and Levy-Lebeyer, 1981; Lee, 1989, pp. 513–14; Kennedy, 1996). But this was only because its population had fallen so drastically that its per capita income levels were respectable by European standards. Per capita income levels were further distorted because the distribution of incomes was still highly uneven due to Ireland's structure of land tenure.

3. Frank (1969) has referred to 'subordinate metropoles' or 'metropoles of satellites' to describe the position of relatively developed cities within peripheral regions. Wallerstein (1988) argues that a primary characteristic of world-system incorporation and peripheralisation is the creation of 'larger units of economic decisionmaking', including productive units and places where goods are collected for trade or shipping.

4. Quoted from confidential Ministry of Commerce memorandum, 'Industrial Development and Unemployment in Great Britain', 15 September 1958.

5. As well as liberalising the North's investment attraction programmes, Britain also considerably increased its subsidies of major Northern manufacturers, such as Harland & Wolff and Shorts. This did not halt deindustrialisation, but was an important way of maintaining support among the Loyalist working class.

6. It should be noted that similar losses were incurred in the Southern clothing and textiles sectors after Britain and Ireland joined the European Community in 1973. The difference, however, was that the South had already broken from its dependence on these sectors with policies that enabled it to attract new US investors, on which it now came to depend.

7. In the 1990s, the English share of inward manufacturing investments in the UK rose to more than 80 per cent, with Scotland receiving about 10 per cent and Wales about 5 per cent (Hamilton, 1992).

8. The head of Hualon Group, Oung Ta-ming, was later found guilty and jailed on charges of defaulting on share dealings. The history of the Hualon affair is a comedy of errors. After Hualon announced its intention to invest in the North, with the aid of a massive 60 million pound IDB grant, British and European textile manufacturers attempted to block the project on the basis that it would distort competition. Although the European Commission decided to let the

project go ahead, a decision partly influenced by post-IRA ceasefire goodwill, this decision was appealed to the European Court. The European Court ruled in early 1997 to allow the project to go ahead, but the decision was appealed by the British Apparel and Textile Confederation. This tactic was expected to delay the investment by an additional 18 months, and possibly lead Hualon to take their investment to Eastern Europe. That British industry would take such a hard and consistent line, without attracting strong opposition from the British government, is a further indication that the Northern economy is essentially a separate and subordinate peripheral economy rather than an integrated region of a 'British economy'.

9. Gross *national* product, however, grew much more slowly than GDP because much of Southern output growth was removed in the form of transnational profit repatriations, which are not a part of GNP. By the mid-1990s, foreign profit repatriations accounted for nearly 15 per cent of GDP.

10. This research was carried out on behalf of the Scottish National Party (SNP), which sought to show that independence was consistent with relative economic prosperity. See the SNP news release, 'Ireland to overtake UK by the year 2000: Scotland can become tiger economy of Europe', which incorporated research by Robert Twigger of the Economic Policy and Statistics Section of the House of Commons Library, 27 September 1996. For further comparative data on economic growth in the Irish economies, see Goodman, 1996, pp. 162–5.

11. See Munck, 1993, Chapter 7 (written with Douglas Hamilton) for one vision of such a semiperipheral 'democratic economy'.

4 Integrating Europe, Integrating Ireland: The Socio-economic Dynamics

James Anderson

The European Union (EU) and Single European Market (SEM) have fostered major new and *non*-nationalist dynamics for the economic and social reintegration of Northern and Southern Ireland. There are compelling socio-economic as well as political-national reasons for the sorts of 'North/South institutions' which were proposed in the 1995 'Framework Document' and then emerged in diluted form in the 1998 Northern Ireland Peace Agreement. The fact that economic development has substantial dynamic potential to integrate North and South was indeed reflected in unionist insistence, and to some extent success, in minimising the 'economic' remit of the 'North–South Ministerial Council' and sectoral 'implementation bodies' as specified in the 'Agreement'. These bodies are clearly inadequate for realising the full economic, social and political benefits of integration, as is argued in Chapter 13. On the other hand, the socio-economic dynamics already in operation and the obstacles to them, as outlined in this chapter, suggest that there will be continuing pressures to extend the scope and powers of North–South institutions.

Dynamics for Cross-Border Integration

North–South reintegration across the Irish border can be seen in terms of four dynamics and their sometimes contradictory inter-relationships. The most familiar is the Irish nationalist demand for the reunification of Ireland. This dynamic and opposition to it by British nationalists/unionists is central to the conflict over the territorial sovereignty of Northern Ireland. It is reflected in the British and Irish government view that 'parity of esteem' for

Northern nationalists and institutional recognition of their 'Irishness' in the form of 'North–South' institutions of governance are central to conflict resolution. A bridging of the disputed border to produce a 'compromise' between the mutually contradictory 'zero-sum' alternatives of exclusive British or exclusive Irish sovereignty is essential to a settlement. And the conflict, paradoxically or in counter-productive fashion, is an obstacle to the other three 'dynamics', though ultimately they all point in the same integrative direction.

The second dynamic, less familiar than the 'national' one, is the pressure from business North and South for the creation of a 'single island economy' to meet the new opportunities and threats posed by the establishment of the Single European Market since the late 1980s. This 'economic' dynamic is now probably the most important new element in the traditional equation of North–South relations (Anderson, 1994; Bradley, 1996). It could of course be thrown into reverse by further European integration to monetary union with the South joining the EMU while the North, as part of the UK, initially stays outside, just as in the 1970s divergent British and Irish responses to 'Europe' led to the Irish pound leaving the sterling area. Though such a reversal may be only temporary, it highlights the fact that European integration does not necessarily or automatically translate into Ireland's reintegration.

Even less familiar and more nebulous, but potentially of at least equal importance, is a third, 'social', dynamic whose logic is a 'single island society'. This is implied in the 'single island economy' – one 'economy' but two 'societies' is hardly practical – but the 'social' dynamic is also made up of a wide range of *non*-economic pressures for more or closer social interactions across the border. While encouraged by European integration, its basis and motivations are much wider. Indeed many of them pre-date not only the European Union in its various guises since the 1950s but also Partition itself.

While the Partition of the island in 1921 severed most of the political links between North and South, and did lead to the creation of two more or less separate 'economies' and 'societies' by the 1930s, an impressive array of pre-existing 'all-Ireland' institutions, particularly but not exclusively in the social and cultural spheres, have continued to operate on an island-wide basis. They include, for instance, the four largest churches, and also most of the major sporting bodies, not only the essentially nationalist and socially hegemonic Gaelic Athletic Association but also bodies covering such sports as rugby, hockey, cricket and boxing which have large unionist affiliations. They include too, much of the banking system and other commercial operations which pre-date Partition, though some of the border-crossing institutions have internal 'federal' structures to cope with the problems of operating in two jurisdictions. In addition they were joined by some other important organisations established since Partition, most notably the Irish Congress of Trade Unions. Thus writing about the situation in the early 1970s – before the newly-joined 'Common Market' had much impact on the Republic of Ireland or the United Kingdom – Whyte (1983) concluded that the Irish border was perhaps the most permeable in Western Europe, and that is equally if not more true today even allowing for the progress in cross-border integration elsewhere in the European Union. Not only are there more border-crossing institutions, including more private sector firms, but there have always been various forms of cooperation between separate Northern or Southern bodies and their cross-border counterparts, and these too have increased since the 1970s. Some of this increased social interaction is a 'spin-off' from increasing economic integration, but it has also been stimulated by European integration defined more broadly (and more accurately) in political terms.

Thus increased cross-border contact is particularly marked among some campaigning groups involved for instance with problems of poverty, unemployment, women's rights or gay rights, and to varying degrees EU legislation and lobbying networks have facilitated or provided a common focus for joint North–South activity. This, in turn, has stimulated what can be considered a separate 'democratic' dynamic.

One of the more general concerns of campaigning groups is for a democratisation of the emerging North–South policy agendas. These can be seen as overly dominated by the business lobby and by official 'neo-functionalism' (see Chapter 1), both heavily constrained by the national conflict, secretive or 'depoliticising' and in effect anti-democratic. It is thus useful to specify a fourth, overarching 'democratic' dynamic which goes beyond the functional aspects of the 'economic' and 'social' dynamics and the more narrowly conceived politics of the 'national' dynamic. It is overarching in the sense that the economic, social and political potential of the other three dynamics can only be realised if North–South relations and processes are radically democratised – an argument further advanced in Chapter 13.

The four dynamics – the 'national', 'economic', 'social' and 'democratic' – all point to increasing integration, but the relationships between the 'national' dynamic and the other three have been contradictory, particularly because of the national conflict taking the form of armed conflict. The economic and social reintegration of the North and South has been actively hampered by the national struggle for unification in its military phase, a contradiction epitomised by the IRA 'logic' of fighting for a united Ireland by blowing up the only North–South railway line linking the country's two main cities. The military conflict not only fed the traditional intransigence of Northern unionists and the reinvigorated British nationalism of their right-wing Tory allies, incensed too by a loss of sovereignty to the EU (see Chapter 6), it also deepened the 'Partitionist' attitudes in the South and further encouraged the development of a 'partitionist' Irish nationalism sometimes referred to as 'revisionist 26 county' nationalism (see Chapter 5). Coupled with the obvious fact that while the IRA might not be beaten it could not force the British state to withdraw from Ireland, it seems highly likely that an unadmitted realisation of militarism's counter-productive effects within Ireland helped convince the Sinn Fein leadership of the need for an alternative political strategy (see Chapter 10).

However, while the national conflict has hampered the 'economic' and 'social' dynamics for reintegration, as we shall see, these two dynamics are pushing in the same direction as the 'national' dynamic, towards the island's reunification, albeit for quite different and independent reasons. Ironically, it is precisely this coincidence which has forced business people to adopt an aggressively 'non-political' stance, in an environment where 'politics' is all too readily taken to mean simply nationalist politics, whether of an Irish or British colouring. The muted lobbyists for a 'single island economy' have as it were 'tied one hand behind their back', adopting the self-denying ordinance of avoiding the 'politics' of cross-border integration lest they be thought to have a nationalist 'hidden agenda'. Even so they have predictably been attacked by unionist politicians as if they had.

This is at least partly because the governments' essentially weak 'neo-functionalist' response to containing and managing the 'national' dynamic has rested largely on supposedly uncontentious cross-border cooperation on economic matters. While their main reason for establishing North–South institutions of governance is to give institutional recognition to the political identity of Northern nationalists and at least symbolically breach exclusive British sovereignty, they have studiously avoided admitting any change in sovereignty in order to minimise unionist reaction. Instead, the emphasis has been on 'non-political' functional matters such as coordinated tourist marketing for the whole island and the technical cross-border concerns of particular economic sectors or industries such as transportation and energy supply. How the 'economic' and 'social' dynamics operate, however, cannot be understood in isolation from the 'national' dynamic, as was made particularly clear by – paradoxically enough – the most determinedly 'non-political' respondents. Trying to avoid the all-pervasive politics of the border requires 'political gymnastics' of a high order.

How these dynamics operate, the obstacles to them, and the consequent *non*-nationalist reasons why North–South institutions are needed, can now be clarified on the basis of in-depth interview surveys in Belfast and Dublin and an overview of more detailed analyses (Anderson, 1994; Anderson and Goodman, 1997a and 1997b). A wide range of representatives of business, the trade unions, civil service departments, cultural institutions, the voluntary sector, campaigning groups and other organisations in both cities were questioned about the implications of European Union integration for Ireland, the problems and prospects of cross-border development, its institutional forms and socio-economic motivations. The interviews were semi-structured to elucidate the respondents' own concerns and priorities and to explore the 'apolitical' argument that economic integration can proceed without significant political integration.[1]

The EU and Socio-economic Integration

Hopes that European integration would transcend Partition, reunite the country and finally solve Ireland's 'Troubles' go back to the 1950s. In the 1960s convergent tendencies in the Northern and Southern economies were expected to lead to political convergence. A significant body of Irish nationalist opinion invested in this 'technocratic anti-partitionism' (Lyne, 1990; and see Chapter 5). But instead the current 'Troubles' escalated, and when the Republic and the UK joined the EEC in 1973 there was if anything divergence, particularly after 1979 when the Irish pound was decoupled from sterling. Most economic linkages were arguably *weaker* in the 1980s than in the pre-EC 1950s and 1960s. Rather than the EU being an unproblematic agent of integration, divergent relationships and responses to it by the two states have in the past increased the gap between North and

South and in the short term could do so again with respect to
EMU. However, the fact that the political, and largely rhetorical,
'technocratic anti-partitionism' of the past was ineffectual does
not mean that the present, economically-driven, integration
project will also fail.

EU integration is now much more advanced in political as well
as economic terms, with 'fine-grained' region-to-region integration across state borders, including the Irish border, as distinct
from simply state-to-state cooperation (Anderson and Goodman,
1995). These developments, and in particular the Single
European Market (SEM) formally completed in 1992, are the
main context and driving factors behind the 'economic' and
'social' dynamics for North–South integration.

Externally-based multinational enterprises increasingly see
their Irish operations in island-wide terms. Irish economic interests, South and North, are now backing economic integration,
not for nationalist reasons, but because of the new business
opportunities offered by the SEM and the threats it poses. There
are fears that increased competition threatens 'peripheralisation'
for North and South, particularly as the SEM's 'centre óf gravity'
moves further eastwards and as less prosperous East European
countries join the EU. Indigenously-owned small and medium-
sized enterprises in both parts of Ireland are seen as particularly
vulnerable to external competitors. Against this, North–South
integration and the creation of all-Ireland markets are widely seen
as a means of countering this threat and promising 'economic
growth for the island as a whole'.

The dramatic new enthusiasm of Northern business people for
economic integration with the Irish Republic, particularly ones
from unionist backgrounds traditionally dismissive of the supposedly 'backward' South, is one of the most remarkable
developments in Northern Ireland in the 1990s. Although no
doubt encouraged by the contrast between the Republic's
economic success and the North's chronic Mezzogiorno-like
dependency on Britain's taxpayers (see Chapter 3), the enthusiasm clearly pre-dates the 'Celtic Tiger' hype. Significantly, it
also clearly pre-dates the various paramilitary ceasefires – its
motivation or dynamic is independent of the national equation.

The vulnerability of two small, open economies has concentrated minds on the need for economic cooperation, a pooling of
resources and policy coordination across the island. The general
similarities of Northern and Southern problems – including relatively high unemployment, relatively low overall productivity, and

an over-reliance on traditional agriculture, foreign investment and external subsidies – leads logically to sharing common solutions. While increased border-crossing is part of wider European and 'globalisation' processes, and also applies to relations between the South and Britain, for many interviewees (including civil servants, employers and trade unionists) the potential for economic synergies across the island is greater than across the Irish Sea, the North's interests in the EU are more similar to the South's than to Britain's, and Westminster priorities often conflict with Northern needs.

Partly in response to European integration, the Irish Congress of Trade Unions and individual unions took the lead in arguing for economic integration from the mid-1980s, but more recently the lead has been taken by business people. Dr George Quigley, Chairman of the Ulster Bank and also then of the Institute of Directors in Northern Ireland, called for a 'one island economy' in a key speech to the Confederation of Irish Industry in Dublin in 1992. He proposed that 'Ireland, North and South, should become one integrated island economy in the context of the Single European Market'; that this unified economy should be supported by the EC with a special fund for projects agreed with the British and Irish governments; that this would in time ensure a direct route to Brussels for a devolved Northern Ireland government; and that a Belfast–Dublin 'economic corridor' would further increase economic development North and South (Quigley, 1992). Subsequently a much wider range of employers' bodies, Chambers of Commerce and trade organisations have joined this integrative movement. There has been extensive lobbying for the public provision or promotion of such things as training, research, transportation, tourism and environmental improvement on an all-island basis. EU funding regimes are stimulating transnational lobbying networks. Together with the new North–South reorientations in the private sector, these developments are encouraging the emergence of island-wide policy agendas both for the two states and within civil society.

Crossing territorial state frontiers is facilitated by the EU in a variety of ways, ranging from the ideological legitimation of partially shared sovereignty to such practicalities as no longer having to pay sales and excise tax on the border. The benefits of North–South links vary widely from one enterprise or institution to the next, both in quantitative and qualitative terms, and it is realised that there are also losers from cross-border competition and rationalisation. But the interviewees in Belfast and Dublin generally stressed the mutual advantages of integration which included minimising unnecessary duplication in public services; gaining economies of scale in island-wide stockholding and distribution; economies in administration, technology innovation and price harmonisation; enhanced leverage in overseas markets; and greater influence with governments and EU institutions. Selling across the Irish border was seen as providing a good international training ground for small inexperienced exporters not yet ready to explore markets in Britain or further afield.

While actual cross-border links remain uneven and in some areas very patchy, there have been remarkable developments in the public and particularly the private sector. For example, the respective farmers' unions now hold regular meetings at board level and systematically coordinate their activities, especially with respect to the EU. Multinationals selling into Ireland have reorganised on an island basis, while producers and retailers have constructed North–South partnerships. There has been a surge in North–South merger activity, with corporate concentration both by indigenous and foreign-owned firms. There has been a substantial rationalisation of agribusiness on an island-wide basis, with the large Southern conglomerates, Golden Vale, Kerrygold and Waterford, all absorbing Northern dairy businesses since the early 1990s. The number of Northern private sector employees now working for all-Ireland companies has grown significantly (Anderson and Goodman, 1997a, 36). The tourist industry has set up an all-Ireland coordinating body, 'Hospitality Ireland', and the respective tourist boards now have relatively integrated marketing and development programmes with the possibility of an all-Ireland tourist board being established as a consequence of the Peace Agreement. Ironically – on two counts – the examples of closer working relationships across the border include the Southern and Northern electricity suppliers holding regular joint meetings on technical and training matters and cooperating to restore the North–South electricity connector. The connector had been blown up by the IRA, and 'Energy', presumably because of its strategic economic importance, was one of the matters for North–South bodies which unionist negotiators succeeded in having excluded from the 'Agreement' – a case perhaps of closing the stable door when the horse is already on its way.

The recentness of these cross-border developments is worth stressing.[2] It was only in the late 1980s that the Northern Irish Tourist Board opened an office in Dublin, despite the fact that a majority of foreign tourists to the North come via the South; only in 1990 that the main Northern and Southern employers' organisations held their first joint meeting; and only since 1991 that business organisations have lobbied the two governments to coordinate their respective plans for spending EU structural funds. The respective development reports for 1994–99 were the first to include a jointly written 'North–South' chapter.

While business organisations have recently been setting the pace, trade unions and groups campaigning around such issues as unemployment and women's rights are also increasingly active in North–South integration. There has been some growth in non-national struggles on a cross-border basis (Anderson and Goodman, 1997b). The economics of the SEM constitute the most important new dynamic for cross-border development, but European integration has increasingly taken on new political, social and cultural dimensions which feed the 'social' dynamic for North–South integration. EU-wide networks such as the European Bureau for Lesser-Used Languages, the European Network for the Unemployed, the European Women's Network and the European Anti-Poverty Network were seen to have directly stimulated North–South cooperation and the development of common policy agendas.

While some of these networks are concerned with economic matters, their interests extend well beyond the economic. There is indeed a wide range of reasons or common bases for joint North–South working, including the different class interests of capital and labour, the common interests of women, the similar problems faced by various oppressed minorities, and shared interests in protecting the environment.[3] These and other issues have the potential to unify people across and despite the national and jurisdictional divides. The women, or environmentalists, or gay rights campaigners, who are developing North–South cooperation and mutual support are not motivated by the SEM (much less by nationalism). Indeed their motivations may have little or nothing to do with the EU. Thus cross-border integration is important for unions which have members North and South, as for those sporting and cultural bodies which have always been all-Ireland operations. Strengthening the 'cultural community' through increased contacts and the pooling of expertise in various fields across the religious, national and state divides has a wide variety of motivations. However, the social and cultural policies and practices which have been instituted to stimulate and legitimise EU integration have generally encouraged a more cross-border approach. The nationally 'neutral' EU context was felt by some to be a crucial factor in getting together groups which would otherwise have been hostile to cross-border cooperation.

In summary, there is great unevenness in cross-border cooperation, ranging from full institutional unification to mere 'social get-togethers' to non-existence, but the overall thrust is towards greater integration. Amongst firms, semi-state bodies and professional associations, and campaigning, social and cultural organisations, there has recently been a very significant growth in the number, range and capacities of cross-border and all-island institutional arrangements. On the spectrum from full institutional integration to merely social contact, the former is generally more likely the less state-oriented the organisations. The growth in integration has been noticeably strongest in the business sector, but other types of organisation are also becoming increasingly concerned to redefine their goals on an island-wide basis. In addition to the 'normal' problems in crossing state borders, strategies for integration often have to cope with the problems of avoiding or minimising unionist opposition. Here the EU can be useful as a 'neutral' third party facilitator and funder which legitimises cross-border projects in line with its own agenda of encouraging European integration.

Overcoming the Obstacles to Integration

The interview surveys not only indicated the strength of the 'economic' and 'social' dynamics for Ireland's reunification, they also clarified the formidable obstacles to 'a single island economy' and 'single society'. Unionist opposition and the national conflict inhibit cross-border cooperation in various ways, in addition to the practical problems of working in two separate jurisdictions.

Since Partition nearly 80 years ago, South and North have developed different institutional arrangements, party systems and clientalist networks. In short, there are different political cultures which feed the 'Partitionist' attitudes not only among pro-Partition unionists but also among Irish nationalists, particularly in the South. The main obstacles to integration stem from administrative, policy and political differences. The separate civil services respond to different, and generally territorially-delimited, vested interests, and the state bureaucracies still tend to downgrade cross-border initiatives. For most government departments in Dublin, as in Belfast, involvement with another jurisdiction is at the very least 'non-standard', and can be seen as upsetting long established procedures and power relationships.[4]

Cross-border developments are hampered by differences in taxation and currencies North and South; a lack of informal contacts among business people; and a lack of coordination in the economic policies and plans of the respective administrations. Taxation differences have been reduced, but large differentials remain with generally higher labour costs in the Republic. No matter how close the relationships between Northern and Southern arms of the same organisation, in legal and fiscal terms they are separate entities. Even where North–South differences are small, it is still necessary for organisations to have separate financial accounts for each jurisdiction. Fully integrated cross-border operations are thus difficult to construct, particularly in the business sector. Furthermore, increased North–South contact can mean increased competition as well as increased cooperation. Both parts of the country struggling for the finite amounts of potential inward investment available is recognised as a potentially damaging 'zero-sum game'.

The institutional divergence from eight decades of Partition means it can be difficult to 'match up partners' for North–South projects because they operate differently, or are weak or nonexistent in one or other jurisdiction. Even with compatible interests and institutions, cooperation may be obstructed by mutual suspicions and stereotyping. In the decades of largely separate development and 30 years of military conflict in the North, Southerners and Northerners have solidified a range of myths about each other.

Deeply ingrained Partitionist attitudes in the South mean that public discourses about its relations with Britain and with the EU are generally separate from and do not take into account the discourse about North–South relations, thereby obscuring possible trade-offs and contradictions. For example, some Southern interests see the EU as an opportunity to escape relations of dominance and dependence with Britain and British markets, but any 'distancing' from Britain can also create a gulf with the North as part of the UK. It can be detrimental as well to other Southern interests which remain tied to British markets, for despite very substantial diversification, Britain remains the South's most important export market. While Northern Ireland issues are followed and discussed in the South with notably greater interest and thoroughness than in Britain, the discussions often seem to exist in their own cocoon, quite separate from

debates on the South's other cross-border relations, the participants seemingly oblivious to the North–South implications.
Contrary to unionist fears of 'Southerners taking over the North',
many Southerners have 'bigger fish to fry' elsewhere.

Economic and social integration are to some extent paving the
way for a political settlement, but they are at the same time
obstructed by the national conflict, by unionist opposition or by
having to circumvent what are euphemistically referred to as
'unionist sensitivities'. Potentially hostile Northern interpretations of 'Southern takeover' are deflected by hiding or playing
down the 'Irishness' or Southern base of parent companies; local
management structures may be left undisturbed for political
rather than economic reasons. For example, the Allied Irish Bank
treats the whole of Ireland as a single entity, but when it acquired
the Trustee Savings Bank in the North in 1991, it did not simply
absorb it into the existing AIB (NI), or trade under the 'AIB' label
as in Britain; instead, it created an autonomous Northern
subsidiary with a new, neutral identity – 'First Trust Bank' which
if anything sounds North American![5]

The armed struggle for reunification has driven wedges
between North and South – epitomised by the IRA in its political wisdom blowing up the rail link between Dublin and Belfast,
and contributing to the growth of Southern 'Partitionism' since
the 1970s. But it has also constituted a more subtle barrier to
cross-border development. The need to circumvent the national
conflict has encouraged counter-productive 'non-political'
stances to integration. Some business attitudes reflect a neo-
liberal anti-statism, but the claims to be 'non-political' mainly
reflect an understandable desire to 'distance' their economic
integration agenda from the traditional reunification goal of Irish
nationalism, precisely because the logic of their economic
strategy points in the same direction. As Quigley (1992) put it,
'making a reality of the island economy is dependent on there
being no political agendas, overt or hidden'. However, the
responses from unionist politicans were predictably critical,
precisely because they did see, if not a political agenda then
certainly political implications which they did not like. While
economic integration is not driven by political, much less nationalist, motivations, it clearly cannot be divorced from political
means and political effects. Ultimately, those asserting that integration across state borders is 'non-political' succeed only in
hampering their own cause. Their claim is counter-productive to
the extent that 'depoliticisation' has weakened and delayed the

pressures for establishing the political institutions needed for cross-border integration.

The end result of 'politics' lagging behind 'economics' is a very uneven, *ad hoc* and stunted pattern of integration, sorely lacking in coherence, coordination and accountability. Economic cooperation and integration have generally followed lines of least resistance, dodging rather than transcending the political obstacles. Overcoming all the obstacles – the unevenness of existing linkages, the institutional mismatches, the Partitionism both in civil society and the state administrations, and the problems of national conflict, of meshing the economic involvement of two states, and of accountability to two separate electorates – all suggest that North–South institutions are urgently required. Integrating the two separate economies in two different states will require proactive and concerted political management; and that will be even more the case with the (probably short-term) disruption of the North's delayed joining of the EMU some years after the South.

Neither ostensibly 'non-political' integration in civil society, nor orthodox diplomacy and cooperation between separate sovereign state entities, is up to the task of securing the island's future. Civil society needs state help and the state help needs to be coordinated rather than *ad hoc*. Particularly given the economic importance of the state sectors, integration cannot be left to private business or the workings of the market. Private business interests cannot achieve economic integration on their own, partly because of the importance of the public sector, and besides it is too important to be left to them.

Representatives of the trade unions and other campaigning and voluntary sector groups all stressed the need to widen access to all-island policy formulation and decision-making. The 'depoliticisation' of integration is seen by some organisations as tied in with the dominant role being played by business people, and there is now a growing number of North–South community, cultural and campaigning networks which are calling for more popular control of integration. Perhaps the biggest obstacle to economic integration has been the lack of an adequate institutional framework and political programme.

As the various strategies adopted to 'dodge the national question' paradoxically indicate, political considerations are in practice inextricably part and parcel of supposedly 'apolitical' economic initiatives. In fact, despite the prevalent 'non-political' public stance, most business interviewees wanted a firmer partnership between themselves and government agencies, North and South. There was a general consensus that North–South bodies were required and that, in time, some form of all-Ireland political body to oversee North–South integration should and would be established. Here several respondents stressed the urgent need for more proactive government encouragement, and for the EU to take a more explicitly political role and treat North and South as a single entity.

Conclusions

Despite its foundation in the substantial North–South linkages which pre-date Partition, and the very significant developments of the 1990s, cross-border integration is very uneven. It faces deeply ingrained Partitionist attitudes and in many cases remains weak and stunted. This has been partly because of the absence of democratic North–South institutions, itself a function of the national conflict and the lack of democracy in a North under 'direct rule' from London.

However, even before the 'Framework Document' appeared in 1995, a limited and *ad hoc* North–South framework in civil society was already being constructed 'from the bottom up', rather than awaiting concerted state action or a settlement of the national conflict. Its main dynamics come from elsewhere – from more global processes of transnationalisation which encompass Ireland, Britain and the EU. But economic and social integration between North and South cannot proceed much further without significant political integration within Ireland. Socio-economic integration requires proactive state involvement – not least because the economics of civil society are closely entwined with the state in both parts of the island. Integration requires concerted political management by joint North–South institutions which are legitimised by democratic involvement and political accountability. And now, building on the Belfast 'Agreement', business groups, the trade unions, campaigning and other organisations will hopefully feel freer to lobby for the necessary cross-border institutional support (see Chapter 13), and not least on the 'economic' matters which unionists strove to exclude from the 'Agreement'. This will become all the more important if a return to more peaceful conditions means that the North can no longer expect the same degree of generosity in its presently huge economic subsidy from Britain.

The 'single island economy' implies an 'all-Ireland civil society' and both imply a political 'bridging' of the border for reasons which are independent, though supportive, of defusing the national conflict in the North. This entails moving away from the outdated idea that exclusive national sovereignty is sacrosanct, a movement in line with contemporary global trends. While 'the death of the nation state' has been greatly exaggerated, the ground is shifting under conventional political institutions and concepts (Anderson, 1995a and 1996). In reality sovereignty has already been substantially altered across Europe by EU integration, and also by the Anglo–Irish Agreement and the 'Peace Agreement' in Ireland – and in Ireland it needs to be further altered in order to realise the potential benefits of socio-economic integration. Without a 'political' agenda' of significant institutional innovation, there will still be two separate economies and limited scope for mutual help and development. Socio-economic integration is already building bridges between North and South, but making a reality of the 'single island economy and society' is dependent on the building of political bridges.

Notes

1. In Belfast interviews were conducted with representatives of over 30 bodies, including ten government departments and agencies, three employers' organisations, six particular firms, three professional associations, four trade union bodies, four voluntary organisations and various other cultural and social groups. The Dublin survey included 13 private sector firms and semi-state organisations, eight professional and business associations, six cultural and sporting organisations, five government departments, six trade unions and campaigning organisations, and five other organisations which promote North–South links. The interviews, which on average lasted an hour and a half, were loosely structured around open-ended questions about advantages and disadvantages of EU membership, hopes and fears about future EU-related developments and the benefits and problems of North–South integration. The format allowed the interviewee to specify and address the issues which he or she thought most important; and it allowed the interviewer to cross-check information from different sources.
2. Other recent cross-border developments include the establishment in 1994 of a joint project team to manage the upgrading of the Dublin–Belfast railway line; and Northern and Southern broadcasting organisations increasingly collaborating on joint productions.

3. Examples of joint working include the granting of full affiliation rights for Northern unemployment groups in the Dublin-based Irish National Organisation of the Unemployed. Other bodies have similarly been coopting Northern representatives and initiating joint training, research and lobbying. The South's Community Workers Cooperative has begun working with the Northern Ireland Council for Voluntary Action; the National Social Services Board has produced joint reports with the Northern Citizens' Advice Bureau; the Federation of Youth Groups has begun meeting regularly with the Northern Ireland Association of Youth Clubs; and a number of childcare organisations have begun producing joint reports. Women's organisations have developed reciprocal linkages since 1990, running annual joint conferences and in 1995 they presented a joint submission at the Dublin Forum for Peace and Reconciliation.

4. In many sectors separate development and 'Partitionism' still dominate. For example, major law firms in Dublin might have offices in London or Brussels but not Belfast, and there is little direct connection between the Southern and Northern legal bodies. In the Southern state sector, the officials responsible for North–South cooperation in Bord Tráchtála, the Trade Board, had to argue their case that Northern Ireland should not be treated as an 'overseas market'(!), reflecting tensions between the demands of North–South cooperation and more narrowly defined 'Southern interests'.

5. Similarly, the Dublin-based Irish Distillers when it took over the Northern firm Hazletts, stressed that Distillers was itself a subsidiary of Parnell Ricard so the takeover was 'French' rather than 'Irish'. In the Northern construction industry the pattern of takeovers through chains of subsidiaries means that there is little public awareness that many Northern building companies are owned by the Southern-based Cement Roadstone Holdings, despite the fact that in 1994 it combined all its Ireland operations under one regional director.

5 The Republic of Ireland: Towards a Cosmopolitan Nationalism?

James Goodman

State-sponsored nationalisms, what Benedict Anderson (1991) calls 'official' nationalisms, are grounded in a particular set of political imperatives. In contrast to nationalist movements in search of a state, 'official' nationalism is promoted by national leaders already in power. It is an ideology of the empowered, often geared to legitimising their role as much as any wider transformative social objectives. Given the role of the state in capitalist society, these dual roles of official nationalism are invariably in conflict. While state elites may seek radical social transformation, this objective cannot be permitted to disrupt the social order. Official nationalisms then, are often ambivalent, caught between legitimation and transformation.

Official variants of Irish nationalism, emerging from the 1920s in the aftermath of Partition, are no exception to this general rule, despite the 'unfinished business' of the North. Southern nationalism is both an ideology serving state elites, consolidating their claims to rule in the 26 Counties, and a vehicle for popular, national self-determination in a post-colonial 32 County Republic. There is a constant tension between these two components, which are in many respects mutually interdependent. Aspiration to a 32 County unified Ireland is often sacrificed for greater stability and independence in the 26 County Republic. Yet the legitimacy of the Southern state, the rationale for its existence, hinges on the nationalist aspiration for a 32 County Irish Republic. This tension, between state and nation, is reflected in disputes between partitionist nationalists and irredentist nationalists, in which independence for the 26 County unit is set against all-Ireland unity. Irish governments have at times sought to escape this either/or dilemma, and have instead encouraged relationships and structures that supersede the conflicting national claims.

In the 1990s, prospects could be improving for this 'cosmopolitan' mode of official nationalism, especially in highly internationalised societies like the Republic. Increased pan-European and global pressures are immersing national identities in a range of transnational relations. Irish society does not end or begin at its 'passport control' – neither does the influence of other societies. Some argue this heralds a move away from nationalism, and into regionalism or 'post-nationalism' (Kearney, 1997). But the transnationalising pressures are emerging in tandem with state structures and national identities – not against them. In many ways the two sources of authority are mutually constitutive: as transnational forces side-step state structures, national states strengthen their authority; as transnational identities become more important, nationalisms are re-geared to meet new, more 'externally'-driven aspirations. Paradoxically then, transnational pressures may broaden the options for official Irish nationalism, not close them off.

Ireland's place on the global semiperiphery accentuates these pressures (see Chapter 3). Societies or social groupings in this position are caught in a flux of pressures between core and periphery, and can play key and strategic roles as channels or mediators. The social or spatial semiperiphery has historically constituted a crucial site for reclaiming democratic rights; the 'creole pioneers' of Anderson's first nationalist 'imagined communities' in the early nineteenth century, and the 'Third World' elites that led the wave of national liberation movements in the middle of the twentieth, for instance, both existed on the semiperiphery (1991). In Ireland, this international positioning allowed Irish Republican and nationalist revolutionaries to initiate the implosion of the British empire in the opening decades of this century. The movement for Irish independence became a 'headline for the so-called third world' (Cronin, 1980, p. 217), and the Irish Republic was one of the first ex-colonies 'to walk in darkness down what is by now a well-lit road' (Kiberd, 1997, p. 81).

In the 1990s, socio-economic dependency and unfulfilled national aspirations may link the Republic to the post-colonial periphery (Coulter, 1990), but on the other hand, it also aspires to membership of the ex-imperial core, centred on the European Union (EU) (Kennedy, 1996). Accelerated transnational integration, and the increased political multipolarity that came with the end of the Cold War, have increased the political significance of such mediators. The Republic's political leverage with the US presidency, for instance, has been a product of the enhanced symbolic costs of conflict between the IRA and the British Army. There are also powerful pressures for greater social and economic integration between the Republic and Northern Ireland, as both the UK and the Republic participate in the European Union's economic and monetary union (see Chapter 4). In the North, economic linkages with Britain have begun to hold fewer discernible attractions; in the South, concepts of national reconciliation have entered into official parlance as political elites have sought to define a more inclusive state legitimacy.

This chapter is divided three sections. Section I examines varieties of official nationalism, contrasting irredentist and cosmopolitan forms. Section II examines two historical examples of cosmopolitan nationalism – De Valera's concept of 'external association', pursued in the early 1920s, and Lemass's 'technocratic anti-partitionism', developed in the 1960s. Both of these failed in the face of British and unionist opposition, and Section III analyses the contemporary politics of 'cosmopolitan reconciliation', asking whether it has more chance of success. The chapter conclusions outline some dangers of relying on a cosmopolitan framework to pursue nationalist goals.

I. Varieties of Official Nationalism

Irish nationalism is rooted in an anti-colonial struggle against British claims to rule in Ireland. It involves the aspiration to independent statehood for the Irish people, including the one-third of the population who live in Northern Ireland. There are two barriers to the realisation of this aspiration – first the preferred nationality of some 700,000 Northern unionists, and second the British guarantee of that nationality. If it is assumed that these barriers are relatively immovable, then there are two options. The first is a form of partitionist nationalism: a 'completed' 26 County Southern unit, perhaps having greater links with the North, as a foreign state. The second option is a form of irredentist nationalism: an Irish nation living in the hope of eventual unity, but unable to achieve it.

Official nationalists in the South have generally pursued the irredentist option, at least at the level of rhetoric, hoping that with time the unionist and British barriers will be overcome. This defines Irish independence against British rule, and against

Northern unionist preferences, and is expressed in a formal constitutional claim on the 6 Counties of Northern Ireland. But constitutional irredentism, primarily confined to rhetoric, has not secured a 32 County unit – not least as the Southern claim legitimises Northern unionism, and underpins the British guarantee. This is then presented by partitionist nationalists as an argument for down-playing the aspiration to unity: Northern unionists are not seen as a movable barrier, but as a fixed reality; it is the Irish nationalists who should be prepared to subordinate their aspirations to the overall objective of securing a peaceful future.

In this respect, irredentist and partitionist nationalists disagree on which national identity – Irish nationalist or unionist – is relatively fluid, and which is fixed. Irredentists assume the existence of a singular Irish national identity spanning North and South, and define unionism as an aberration created and sustained by the British state. Partitionist nationalists stress the fixed nature of unionist identity, defining Irish nationalist identity as relatively fluid, and capable of accepting Partition.

Confronted by the apparently zero-sum conflict between nationalism and unionism, Irish governments have on occasion sought to develop an alternative, 'cosmopolitan' form of nationalism. This is in part derived from the traditional Irish Republican aspiration to overcome religious divisions, and to build an independent Ireland in the name of the Irish people as a whole. Irish independence is defined inclusively, in terms of common secular and 'civic' interests, rather than in terms of exclusive identities or sectional interests, and neither unionist nor nationalist national identity is assumed to be fixed in stone. Both are defined as context-bound, and open to political options which serve mutual interests on the 'island of Ireland'.

This is combined with a faith in the international context as a basis for realising these interests and securing the necessary political changes. While some Republican nationalists believe that political violence is required to bring about these political changes, cosmopolitan nationalists rely on the international context to bring it about. The aspiration to independence through national statehood is retained, although it is submerged in a range of international linkages that transform national divisions into common interests. In this way, nationalism is broadened and extended beyond the purely national framework, although statehood is retained as a primary political objective.

For Southern state elites this has proved a particularly useful mode of nationalism. It enables a simultaneous commitment to

32 County national unity and 26 County state legitimacy, in a convenient conjunction of aspiration and authority. It offers Northern nationalists an alternative to Republican irredentism, and enables Southern nationalists to distance themselves from 26 County partitionist nationalism. The success of this approach hinges on the possibility of a parallel redefinition of nationalism in Britain, and its unionist variants in Northern Ireland. But British nationalism rests on an imperial history, and, as a 'core' nationalism, it is not so pliable – primarily because, perhaps until recently, there has been no imperative forcing redefinition. Official Irish nationalism has been highly adaptive because it is subordinate; British and unionist nationalisms are inflexible because they are in mutually supportive, dominant positions (see Chapter 6).

As well as these formidable 'external' obstacles, the strategy is also vulnerable to disruption 'from within'. Official accounts of cosmopolitan roads to national unity are open to challenge from irredentist nationalists who may define international linkages as a betrayal of aspirations for national independence. Alternatively, partitionist nationalists may argue that official cosmopolitanism is wedded to aspirations for independent 32 County statehood, against the wishes of Northern unionists. Not surprisingly, the two historical examples of official cosmopolitan nationalism have stumbled on the 'external' British and unionist obstacles, and have imploded under the resulting 'internal' pressures. This historical experience reveals the barriers to cosmopolitan nationalism, yet it also highlights contemporary possibilities, which are outlined in the final section.

II. Historical Lessons

The history of the Southern state demonstrates the problems of developing and implementing a cosmopolitan nationalism. De Valera's concept of 'external association', a form of independence within the British empire, was pursued in the early years of the Dáil, but in the face of British opposition fell back into more traditional irredentist approaches. From the mid-1960s there was increased rejection of rhetorical irredentism, with increased in-practice commitment to reunification, embodied in Lemass's 'technocratic anti-partitionism', which pre-dated and encouraged the Northern civil rights movement (Lyne, 1990). This faced opposition from Northern unionism and loyalism, which remained firmly committed to 'all or nothing' conceptions of national identity. Partly reacting to this, and also reflecting a growing Southern rejection of the war focused on the North, from the mid-1970s there was a return to more traditional irredentism.

'External Association'

In June 1921 the British monarch opened a Northern assembly with the right to remain in the UK, separate from the home rule 'Free State' in the South. In response, President De Valera argued that Ireland should be granted fuller independence, in exchange for recognising Northern autonomy. Northern counties would have the right to form a local assembly with local representation, in addition to sending national TDs to the Dublin Dáil (rather than MPs to Westminster). This formed part of De Valera's proposal for 'external association' between Britain and Ireland, in which the unified Republic would be independent but linked to Britain through a 'Treaty of Association', as an equal partner rather than a subordinate dominion. Ireland would retain sovereignty in domestic affairs, with British 'reserved' powers transferred to the Dáil, but would be 'associated' with Britain in external affairs. These proposals sought to bridge British and Irish jurisdictions through a form of 'independence in unity', that would both supersede unionist fears and satisfy Republican aspirations.

However, the British government responded by insisting that the northern counties remain in the UK if they wished, and that the Free State should remain in the Empire, threatening that repudiation of the Crown would lead to a resumption of the Anglo–Irish war. In perhaps the clearest possible statement of British sovereignty, the British government went on to spell out that 'no man can be a subject of two States. He must be either a subject of the King or an alien, and the question no more admits of an equivocal answer as whether he is alive or dead' [sic] (quoted in Coogan, 1993, p. 269). The British, and their representatives in the 'dominions', were determined to preserve absolute definitions of British sovereignty and monolithic conceptions of British state power, and this meant refusing the possibility of 'external association'. With this, Northern unionists were assured of British government backing, and the Southern Dáil began to accept the de facto existence of Partition.[1]

In this context the Southern Dáil defined institutional linkages between North and South as British or unionist interference. The Council of Ireland, which was set up as a link between North and South, was seen as involving implicit recognition of Partition. In

1924 the British proposed the creation of a North–South legislative body to exercise powers that had been 'reserved' for the Council, and this was rejected by the Dáil as it would have given 'the northern parliament a veto on our legislation'; the Council was dissolved in 1925, removing the 'last formal bridge between north and south' (Phoenix, 1994, pp. 299 and 332); Northern nationalists complained, and attempted to get a hearing in the Dáil, only to be told they should direct their energies on the Northern Assembly (O'Connor, 1993, p. 229). In what followed, reaction justified reaction in a spiral away from progressive politics, North and South – the 'carnival of reaction' predicted by James Connolly (Beresford Ellis, 1988, p. 275). In the North the Unionist Party set about constructing a 'Protestant parliament and a Protestant state', as James Craig put it in 1934; in the South, as Coogan has argued, the Dáil approved 'a Catholic Constitution for a Catholic people' (Coogan, 1993, p. 695). Appeals that the Constitution be directed at combining 'our national traditions and aspirations so as to fuse them into one national consciousness' were rejected by the Dáil (Frank MacDermot (TD) quoted by Bowman, 1989, p. 152). Instead, the Catholic Church was granted a 'special position', and the new Constitutional Preamble read more like a religious dedication than a republican claim to self-determination. Indeed, many of its clauses could have been deliberately written to flout the 1916 Republican Proclamation, that the Republic would guarantee 'religious and civil liberty, equal rights and equal opportunities to all its citizens ... cherishing all of the children of the nation equally'. Hardly surprising, in July 1937, the new Constitution was only very narrowly endorsed by Southern voters.[2]

The Republic's legitimacy now rested on the 'sovereign' rights of the 'Irish nation' (Article 1) within the 'national territory', defined as the 'whole of the island of Ireland', including the North (Article 2). In the meantime, 'pending the re-integration of the national territory', the 'extent of application' of laws enacted in the Irish parliament would be limited to the 26 Counties (Article 3). This placed a deep barrier of legal principle between North and South, and for nearly 30 years was to rule out any recognition of the Northern statelet – or any behaviour that implied recognition. The tactic of weakening the North through economic boycott, implemented in 1921–24, was translated into an official policy of non-recognition. Residual North–South co-operation for instance in fisheries management and rail transport continued in spite of, not because of Southern policy.

The slide from a form of attempted cosmopolitan nationalism
into irredentist nationalism was complete: state-building as an act
of domination in the North was twinned with state-building as an
act of forgetting in the South. The British doctrine of Crown
sovereignty had written off the possibilities of 'independence in
unity', both by guaranteeing unionist preference for subjecthood
under an English monarch, rather than a looser citizenship in
'association' with it, and by British and colonial refusal to accept
such an implied redefinition of the empire (Hachey, 1989).

The new Southern strategy was neatly summarised by De
Valera during the 1957 election campaign, where he asserted that:
'if we make sure that this five sixths is made really Irish we will
have the preservation of the Irish nation in our hands', adding
that 'time will settle the other thing' (quoted in Bowman, 1989,
p. 312). But Partition proved signally resistant to time's healing
effects. Political masters of the 'other thing', and their British
allies, would not lightly give up their monopoly of power – which
only found greater self-justification in the face of the South's
increasing 'Irishness'.

'Technocratic Anti-partitionism'
From the 1960s, principled non-recognition of the North was
undermined by increased North–South economic cooperation.
The Southern government began elaborating a new mode of
cosmopolitan nationalism, 'which depended on modernisation of
the Irish economy in order to present an attractive image to the
inhabitants of Northern Ireland' (Lyne, 1990, p. 420). In 1965,
30 years after De Valera's 'economic war' with Britain, the
Republic signed the Anglo–Irish Free Trade Agreement, and
began meeting with the Northern O'Neil government to explore
the possibilities of North–South policy coordination. There had
been rapid convergence in economic orientations and employment structures, as both economies gained a large
multinational-controlled sector producing consumer goods for
export. Reflecting international trends, the Republic had moved
from national autarchy to economic 'openness', and in both parts
of Ireland there was an attempt to 'hook on to' the 'Fordist' wave
of production from which both had been largely excluded
(Mjoset, 1993, p. 272).

Economic cooperation was seen as helping to build the conditions for reconciliation, and some form of eventual unity.
Reflecting this, there was open reassessment of the Republic's
non-recognition of the North. In 1967 Lemass established a Dáil

Committee on the Constitution, and broached the question of whether the South should offer *de facto* recognition of the *status quo* as a firmer basis for joint working. Taking this position, the Committee stated the jurisdictional claim in Article 2 should be revised to express the Republic's 'firm will that its territory be reunited in harmony and brotherly affection between all Irishmen' [*sic*]; as evidence of this 'affection', it argued the 'special position' of the Catholic Church should be removed and divorce decriminalised.[3] This was reiterated in 1972 by an Inter-Party Committee on the Implications of Irish Unity, attended by the new Northern nationalist party – the Social Democratic and Labour Party – and by some unionist representatives. Again, recognition of the need for nationalist–unionist accommodation was presented as a requirement of North–South integration. Reflecting this, the government began favouring an interim 'internal' power-sharing solution to the Northern conflict, as part of the wider process of North–South 'detente' (Herz, 1986).

These developments, and the emphasis on economic reintegration as the prelude to political reintegration, dovetailed with debates about the South's imminent membership of the European Economic Community (along with Britain and Northern Ireland). From as early as 1962 Garret Fitzgerald had promoted EC membership as a means of reducing the 'economic differences that divide North and South', while also freeing the South from dependence on Britain. This approach became official policy in the late 1960s, and was detailed in the Taoiseach's statement to the Dáil during the debate on EEC membership in March 1972, in which he argued that a 'no' vote on membership would 'confer on the border the status of a frontier ... thereby "copper-fastening" Partition'.[4] Integration into a transnational, pan-Irish and pan-EEC economic space was seen as both encouraging reunification and enhancing independence, in a happy 'conjunction of the interests of the pocket with certain predispositions of the spirit' (Coakley, 1983, p. 64).

The British government, meanwhile, had shifted from defending its 'Crown territory' to presenting itself as a neutral arbiter between nationalist and unionist aspirations. Initially, in 1969, it had rebuffed Southern concerns about the intensifying conflict, stating that 'responsibility for affairs in Northern Ireland is entirely a matter of domestic jurisdiction'.[5] But as the crisis deepened and Direct Rule was imposed, the British government began meeting with Irish officials, and under the Sunningdale process of 1973–74, agreed to the Republic's involvement in a new North–South Council of Ireland. This was agreed on condition there would be no change in the constitutional status of Northern Ireland without the consent of a majority of its inhabitants, with the Republic declaring that the 'only unity' it wanted to see was a 'unity established by consent', reflecting the 1967 Dáil Committee's suggestions, and in effect recognising the *de facto* existence of Partition.[6]

The 'largely symbolic' Council framework (Lee, 1989, p. 444) had gained the support of constitutional nationalists, but faced opposition from unionists. The Ulster Unionist Party rejected it and joined Loyalists in an anti-Agreement Alliance, which gained 51 per cent of the Northern vote in the 1974 General Election.[7] Under pressure from this grouping of 'mainstream' unionists, Loyalists and paramilitaries, the British government reneged on the Agreement (Millar, 1978). This broke the Southern consensus on the need for Northern reconciliation as a prelude to unity. In 1975 Fianna Fáil returned to the more irredentist position that a British declaration of an intention to withdraw was the necessary precondition of conflict-resolution; Fine Gael remained committed to North–South rapprochement as a route to a preferably federal Ireland, but given unionist and British intransigence this quickly translated into an appeal for Southern 'pluralism' and nationalist 'revisionism'. In 1977 the Fine Gael Coalition government was soundly defeated at the polls, at least in part due to its position on the North. Meanwhile, the economic road to North–South detente – Lemass's technocratic anti-partitionism – was forced into abeyance as the British government opted for purely 'internal' solutions to the conflict.

III. Contemporary Reconciliation

In the 1920s the British government threatened to resume the Anglo–Irish war rather than accept proposals for 'independence in unity'; and in the 1970s unionist leaders mounted a paramilitary blockade against North–South 'detente' based on a revived Council of Ireland. By the 1990s such British and unionist opposition was weaker, suggesting it could be 'third time lucky' for cosmopolitan nationalism. There are at least three positive reasons for thinking that such efforts may now have greater mileage.

First, from the early 1990s there are signs that traditional North–South divisions are becoming unsustainable. Facing the decline of indigenously-owned industry, economic elites have begun to suggest that the answer to Ireland's vicious cycle of dependency and unemployment lies in greater North–South integration.

Socio-economic differences between North and South narrowed in the 1980s and 1990s, and employment patterns converged as the North deindustrialised and the South became an 'export platform' for multinationals trading into the EU (OECD, 1985). Unemployment rose dramatically and overall levels of disposable income converged; both parts of Ireland remained heavily integrated into the British labour market, with rates of migration unparalleled in the EU. Meanwhile, dependence on external subsidies escalated, particularly in the North which relied on Whitehall for one-quarter of regional GDP, while the South received 5–6 per cent of GDP from the EU.

EU integration has played a central role in this convergence, primarily through policy harmonisation – of taxation rates, interest rates and exchange rates. Intensified competition from larger pan-EU producers poses a shared problem; in 1992 the Southern government identified the task of creating a viable indigenous sector as 'the main common challenge facing indus-trial development, North and South' (DSO, 1992, p. 41); and in the North there was a parallel reorientation, with business leaders calling for a 'single island economy'. By the mid-1990s the need for an all-Ireland economic strategy had virtually become conven-tional wisdom (see Chapter 4), though, as the 1998 'Agreement' reflects, unionists remain determined to delay developments towards the 'single economy'.

The second 'motor' for cosmopolitan nationalism is an increased realisation that Irish nationalism and republicanism have to strengthen all-island perspectives, and embark on a process of 'national reconciliation' that can encompass Northern unionists – as expressed in the deliberations of the Forum for Peace and Reconciliation. The emerging all-Ireland economic pressures 'highlight the extent to which the continuing existence of the border [is] determined by political and cultural forces' (Hickman, 1990, p. 21), and this forces Southern nationalists (as well as Northern unionists) to more effectively address the difficult ideo-logical questions raised by increased North–South dialogue.

In many respects these dialogues are (still) patterned by sectar-ianism. Unionist assertions that the Republic is a 'theocratic state' and that Irish unity would impose 'Rome Rule' on Northern Protestants were, and are, used to justify the 'defence' of

Protestantism through sectarian practices in the North. In the South, explicit reference to the 'special' Catholic role in the 1937 Constitution was removed in 1972, but this has not been replaced with a commitment to secularism, and the Church's 'special' administrative and legal role remains in place.[8] The Constitution claims authority from the Church and the Irish nation – and there remains some doubt which takes precedence, as the Church has actively involved itself in popular referenda, for instance on abortion in 1983 and 1993, and on divorce in 1986 and 1995.

There have been powerful challenges to these divisions, and to the social conservatism that sustains them. The challenge to Protestant domination in the North intensified with the 1960s civil rights movement, and has continued since. From the late 1970s there have also been stronger challenges to the 'authoritarianism of Irish political culture' in the South (Boyce, 1995, p. 429), culminating in campaigns around abortion, contraception, divorce and control of education. Significantly, these campaigns are increasingly fought on an explicitly all-island basis; while in 1974 church-based organisations were still the strongest North–South social institutions, by 1990 campaigning and advocacy organisations had taken the lead in building cross-border links, primarily to increase their political leverage (Whyte, 1983; Murray and O'Neill, 1991). Often speaking from the social and political margins, such groupings challenge the definition of North–South relations in sectarianised terms. As a result, all-Ireland unity around issues such as labour and trade union rights, environmental protection and women's rights, has begun to emerge, along with greater North–South cultural interaction.

Partly reflecting this, there has been considerable ideological convergence between Northern-based Republicans and Southern constitutional nationalists. Beginning with the Hume–Adams talks in 1993, and leading to events such as the Dublin 'Forum on Peace and Reconciliation', this has encouraged the emergence of an all-Ireland 'public sphere'. At the Forum, Irish nationalists and Republicans were at one in recognising the need to accommodate Northern unionist opinion, and in their willingness to accept linkages with the British state to achieve this. Their agreement with liberal unionists at the 1996 Forum on Peace and Reconciliation mapped out a possible agenda for North–South reconciliation – 'not simply based on majoritarianism ... [but] on a balanced constitutional accommodation'. The joint Report signed by all constitutional nationalist parties, the Irish Labour Party, Sinn Fein, the Workers' Party and the Alliance Party, asserted that these 'constitutional changes should be such as not to diminish in any way the existing citizenship rights [of the people of Northern Ireland], and their birthright to be accepted as British or Irish – or both'.[9]

Third, in tandem with these ideological shifts, the Irish government has been reinterpreting its constitutional commitment to unity. A central factor in this is the increasing British reliance on joint management of the conflict with the Republic: the two states, British and Irish, have discovered a joint interest in containing the conflict, with both standing to benefit from establishing Anglo–Irish and North South institutions to manage their common political agendas.

This Anglo–Irish convergence has required a reinterpretation – or clarification – of the Southern claim to unity. Under the 1973 Sunningdale Declaration and the 1985 Anglo–Irish Agreement (AIA) – both of which sought to establish intergovernmental structures to manage the conflict – the Republic recognised that Northern consent was a precondition of Irish unity, while stopping short of recognising Northern Ireland's constitutional status as part of the UK (Coughlan, 1992). To bring this position into consistency with Articles 2 and 3, in 1990 the Irish Supreme Court ruled that Southern politicians were required to work for reintegration – and hence for Northern consent – as a 'constitutional imperative' (Donoghue, 1993, p. 17).[10]

One way of reading the 'imperative' is that it requires politicians to act as advocates for 'their' minority in the North. This was reflected in AIA, which was presented by the Taoiseach in November 1985 as establishing structures 'capable of eroding the alienation of the nationalist minority'.[11] This pandered to irredentist nationalism and (ironically) was underpinned by the British government's 'two-nations' or 'double minority' interpretation of the conflict, along with its need to recruit the South as a 'partner' in winning over Northern nationalists. In this respect, the AIA simply 're-partitioned' the island, as the two governments recognised each other's sphere of communal influence.[12]

An alternative, more positive reading of the nationalist 'imperative' suggests that Southern politicians should be seeking to rebuild reciprocal and symbiotic North–South relations. These could encourage unionists into a reintegrated Ireland, rather than encourage them to see the British government as 'their' advocate (as under the AIA). With the Hume–Adams, SDLP–Sinn Fein talks process, and in the subsequent lead-up to the IRA ceasefire, such agendas began to gain ground. From 1990 the British government had claimed it was neutral on the question of the Union, and in December 1993, under pressure to secure an IRA ceasefire, it joined the Republic in signing the Downing Street Declaration, which defined unionist–nationalist reconciliation as a North–South concern as much as an 'internal' Northern Ireland concern.

This opens up the possibility of superseding unionist–nationalist divisions, rather than simply managing them: if confined to the North, reconciliation simply requires Southern input to balance Northern unionist hegemony; in contrast, North–South reconciliation requires joint institutions founded on common, island-wide interests. To a significant degree the Southern government was reasserting the New Ireland Forum goal of unity by 'agreement and consent, embracing the whole of the island of Ireland and providing irrevocable guarantees for the protection and preservation of both the nationalist and unionist identities' (NIF, 1984, para 5.7).

The three factors – socio-economic, ideological and constitutional – are laying the groundwork for a positive-sum means of overcoming national division. Not surprisingly this has reinvigorated debate in the South about a possible rewording of Articles 2 and 3. After the AIA the position was simply that Partition could be recognised *de facto*, but not *de jure*, and this was already a pragmatic rather than an 'in principle' position. As Taoiseach in 1990 Haughey opposed a proposal that the Constitution be amended to revoke the *de jure* claim, arguing that if constitutional nationalists dropped 'the claim to nationhood', it would immediately 'become the exclusive property of the men of violence'; only in the context of a wider settlement could the issue of altering Articles 2 and 3 be put to a referendum (Speech to the Dáil, *Irish Times,* 6 December 1990). This position – that the territorial claim was essentially an 'opening gambit' – remained in place through the 1990–92 inter-party talks (which excluded Republicans and Loyalists linked to paramilitaries), with both Albert Reynolds and Dermot Ahern reiterating that Articles 2 and 3 had to be kept in place until a wider settlement had been negotiated (*Irish Times,* 4 March 1993).

The position began to change in 1994, as the Irish government outlined the implications of such a settlement for Irish unity, for instance arguing that 'between the traditional poles of belonging to a sovereign UK and a sovereign united Ireland, there is large room for compromise and mutual accommodation, and for a step-by-step approach to building confidence and promoting national reconciliation and cooperation' (Albert Reynolds,

Taoiseach, *Irish Times,* 18 April 1994). Initially this was defined as requiring mutual compromise, essentially a constitutional quid pro quo. At the Forum for Peace and Reconciliation, in November 1994, Fine Gael asserted that 'change is required both in the Government of Ireland Act and in Articles 2 and 3 of the 1937 Constitution', adding that such change 'could help to transform the situation and make positive gains for both communities'; Fianna Fáil made similar suggestions, albeit less clearly defined, in arguing for 'accommodation ... of fundamental and legitimate constitutional differences' (FPR, 1995, pp. 9 and 22). The 1995 Framework Document committed both governments to making such constitutional changes, but failed to state the precise extent of rewording that would be required.

In this relatively fluid context, the Irish government has embarked on a process of realigning Irish nationalism. As in the previous attempts at delineating a compromise 'cosmopolitan' nationalism, these discussions are bounded by the twin constraints of popular aspiration and state legitimacy. Constitutional change may stabilise jurisdictional authority, and help to facilitate negotiations on the future of Northern Ireland, but to go ahead it would have to attract majority support in a referendum. Reflecting these twin imperatives, the government has begun elaborating a 'one nation, two jurisdictions' model, which involves recognition of Partition, paired with the demand for self-determination. Significantly, this is founded on a reinterpretation of the historical record: as the Taoiseach stated in 1996 – 'while we consider that Partition was a grave injustice and contrary to the principle of self-determination, if correctly observed at the time, we cannot ignore the lapse of time and treat Northern Ireland 75 years on as if it had never existed' (Bertie Ahern, *Irish Times,* 14 February 1996).

The central innovation in the emerging position is a significant redefinition of the *de jure* claim, towards *de jure* as well as *de facto* recognition of Partition, conditional upon the continued aspiration to overcome it. The legal logic of this apparent contradiction was explored by an international lawyer, Professor Eide, in a Report commissioned for the Forum for Peace and Reconciliation in 1996. He argued that the 1920 Partition had breached an international norm, of the right of colonial peoples to self-determination, but had not breached international law, as the right to self-determination only gained the status of law in 1966 (Eide, 1996). While the right to self-determination existed from at least 1919 when the concept was deployed in the Versailles

Treaty process, and while the British government's decision to create a colonial enclave in the North flouted such norms, Eide argued that Partition was technically legal at the time. This suggests that a *de jure* right to territorial unity does not exist, although the *de jure* right to all-Ireland self-determination does, hence the apparent contradiction: Partition flouted norms that later became international law, and it is the Southern government's responsibility to correct this injustice, and work for unity.

By accepting these arguments, and offering the model of 'one nation, two jurisdictions', the Irish government is attempting to separate the claim to territorial jurisdiction from the claim to self-determination. This new form of cosmopolitan nationalism is associated with suggested amendments to Articles 2 and 3, and is aimed at creating a 'middle ground' between British and Irish jurisdictions in Ireland (see Chapter 7). The two states are not relieved of their responsibilities; the pre-existing and still-prevailing right to self-determination for the Irish nation imposes a burden of responsibility on the two states – on the Northern Ireland jurisdiction as much as on the Southern state. This is expressed for instance in commitments to cross-border 'parity of esteem', and to the creation of North–South institutions. These are to be founded on popular aspirations, notably for reconciliation on the 'island of Ireland', not territorial or jurisdictional claims. The states acquire a central role in developing this all-Ireland civic 'space', and this finds its primary legitimation in the global civic norm of the right to self-determination for colonised peoples.

As in the 1920s and 1970s, this new mode of official cosmopolitan nationalism directly raises the question of the British position: in 1996, Martin Mansergh, head of research for Fianna Fáil, argued that 'the refusal to accept any mid-way between union and separation ... finished the Union in the rest of Ireland. Similarly, an inability to accept a middle ground between integration with the UK and a united Ireland, if persisted with, will, I believe, be damaging to the prospects of the Union in the longer-term' (1996b, p. 9). It will also – as suggested by the historical record – be damaging to the prospects for peace.

Conclusions

Since their earliest days, Irish nationalists have attempted to overcome Protestant–Catholic and Irish–British divisions. In doing so they have often sought to move beyond the zero-sum hierarchies of colonialism, towards more positive-sum relationships. Such 'cosmopolitan nationalism' defines an inclusive national identity and offers Southern politicians an alternative to irredentism and partitionism. But nationalism is never developed in isolation, it is always in some way relational; and in the Irish case it is the colonial–imperial relation that dominates. The emergence of cosmopolitan nationalism in the Republic, and indeed its potential success, hinges on the possibilities that have opened up as British nationalism has been forced to adapt to post-imperial realities.

British nationalism is peculiarly brittle and resistant to change, especially in its unionist variants. The historical experience, from the 1920s and 1970s, amply illustrates the barriers to cosmopolitanism, first erected by British nationalists in London, and then by unionists in Northern Ireland. In the 1990s a revival of Southern cosmopolitan nationalism is under way as Partition faces formidable challenges 'from within', with increased cross-border linkages, a challenge to social conservatism North and South, and a redefined state legitimacy, expressed in the British–Irish 'peace process'.

In response to these pressures there has been a significant realignment of official Irish nationalism, leading to proposals for a redefinition of the Southern state's constitutional commitment to national unity. These proposals do not fall into the partitionist mould, as the claim to national self-determination remains paramount; neither do they fall under the heading of irredentist nationalism, as the territorial claim is increasingly discarded in favour of national reconciliation. Instead, they mark out pathways for a cosmopolitan nationalism. In doing so, they define new political possibilities, for constitutional change in Northern Ireland and the Republic, North–South institutions, for reconciliation and 'parity of esteem' on an island-wide basis (see Chapter 13).

Whether these possibilities are realised depends in large part on the British government. As noted, the British state has moved away from its 'all or nothing' stance on Northern Ireland, and has been increasingly willing to work jointly with the Republic in managing the conflict to secure a broadly acceptable peace settlement; yet despite these commitments the British government is still wedded to the majoritarian constitutional guarantee. Whether there can be substantive redefinition of British sovereignty in the North, including the repeal of Britain's constitutional claim, and the creation of North–South institutions, remains to be seen. The possibility of progress also depends on the position of unionist and Loyalist politicians in Northern Ireland. Again the prospects are mixed; while some sections of unionism now see the symbolic and practical value of North–South institutions, there remain significant sections opposing any Southward integration.

The strategy remains vulnerable to British nationalism and to unionist obstructionism; and given such threats it also remains vulnerable to implosion from 'within', as the contending demands of irredentists and partitionists threaten to engulf the more positive-sum alternatives offered by cosmopolitan nationalism. Yet still it is fair to suggest that the balance of forces has now significantly shifted against a continuation of the *status quo*, and towards the possibilities offered by cosmopolitan nationalism. The historical record and contemporary conditions suggest that it indeed may be 'third time lucky' for Ireland's cosmopolitan nationalism.

Notes

A version of this chapter was presented to the International Sociological Association Research Committee on Racism and Ethnicity held in Manila in May 1996. My thanks to participants for comments.

1. De Valera's alternative to the 1921 Treaty, the 'Document No. 2', persisted with 'external association' to bridge the clash of claims although it granted *de facto* recognition of Partition. The civil war that ensued centred on the question of whether there should be *de jure* recognition of the North, and independence from the British Crown for the 26 Counties (Mansergh, 1981, p. 19; Bowman, 1989, p. 77).

2. An election to the Dáil was held on the same day of the referendum and attracted a 74.7 per cent turnout. Only 68.4 per cent also voted on the Constitution – 685,101 votes in favour, 526,945 against and 170,000 spoiled votes (Bowman, 1989, p. 160). The Constitution claimed legitimacy 'in the name of the most holy Trinity from whom is all authority and to whom in our final end all actions both of men and states must be referred'; equal rights before the law were asserted subject to 'differences of capacity, physical and moral and of social function'; Article 41 established the 'family' as the 'necessary basis of the social order' and pledged the state to protect women's 'life within the home'; civil liberties were subordinated to 'the preservation of public peace and order', allowing recourse to non-jury courts.

3. See *Report of the Committee on the Constitution*, DSO, 1967, p. 44.
4. *Dáil Debates*, 21 March 1972, Motion on membership of the European Economic Community.
5. Harold Wilson's 'Downing Street Declaration', *The Times*, London, 20 August 1969, quoted in Hepburn, 1980, p. 198.
6. For the British government, the new North–South structures were explicitly aimed at 'binding the minority to the support of new political arrangements', *Communique issued after the Conference between the Irish and British governments and the parties involved in the Northern Ireland Executive*, 6–9 December 1973.
7. Members of the alliance joined with Loyalist workers' associations and paramilitaries to organise a two-week stoppage against the Agreement, in which paramilitaries mounted street barricades, often with the active encouragement of RUC officers (Fisk, 1975). Anti-Agreement Alliance representatives were later voted into 11 of Northern Ireland's 12 Westminster seats.
8. As a Supreme Court judge clarified in 1995, R. O'Hanlon, letter to the *Irish Times*, 1 March 1995.
9. Agreed at the Forum on Peace and Reconciliation, Dublin, 2 February 1996.
10. This limited commitment to Irish unity can be compared with the commitment to German unity inserted in the Constitution of the Federal Republic of Germany by the Western allies in 1945. It was designed to express the aspiration to Irish unity amongst nationalists, North and South, and it remains the preferred option for the overwhelming majority on the island as a whole. In fact, support for this constitutional commitment increased in the 1980s and 1990s as Irish nationalism, and later republicanism, began to more actively pursue North–South integration as a joint endeavour (Goodman, 1996).
11. Garret Fitzgerald, Taoiseach, announcing the AIA, *Dáil Debates*, 19 November 1985. North–South institutions remained on the agenda, but only as a threat to persuade unionists into a power-sharing Northern assembly
12. O'Mahony J. (1989) 'Hillsborough and Sunningdale, Ireland, the socialist answer', *Socialist Organiser*, 22–3.

6   Constituting Division, Impeding Agreement: The Neglected Role of British Nationalism in Northern Ireland

Liam O'Dowd

While Irish nationalism is universally recognised as an integral part of the Northern Ireland conflict, the role of its British counterpart is generally ignored. This is one manifestation of a broader asymmetry. While Northern Ireland has little obvious impact on overall British politics, the British state has an enormous impact on Northern Ireland politics. Since British nationalism is 'state-led' rather than 'state-seeking' any analysis of the conflict or of the prospects for a political settlement that fails to problematise British nationalism is seriously flawed.

Ulster unionism is an amalgam of various strands of British nationalism, many of them archaic, such as popular Protestantism and identification with the monarchy and the ancient British constitution. As the UK has moved from an imperial state to a member state of the EU, British nationalism has also changed. More secular than in the past, it still identifies with the peculiar form of civil religion surrounding the monarchy (Nairn, 1988). It draws on collective memories of war and Empire. It is informed by contemporary concerns about preserving the British state in the face of minority nationalisms in the British Isles, a larger and more diverse immigrant population and the threat of Europeanisation.

The trajectories of state nationalism in Britain and Northern Ireland have differed, however, even if they intermesh in complex, and often contradictory ways. The 'relentless reciprocity' of Irish nationalists and Ulster unionists is no longer central to nationalism in Britain. Ulster unionists' frequent over-identification with British nationalist symbols has led to them being characterised as outside the realms of normal British politics. For many nationalists in Britain, unionism is an unwelcome reminder of the past – of the coercive nature of British state formation, of the role of militant Protestantism and of a fixation with Irish nationalism which seems irrelevant in contemporary Europe. At the same time, since the 1970s, the British state has become embroiled in the day-to-day management of the Northern Ireland conflict, becoming inevitably a protagonist in it. Against this background, unionists and some other British nationalists have sought to forge alliances in ways which have had a significant impact on the evolution of the conflict and on the prospects for a settlement.

This chapter interrogates the role of British nationalism in the conflict under four headings:

1. the factors which have revitalised British nationalism throughout the UK in the last three decades;
2. patterns of ambiguity and denial which fail to recognise British nationalism as an integral element of the Northern Ireland conflict;
3. the development of British nationalism through conflict with the 'collective other' of Irish nationalism or republicanism;
4. the impact on the conflict of the complex reworking of the frequently contradictory and ambiguous relationship between unionists and other British nationalists.

A New Context for a Revitalised British Nationalism

At one level, contemporary British nationalism is a reaction to the relative decline of the British state from imperial power to its reduced status as a member-state of the European Union. 'Post-hegemonic trauma' (Taylor, 1991) is a response to threats to British state sovereignty from within and without. As a political project, the revitalisation of British nationalism has involved an attempt to protect the integrity of the British state and its core institutions in a period of rapid change. Nationalists seek to defend these institutions as the defining symbols of British nationhood.

Nationalism is not necessarily a pervasive or continuous ideology within any population. But it is possible to identify strong and weak variants in the British case. The strong variant of the nationalist project is Conservative and stresses the need to preserve the archaic institutions of the British state and the memory of wars and conflicts through which British identity was forged (Colley, 1992). In the case of traditional 'one-nation' Toryism, it seeks to defend traditional ethno-national and class hierarchies focused on the master symbolism of the monarchy. Alternatively, it may seek to modernise these hierarchies as in the Thatcherite project. The latter revealed starkly the old elision between British and English nationalism and, accordingly, had little appeal on the Celtic periphery.

Thatcherite conservatism itself is just a part of the strong variant. It is linked in various ways to the legacy of Enoch Powell, the ragbag of right-wing pressure groups opposing European integration, immigration and the IRA *inter alia*. This form of nationalism advocates a 'strong' law and order state and a neo-liberal economic programme. It seeks to combat the 'enemies within' be they socialists, trade unionists, anti-state nationalists such as the IRA, or immigrants diluting traditional English/British culture. Abroad it means 'standing up for Britain' against foreigners be they 'European', Argentinian or Libyan. Sympathisers are to be found in aristocratic, military and business circles. Its most frequent ideological expression is to be found in the overwhelmingly conservative national press, ranging from the tabloids to *The Times*, *Sunday Times*, *Daily* and *Sunday Telegraphs*. It is within this strong, revitalised British nationalism that Ulster unionism feels most at home.

There is a 'weaker' variant of British nationalism, however, which has found its most recent expression in Blair's New Labour. Its commitment is also to maintaining the integrity of the British state. But, it seeks to be less confrontational and more inclusive in terms of class, nation, culture and ethnicity. Its means and its rhetoric are different from the strong variant in that it emphasises 'constitutional reform' and the 'modernisation' of British state institutions. Its devolutionary proposals are a hesitant move to a new form of British federalism and it is less sceptical of European integration. The rhetoric is that of 're-branding' Britain, a new corporate British image, which is competitive in the global order while retaining a human face. In contrast to the 'strong variant' it seeks to celebrate change and multi-culturalism within Britain. While its emphases are different, it shares much with its strong variant: appeals to British national pride, a rejection of a European super-state and shared collective memories of war and the evolution of British institutions. Like the strong variant, it shares a historical sense that Britain has a universalistic mission, an idea quite widespread even on the Left. Thus, it fails frequently to recognise the particularism of its own ideology or that it is a nationalism at all.

The political project of British nationalism is, like that of other nationalisms, diverse and sometimes internally contradictory. Moreover, it is a state nationalism, in that it seeks to use an existing state to create (or maintain) the 'nation' while seeing that state as an expression of a British nation. As such it must be distinguished from 'nations' or national movements seeking states which not do exist as yet.

British nationalism, like the Spanish, Italian, French and German, is one of several state nationalisms in Europe confronted by internal and external threats to national identity and sovereignty. The revitalisation of British nationalism, however, feeds off the particularly severe challenges it faces. For institutional and historical reasons, the UK remains a multinational state in a sense which is now very rare in Europe. The UK risks succumbing to the forces which have fragmented the huge multinational empires over the last two centuries (including the British and, most recently, the Soviet empires) (Anderson, 1992). This process has culminated in the disintegration of the USSR and the breakup of smaller multinational states such as Yugoslavia and Czechoslovakia. The volatility of state borders is reflected in the fact that of the 48 sovereign states comprising Europe in the 1993, 36 have come into existence in the twentieth century (Davies, 1996).

Until 1950, interstate war had proved to be the greatest means of sustaining the nationalism of existing states, of bringing new states into being, and of modifying the borders of existent states (Balakrishnan, 1996). The Second World War, however, clearly distinguished the UK from other big states in Europe. For the latter, the war undermined the ideal of the nation state and of building state nationalisms. In Britain, however, the war affirmed the value of a British nationalism, across the political spectrum, in the face of fascist and communist nationalisms in Europe. While the war confirmed the integrity of the UK state, it undermined that of Germany, Italy and France. Twentieth-century British nationalism has been re-forged in wartime coalitions and in the popular memory and experience of both world wars. Here both strong and weak variants share common ground with Ulster unionists.

But wars have lost much of their capacity for mobilising state nationalisms. For the past half-century interstate wars in Europe have become impractical given that it is no longer possible to defend state borders against nuclear attack. This has not prevented the UK from mobilising nationalist sentiment for involvement in extra-European wars as in Suez, the Falklands and the Gulf. Interstate wars have been replaced by civil wars or conflicts which threaten the integrity of states from within (O'Dowd, 1998b). Unlike interstate wars, these conflicts undermine pro-state nationalisms while often strengthening secessionist or autonomist national movements. National consciousness has to be mobilised now either against the 'enemy within' or against the more insidious, if broad-based, moves towards European integration.

But British nationalism, like other state nationalisms, is not merely a question of conscious political projects. It also takes the form of what Michael Billig (1995) has termed a banal (if not benign) nationalism associated with the national symbols and the designation of 'Others'. This is an almost unconscious sense of being British, which informs everyday activity – a sense of imagined community affirmed in reading daily 'national' news, watching soap operas, in being aware of national flags and emblems and supporting British teams in international sport. It frequently draws on popular stereotypes of 'Britishness' while designating what is 'non-British'. Like its more formal political counterpart it frequently elides English and British identity. Ironically, much of the focus for both political and banal nationalism is the British media which are themselves under transnational ownership.

British Nationalism in Northern Ireland: Ambiguity and Denial

Ireland, however, has a somewhat ambiguous place in the discourse of British nationalism. It allows British nationalists to assert their anti-nationalism. However, the anti-nationalist diatribes in the tabloids, the *Daily Telegraph* and *The Times* are aimed only at the minority nationalisms within Britain and Ireland (Lee, 1998). As Taylor (1991: 148) observes, quoting Chadwick, nationalism is seen as 'a kind of political disease which affects foreign nations [including the colonies; Furedi, 1994] and certain parts of our own islands'. By contrast English/British identity is perceived to be remarkably, and uniquely, immune from this disease, a view common on the Right and expressed by some on the Left also.[1] In this view, contemporary Anglo-British culture is seen as the inheritor of the univeralising legacy of Empire. It is portrayed as pluralistic, democratic and civilising, with a history of opposition to nationalism at home and abroad.

The poorer the fit between this rhetoric and the reality of a post-imperial state in 'reduced circumstances', the more vehement the assertion of an anti-nationalistic Britishness. The refusal to acknowledge the existence of a British nationalism implies an ideology of Britishness which is qualitatively different from, and superior to, mere particularistic and secessionist nationalisms such as the Irish. Ulster unionists now see themselves as the main, if not the only, repository of Britishness in Ireland. They willingly identify with the sense of superiority implied in this claim and this lies behind their frequent assertions that Irish nationalism and Ulster unionism are irreconcilable. This helps legitimise the reluctance to negotiate with Irish nationalists *qua* nationalists. To recognise the problem as one of competing nationalisms would justify a common political discourse, and a strategy of negotiation and accommodation.

In the broader context, the role of Ireland in British state and nation building has been contested and ambiguous. The prolonged attempts to integrate the island of Ireland into the United Kingdom were never completely successful. In the process, British national identity came to be defined historically in contradistinction to Irish identity (and vice versa). This remained the case even at the high tide of imperial expansion when Irish unionists and some nationalists came to think of Ireland and Britain as partners in the same colonial enterprise. Yet, the continuous presence of the British state has acted as a focal point for British interest and identity in Ireland.

The Ulster Unionist Party (UUP) remained an integral, if distinctive, part of the Conservative and Unionist Party until the 1970s. All British governments ceded the day-to-day running of Northern Ireland to the majority community as represented by the UUP. This form of pragmatic and ideological distancing of Northern Ireland from British politics became more significant, and more problematical, with the outbreak of the conflict in the late 1960s.

Under Direct Rule, the central British state became more involved in the running of Northern Ireland, and in seeking to reconstitute a broader base for governance there. Official ideology came to portray the state as a 'neutral arbiter' in an inter-communal conflict. The form taken by the conflict seemed to confirm that Northern Ireland was 'a place apart'. It constituted an implicit denial that Northern Ireland was an integral part of the 'British national question'. This distancing coincided with the reopening of the latter in the 1970s with pressures for devolution in Scotland and Wales.

Beyond the realms of official ideology, British state policy was ambiguous in practice, at times managing the conflict on a quasi-colonial basis, at other times seeking to 'normalise' Northern Ireland as a region of the UK. In all this, however, British politicians and administrators portrayed state policy, not as a vehicle of British nationalism, but as a carrier of universal values with a mission to 'restore democracy' and 'law and order' and initiate reform. British policy in Northern Ireland could be justified by the weak variant of British nationalism as an advocacy of 'British values' of tolerance and democracy in the face of violence and sectarianism. On the other hand, 'strong nationalists' could advocate more active, militaristic and pro-unionist policies in the tradition of British counter-insurgency activities in the colonies.

The Conflict with Irish Republicanism and Nationalism

As the conflict became more rooted, it became more difficult for the British state through the Northern Ireland Office to portray its role in universalistic terms. It became more obviously a protagonist in the conflict. One of the ideological successes of the IRA campaign was to create a sense that the core of the conflict was the military struggle between the 'British forces' and the Republican movement. As Greenslade (1996) observes, years of British press coverage have identified 'only one enemy of the British state, the IRA'. IRA bombs, particularly in England, began to awaken more militant anti-Irish sentiment in Britain. The IRA re-emerged to become part of the 'collective other' of both the strong and weak variants of British nationalism. The Northern Ireland conflict now helped reinvigorate British nationalism alongside opposition to European integration, immigration, the Falklands and Gulf war campaigns and the threats to the integrity of the UK in Scotland and Wales.

As the conflict in Northern Ireland persisted, it became progressively more 'internationalised'. Northern Ireland nationalists and Republicans (the latter notably through the hunger strikes) were succeeding in publicising their case abroad, above all

in the USA. From the early 1980s, even the aggressively nationalist Thatcher government began to engage the Irish government
more formally as a consultative partner in managing Northern
Ireland. This was to culminate in the Anglo–Irish Agreement of
1985. From now on, the conflict was increasingly defined as
between two competing nationalist claims for territorial sovereignty in Northern Ireland (McGarry and O'Leary, 1995,
pp. 248–353). Many 'strong' British nationalists, including unionists, saw the issue of territorial sovereignty in zero-sum terms – a
perspective also strongly represented within Irish Republicanism.

More important, however, than the interaction between British
nationalism and Irish nationalism is the former's complex and
often contradictory relationship with Ulster unionism. Certainly,
the vast majority of British nationalists can find common cause
with unionists in their ideological opposition to the IRA, even if
this does not preclude British governments negotiating with
Republicans. In common with many other 'strong' British nationalists, unionists are what Hedetoft (1997, p. 12) terms 'idealists
of sovereignty'. They see British sovereignty as exclusive, indivisible, as something which is synonymous with their core identity.
It is scarcely surprising therefore, that it is in right-wing circles in
Britain, promulgating strong versions of British nationalism, that
the unionists have found their most consistent support.

British Nationalism and Ulster Unionism: Reworking a Complex and Ambiguous Relationship

One of the distinctive features of the Northern Ireland conflict is
the extent, and the frequency, with which the protagonists have
been surveyed in opinion polls. Since 1969, there has been a
growing preference among unionists to define themselves as
primarily British as opposed to claiming an Irish, Northern Irish
or Ulster identity. At the same time, there has been a consistent
preference expressed in British opinion polls for getting rid of
Northern Ireland into an independent Ulster or a united Ireland
(McGarry and O'Leary, 1995; Ruane and Todd, 1996, p. 225).

These poll findings obscure some important contradictions,
however. While the survival of unionism is identified with maintaining the British link, there is widespread unionist suspicion of
the policies and motives of successive British *governments*. On the
other hand, the British preference to leave Northern Ireland,
while a widely diffused feeling, has little political impact.

Northern Ireland is not a major British election issue. The 'Irish Question' has long since ceased to mark a fundamental divide between the British political parties. The Conservative Party is no longer institutionally tied to Ulster unionism and its half-hearted attempts to organise in Northern Ireland have met with little success. British Labour, with even less prospect of getting votes in Northern Ireland, has refrained from organising at all. Northern Ireland is constituted as 'outside normal British politics' even if it has an insidious influence on British human rights, judicial and policing regimes.

While Northern Ireland has little obvious impact on overall British politics, British politics and the British state have an enormous influence on Northern Ireland politics. Two related responses to this asymmetry are of significance in this context. First, Ulster unionists have sought to mobilise support in Britain for the maintenance of the Union from within the British political parties, rather than by embracing any one of them. While their supporters have been mainly drawn from conservative and other right-wing sources, they have also sought support from moderate nationalist defenders of the integrity of the UK in New Labour and the Liberal Democrats.[2] Second, British nationalists have in varying degrees embraced the unionist cause.

By the 1980s, Ulster unionists were coming to terms with the loss of their monopoly of power in Northern Ireland. The Anglo–Irish Agreement of 1985 was proof that it was no longer sufficient to rely on their own political strength in Northern Ireland to protect the Union. Accordingly, they have mounted an ideological campaign to mobilise support in Britain for their democratic right to be recognised as an integral part of the British nation. Attempts to distance the UK or to recognise the specific political dynamic within Northern Ireland are presented as a threat to their democratic rights as citizens of the UK. This is rooted in the assertion that the Partition of Ireland was a democratic resolution of the Irish question which has been resisted for decades by anti-democratic Irish nationalists.

This unionist identification with the British nation goes beyond protecting an electoral majority in Northern Ireland, however. It contains a number of diverse elements which resonate with the various strands of British nationalism. Paisley and the Orange Order appeal to the popular Protestantism which was an integral part of the forging of the British nation in the eighteenth and nineteenth centuries (Colley, 1992). Monarchist and loyal to the 'protestant crown in parliament', these politics find their most characteristic form in marching and other forms of popular expression. Marches symbolically claim the territory of Northern Ireland and symbolise the will to resist Republican and nationalist advances (Jarman, 1997). While central to Loyalism in Northern Ireland, Orangeism and the preoccupation with territorial control find few resonances in contemporary Britain apart from limited localised support in Scotland (Bruce, 1992). Mainstream British nationalists see marching and popular Protestantism as archaic and embarrassing, hence its projection in Britain can be counter-productive for the unionist cause as a whole.

On the extra-parliamentary front, there is evidence of links between Loyalist paramilitaries and right-wing activists in neo-fascist groups in Britain. A number of legal cases have illustrated periodic collusion between members of the British security forces and Loyalist paramilitaries in targeting Republican suspects including Catholics with no paramilitary connections (Tomlinson, 1995a; Ware *et al.*, 1998).

Much more critically, however, in the 1980s, the UUP under James Molyneaux fell under the influence of Enoch Powell, the leading parliamentary exponent of the strong variant of British nationalism. After Powell had become the MP for South Down he pushed the unionists to press for 'full integration' into the United Kingdom. The greatest setback to the Powellite strategy was Thatcher's signing of the Anglo–Irish Agreement which clearly sets Northern Ireland apart as the only part of the United Kingdom where another government has a consultative role in governance.

From the early 1980s, however, a more sustained intellectual underpinning was being developed to press for unionist support in Britain (O'Dowd, 1998a). This was partially located in the Campaign for Equal Citizenship, a group agitating for the extension of the mainstream British political parties to Northern Ireland and for Northern Ireland citizens to be treated in exactly the same manner as all other UK citizens. Its universalistic sounding policies were meant to appeal to both Conservative and Labour supporters in Britain (see Coulter, 1994). The initial appeal of the equal citizenship arguments in Britain was twofold. First, they explicitly rejected the popular Protestantism of Paisleyism and, second, they virulently opposed the claims of Irish Republicanism and nationalism.

The equal citizenship movement in which Robert McCartney (now a UK Unionist MP virulently opposed to the April 1998 Agreement) was involved, was part of a wider attempt to combat the success of Irish nationalists in winning support abroad. It was

specifically aimed at building support for the unionist position in
Britain. Its advocates saw the election of David Trimble as leader
of the UUP in 1994 as indicative of the emergence of a more
modern, articulate and assertive form of unionism (O'Dowd,
1998a).[3] Part of the appeal of the 'new unionism' rests on its
claim to reject nationalism as such. In this, it represents a long-
standing feature of British nationalism – its refusal to see itself as
a nationalism at all. In the words of one of its foremost advocates,
'it is citizenship that matters anyway, a political relationship
which acknowledges ... a diversity of national and cultural traditions within a common (British) institutional form' (Aughey,
1994, p. 148).

The 'new unionism' makes a virtue of its (British) constitutionalism, identifying with the Crown in Parliament and the
politics of the British state. In Aughey's (1995, p.14) terms, this
perspective makes Ulster unionism part of a 'wider concept',
raising it above the 'day to day struggle in Northern Ireland'. Such
self-recognition has the added advantage of underlining unionists'
self-proclaimed qualitative difference from, and superiority to,
Irish nationalists. As carriers of British (and therefore 'universal')
liberal political values, they claim to speak a different (and
superior) political language to their opponents. This conveniently
obviates the need for genuine political dialogue, negotiations or
compromise with Irish nationalists, *qua* nationalists. Unionists
can engage with them as individual citizens, or even as Catholics,
but not as nationalists who contest the legitimacy of the state.
They portray Irish nationalists as mired in the sentimental and
insular language of identity and self-determination. They assert
that the failure of Irish nationalists to recognise the democratic
legitimacy of the Union means that they are not eligible for equal
citizenship. In fact, to offer Irish nationalists such equality is to
infringe the citizenship rights of unionists themselves.

The 'new unionists' make some rhetorical adjustments
appealing not just to Ulster Protestants but to the 'greater number'
of people in Northern Ireland who favour the constitutional *status
quo*. They insist on the zero-sum nature of the conflict and the
impossibility of a compromise over national sovereignty.
Trimble's (1996) assertion that there can be no compromise
between unionism and (Irish) nationalism was elevated by the
'new unionist' intellectuals to the status of a principle of political
philosophy. In many ways, the rhetoric of the 'new unionism'
sought to put old wine in new bottles. Its apparent embracing of
the univeralistic politics of equal citizenship is little more than an

attempt to dress up traditional Loyalist slogans of 'No Surrender' and 'Not an Inch' in a new, more modern and more marketable rhetoric. This rhetoric asserts the inviolability of British citizenship rights and British sovereignty in Northern Ireland. No reciprocal recognition is to be given to Irish citizens in Northern Ireland or to nationalists. Irish nationalism is presented as politically and morally bankrupt and in the case of Republicanism fundamentally violent and anti-democratic.

Clearly such hardline formulations bode ill for the long-term prospects of the settlement reached in April 1998. They informed the thinking of unionists who boycotted the talks process completely. They also sustained the refusal of the Ulster Unionist Party throughout the negotiations to talk directly with Sinn Fein.

One of the few self-critical explorations of the 'new unionism' (Porter, 1996) has effectively undermined the distinction between 'citizenship' and 'identity'. While Porter (1996) too avoids any discussion of British nationalism, he highlights what unites the cultural unionism of Paisley and the Orange Order and the 'new' or 'liberal' unionism of Robert McCartney and the unionist intellectuals. It is the conviction of both that the Union is an end in itself, 'or better, as the end to which all other ends are subservient' (1996, p. 169). The alliance of Paisley's DUP and McCartney's UK Unionist Party in opposition to the 'peace process' negotiations neatly underlines the convergent political logic of 'traditional' and 'new unionism'.

The willingness of the UUP to remain within the Northern Ireland negotiations, however, may also be understood as a response to wider changes within the United Kingdom. Debates over the politics of devolution and of the possible 'breakup' of the United Kingdom have become more prominent. These debates seem to offer unionism a foothold in the political mainstream in Britain. Indeed, the unionist parties reflect within themselves some of the poles of British political argument. On the one hand, the bulk of unionism can identify with the militant opposition of 'strong' British nationalists to devolution and to the forces threatening the unity of the state. On the other hand, it is possible to favour a degree of devolution while promulgating a weaker version of British nationalism. The latter characterises New Labour and Liberal Democratic thinking and favours a quasi-federal state which is more explicitly multinational and multicultural. It nevertheless continues to draw on a British sense of 'banal nationalism' and on historical myths which celebrate the uniqueness, longevity and democracy of the British constitution.

The current reopening of the 'British national question' has encouraged participants in the debate to understand, and even to identify with some unionist preoccupations. The question at issue is whether the British state can survive intact the historic decline of Empire and political Protestantism, the relative decline of its military and economic power and the demystification of the royal family. The prospects for, and likely consequences of, proposed constitutional reform *vis-à-vis* the survival of the UK remain unclear (McBride, 1996, p. 14; Gillespie, 1996) as are the implications for unionism. But, at least, there is here a common language of 'national sovereignty' and 'defending the integrity of the state' in which unionists can speak, and be heard.

In particular, Ulster unionists' tendency to see the 'British constitution' and even the key British institutions as sacred allows them a niche and an audience on the right wing of British politics which has variously included the National Front, Powellites, right-wing Tories, Euro-sceptics and the overwhelmingly conservative national press (Greenslade, 1996). More recently, the Ulster Unionist Party has allied itself with the late James Goldsmith's Eurosceptic party in the EU parliament. Unionists find common ground, therefore, with British nationalists who wish to maintain the integrity and sovereignty of the UK in the face of internal and external threats. These include the EU, Scottish devolution or separatism and the activities of the IRA and Irish nationalists who wish to dilute British sovereignty in Northern Ireland (Bevins, 1996).

In the 1990s, right-wing British nationalists have often adopted the unionist cause as a litmus test of the government's commitment to defending the state, sometimes equating appeasement of nationalists and the IRA to servility to the EU (see Bevins, 1996; Alcock, 1995–6). For example, *Daily Telegraph* editor Charles Moore (1995, p. 5), complains that the British administrative class refuses to accept that Northern Ireland should be unambiguously British, while persisting in perpetuating and institutionalising 'uncertainty about its constitutional status'. He argues that by 'refusing to decide the issue of Britishness they throw it open to ever more dispute'. Implicit in Moore's view is that the British government has the power to decide the nationality question by making Northern Ireland irrevocably British. What British governments have lacked is the political will to make this decision.

Moore (1995, p. 5) favours full integration of Northern Ireland into the UK and sees it as a 'cautionary lesson' against devolution. Remarkably, an editorial in the *Daily Telegraph* (13 July

1996) used the occasion of the Orange Order's 'victory' at Drumcree to call for the scrapping of the Anglo–Irish Agreement and the reassertion of the British government's 'exclusive prerogatives in the loyal province'. Clearly, in this view, compromise between unionism (as British nationalism) and Irish nationalism is both impossible and undesirable.

British nationalists such as Moore find ample support for this position among all strands of unionism in Northern Ireland. Richard English (1994, 1995), for example, one of the most consistent opponents of 'parity of esteem' between the two communities in Northern Ireland, argues that 'parity of political esteem' is 'fundamentally incoherent' in that it accords equal legitimacy to those who would maintain and those who would dismember the state (1994, p. 98). In this view, the political aspiration to Irish unity is practically, morally and intellectually inferior to the nationalist project of maintaining the United Kingdom. It is 'illogical' and 'intellectually threadbare' (Kennedy, 1995, p. 29) or 'entirely without validity because it is self-refuting – its assertion proves that there is no single nation in Ireland' (Roche and Birnie, 1996, p. 15; also English, 1995, p. 138).

British nationalists advocate maintaining the integrity of the UK in the face of threatening change. The more conservative nationalists allow their myths of the durability and longevity of British state institutions to shade over into an ahistorical conception of the existing state as permanent. This resonates with a deep-rooted strand in Ulster unionism. What is remarkable about the 'new unionism' propagated by unionist intellectuals and the circle surrounding Trimble, is that they mirror so closely populist Loyalist attitudes on the fixity and permanence of the Union. The embrace of British nationalism and Ulster unionism generates an illusion of permanence of the 'British constitution' and British state. What is significant is that this 'permanence' is not to be attained by constructive compromise with Irish nationalists but by *fiat* – by an act of political will on the part of both unionists and the British government. Persuasion, negotiation and compromise count for little for British nationalism in its unionist form. To admit their importance would be to allow Irish nationalists a veto on the kind of 'Britishness' possible in Northern Ireland. Yet, nationalists have always had this veto although it has not translated into significant political power.

Of course, the unionist pursuit of permanence is futile. It ignores the dynamic that has always existed in British–Irish relations. Its latest manifestation in Northern Ireland is the growth in

the power, influence and numbers of nationalists and Catholics as
well as the altered role of the British and Irish states internationally (Ruane and Todd, 1996). In rejecting serious accommodation
on the meaning of terms such as 'democratic majority' and
'democratic consent', both 'new' and 'old' unionists confirm what
unionism has always offered to Ulster Protestants – an identity
rooted in permanent beleaguerment.

Indeed, it is this permanent sense of siege and beleaguerment
which distinguishes Ulster unionists from other British nationalists. The latter lack this historical sense because they have not
shared unionists' close historic encounter and the intricate relationships with Irish nationalists and Catholics. In this sense,
British nationalists' resistance to challenges to British sovereignty
from within and without is different from unionists' resistance to
change. There can be collective amnesia about Northern Ireland
unionists, even on the nationalist right of British politics.

Michael Forsyth's celebration of British nationalism in the face
of devolutionary and secessionist pressures is an illuminating
example of ambiguity and amnesia *vis-à-vis* Northern Ireland.
Proclaiming the integrity of the UK to the Tory Party Conference
in 1996, he stated:

> But what was this United Kingdom? ... God has smiled on this island.
> No aggressive neighbour disputes our boundaries: the sea is our
> timeless frontier. Although our liberty has been threatened twice this
> century, the fortitude of our peoples – Scots, English, Welsh and
> Ulstermen – secured for us our way of life. (cited in Millar, 1996)

This exemplifies the ambiguity about Northern Ireland, even
among conservative nationalists in Britain. While Ulster's place in
the nation's war memories is recognised, it is excluded from
territorial Britishness. Unionists are faced with the permanent
task of reminding British nationalists of their Britishness.
Excessive protests to this effect may make their expulsion from
the UK difficult but it also confirms that they are not perceived as
typically British (Loughlin, 1995).

British nationalists do not have to be constantly preoccupied
with Ulster unionism, however, in the way that unionists have to
constantly assert their British identity. Nevertheless, the overwhelming economic and military power of the British state in
Northern Ireland constitutes a permanent advantage to unionists
which is increased when nationalists in Britain intervene in
response to a crisis or to the prospect of negotiated settlement.

Conclusion

British state policy in Northern Ireland has been a mixture of principle, ambiguity and pragmatism. The principle, confirmed again in the April 1998 Agreement, is that Northern Ireland's continued membership of the UK is subject to the wish of an electoral majority in the region. The ambiguity is rooted in the complex historic interrelationships between Britain and Ireland characterised by the failure either to coerce Ireland fully into the UK state or to find a stable consensual basis in Ireland (North or South) for membership of the Union. This has led to a central pragmatism in British policy in Ireland exemplified between 1920 and 1972 by devolving control to one ethno-religious group in Northern Ireland. Since 1972, British governments have been trying to find a more consensual cross-communal basis for the administration of the region. The role of the strong variant of British nationalism, however, has been to stress the necessity for coercive majoritarianism. Even here, however, the ambiguity re-emerges as in the oscillation between criminalising paramilitaries and treating Northern Ireland as a quasi-colonial war situation.

Indeed, the Agreement reached in April 1998 reflects all the elements of British policy, principle, ambiguity and pragmatism, in a new combination. The influence of British nationalism has been to preclude or greatly limit negotiation on British sovereignty. Paisley and McCarthy accomplished this by boycotting the talks. Within the talks process, the UUP constantly sought to limit the scope of negotiation and any accommodation that might ensue. For example, it refused to talk directly to Sinn Fein throughout. The result is proposed structures where the key aspects of sovereignty – taxation and policing – remain with the British government. The powers of North–South bodies are extremely limited and accountable to an Assembly with a unionist majority. Within the Assembly, nationalists (perhaps even excluding Republicans) will oversee the implementation of policies legislated in Westminster. Simultaneously, the Irish government has agreed to a referendum to drop its constitutional claim to Northern Ireland.

Represented in this way the Agreement seems to mark a victory for the central principle of British nationalism – the constitutional inviolability of the Union. It does lean towards the weaker variant of this nationalism in recognising via devolution various regional forms of Britishness. On the other hand, the Agreement is a pragmatic recognition of the growing power of nationalists in

Northern Ireland and of the role of the Irish government. The human rights and equality measures, the proposed release of prisoners, the promise of a commission to reform policing, the North–South bodies and the British–Irish governmental conference greatly limit the capacity of unionists to exercise power within Northern Ireland or to shape the network of relationships which bind Northern Ireland to Britain and the Republic. Unionists certainly prevented North–South bodies becoming an embryonic all-Ireland government. However, the proposed settlement does envisage a structure which would allow a change of constitutional regime in Northern Ireland. Moreover, it enshrines for the first time a set of political rules and pathways through which evolutionary change might be effected.

The prospect of such changes is deeply unpalatable to 'strong' British nationalists. For them, any compromise with Irish nationalism constitutes one of many threats to the integrity and continued existence of the UK in its present form. From the outset, 'strong' British nationalists have opposed every step of the current peace process. They attacked the Hume–Adams talks at the outset and disabled the Major government's (from within and without) attempts to advance the talks process. They remain bitterly critical of the Labour government's dealings with Sinn Fein (Lloyd, 1997; *The Times*, 1997) and continue to advocate the marginalisation of Sinn Fein within the structures proposed in the Agreement. Under the umbrella of an unacknowledged British nationalism, they virulently oppose concessions to Irish nationalists (Lee, 1998).

While the weaker variant of British nationalism as enshrined in New Labour is far more agnostic on partition than is the Conservative Right, part of this agnosticism has been the maintenance of a bipartisan policy on Northern Ireland. Within such a policy, hardline nationalists have considerable leverage in insisting on decommissioning of paramilitary weapons while opposing wider demilitarisation, limiting police reforms and in seeking to ensure that the unionist veto on change (defined as democratic consent) is as extensive as possible.

The promulgation of zero-sum conceptions of British sovereignty via Ulster unionism and British politicians and policy makers on the ground in Northern Ireland will continue to threaten the prospects for peace, progress and reconciliation held out in the 1998 Agreement. One step towards avoiding this possibility is to grasp the extent to which British nationalism is constitutive of the Northern Ireland conflict and to expose its potential to prevent a resolution.

Notes

1. Eric Hobsbawm, a talismanic intellectual on the British Left, is a case
    in point. He begins a recent article with a scathing attack on 'identity
    politics' of all kinds including secessionist nationalisms. By the end
    of the article, he is celebrating, quite unconsciously, the merits of
    British nationalism and identity as an alternative (Hobsbawm, 1996).
    Heathorn (1996, pp. 9–10) points to a 'recent explosion of studies of
    English/British national identity and its varied manifestations'. He
    suggests that historians of the Left have been spurred to re-examine
    the possible sources of nationalist enthusiasm as a response to the
    jingoism engendered by the Falklands War and European integra-
    tion. However, he suggests that there is a deep-rooted tendency
    among historians to treat the English/British case as exceptional and
    to substitute the term 'patriotism' for 'nationalism'.
2. Burnside (1995) lists British audiences sympathetic to the unionist
    case: new Right think-tanks and lobby groups; key newspapers such
    as *The Times*, *Sunday Times*, *Daily* and *Sunday Telegraph* and the *Sun*;
    the Friends of the Union founded in 1985 by Ian Gow, Lord
    Cranborne (Leader of the Tories in the House of Lords) and Sir John
    Biggs Davison, and 'friends in the Labour Party who believe in the
    Union'. At a recent meeting of the Friends of the Union, John Lloyd
    of the *New Statesman* successfully proposed a think-tank to unite and
    inform all strands of unionist strategy, to give in Lloyd's words 'a
    voice to a democratic demand for a settled nationhood' (*New
    Statesman*, 5 December 1997).
3. The attempt to create a 'new' and more articulate unionism may be
    traced to the equal citizenship campaign in which Robert McCartney
    was prominent. This demanded that 'mainland' political parties
    organise in Northern Ireland. Since then, a new and loosely articu-
    lated intellectual grouping has emerged committed to servicing the
    broad unionist movement. They comprise academics, journalists and
    political activists, some of whom supported Trimble's successful
    leadership bid in the UUP. Their common project is to develop a
    more intellectually articulate and positive case for the Union while
    attacking Irish nationalism and republicanism. Their published
    output is represented in pamphlets of the Ulster Young Unionist
    Council and the Cadogan Group, in the Ulster Review, and in a
    series of published compilations, e.g. Barton and Roche (1991) and
    Foster (1995).

7 The Role of the British Labour Party in Ireland

Jerry Fitzpatrick

The Cause of Ireland is the Cause of Labour. (James Connolly, 1913)

The British Labour Party? They won't lift a finger to help us. (James Connolly, 1916)

Whether an 'Agreed Ireland' will be celebrated in the new Millennium depends, in large part, on the British Labour government of Tony Blair. But can it overcome the obstacles to a genuine lasting settlement, including its own history of involvement in Ireland? This chapter suggests the British Labour Party can play a progressive role in helping to deliver an 'Agreed Ireland', but only if it makes a decisive break with British nationalism. The policy being implemented by the Blair government is only the policy devised by previous Tory administrations, albeit one they failed to carry out. However, the endorsement, North and South, of the 1998 'Agreement' does represent a decisive and progressive stage in the development towards the final resolution of the historic conflict. The British Labour government retains the political responsibility to complete the 'unfinished business' between Britain and Ireland. The chapter begins by examining the historical record and outlines contemporary obstacles before discussing how Labour could help to deliver a lasting settlement.

Labour's Record

The British Labour Party has an abysmal record in Ireland: uncritical bipartisanship with the Tories when in opposition and a failure of political will when in government. In truth, Labour and the Tory governments have differed little in their approach to Ireland. There is a consensus within Westminster founded on the determination to keep that 'troublesome subject' from becoming a serious issue within Parliament. Labour policy on Ireland has see-sawed wildly over the decades from nationalist periods while in opposition to decidedly unionist phases in government. It is not just a tale of radical instincts curbed by the exigencies of office but also a tale of political abdication to 'might is right' lawlessness.

Ireland was not debated at the six conferences of the Labour Representation Committee (LRC) from 1900, and did not appear on the Conference agenda of its successor – the Labour Party – until 1918. While the LRC had a policy of 'legislative independence for all parts of the Empire', the Labour leader Ramsay MacDonald could avoid taking a stand on Ireland on the basis that his party had no declared policy.

This abstentionist position appeared to change when the Liberals presented the third Home Rule Bill in 1912. On behalf of Labour, James Parker MP endorsed the Bill stating that, 'so far as the Labour Party is concerned we stand for Home Rule because we believe that the mass of working people of Ireland have a right to decide what form of Government they shall have'. But, in the face of armed rebellion by the Ulster Volunteer Force, led by the unionist Edward Carson, and supported by the British Tory Party and by British Army elites, the Liberals started to accept the possibility of Partition and Labour followed suit. In 1914 Ramsay MacDonald declared 'we will take the position of a detached party', the Liberal Bill was suspended and Britain entered the First World War.

The World War and the 1916 Rising changed the demand in Ireland from Home Rule to Independence. The 1918 General Election results in Ireland represented a landslide to Sinn Fein with the party taking 73 out of 105 seats; Sinn Fein promptly convened Dáil Éireann and declared Irish Independence. Labour MPs meanwhile had sat in the wartime Coalition Cabinet which executed James Connolly and the other leaders of the Easter Rising of 1916. But when the 1918 Labour Conference debated Ireland it carried a resolution recognising the 'claim of the people of Ireland to Home Rule and to self determination in all exclusively Irish affairs', although a radical amendment to delete the proviso, 'in all exclusively Irish affairs', was defeated.

Then when Lloyd George's Coalition government introduced the 1920 Government of Ireland Bill which provided for Partition, Labour roundly condemned the proposals. J.R. Clynes stated: 'we oppose this scheme of self government because it provides a form of Partition founded on a religious basis and

recognises neither the historic unity of the province of Ulster nor
of Ireland as a whole', stressing however that he was 'not arguing
for independence'.

The 1920 Labour Conference strengthened this position and
carried a resolution 'demanding that the principle of free and
absolute self determination shall be applied in the case of Ireland'.
More importantly the qualification, 'in all exclusively Irish
affairs', was rejected. For the first time the British Labour Party
had given unconditional support to Irish self-determination. But,
as is the way with radical resolutions passed at Labour conferences, the policy was not reflected in the activities and words of
its leaders. Although the Parliamentary Party voted against
Partition and effectively boycotted debate on the 1920
Government of Ireland Act, its leaders reverted to supporting
conditional self-determination. Labour leaders welcomed the
1921 Anglo–Irish Treaty signed under duress but hailed by
Arthur Henderson as 'an honourable peace' which 'would open
up a new era of friendship between British and Irish peoples'. The
decades which followed gave their own verdict on the 'new era'.

In 1945 Labour gained a parliamentary majority for the first
time in its history and formed a pro-Partition government.
Deputy Prime Minister, Herbert Morrison, praised Northern
Ireland's loyalty to Britain during the Second World War and
acted as a self-appointed guardian of the Union. In 1948 the
Dublin government announced that Ireland would formally
declare itself a Republic and leave the Commonwealth; Labour
responded with the 1949 Ireland Act which declared that, 'in no
event will Northern Ireland cease to be part of the United
Kingdom without the consent of the Parliament of Northern
Ireland'. Since the Stormont parliament had an in-built unionist
majority this provided a unionist veto on all constitutional
change. Electoral gerrymandering and institutionalised discrimination in all fields of life against nationalists ensured the
maintenance of a one-party unionist state. Labour backbencher
Michael Foot supported the Act but called for an inquiry into
Stormont's 'monstrously undemocratic methods', while Jack
Beattie, the West Belfast anti-Partition MP, warned that, 'when
constitutional reform is refused, the physical force movement
emerges', and more prophetically said that 'so long as Partition
remains, so long will British Governments find it haunting them'.

Two decades later, when the civil rights movement shook
Northern Ireland to its core, the Wilson Labour Ggovernment
sent in the British Army to defend this constitutional guarantee.

The IRA was reborn and 30 years of armed conflict and sectarian violence ensued.

Labour remained in government until 1970 and then from 1974 to 1979. In opposition Wilson called for Irish unity within a 15-year time frame; in government he lowered his sights, to managing the conflict. Labour abdicated to unionist lawlessness in 1974 when the hapless Merlyn Rees gave in to the Ulster Workers Council stoppage, and introduced the repressive Prevention of Terrorism Act, described as draconian by Labour's own Home Secretary, Roy Jenkins.

The Callaghan administration eschewed political initiatives and under Roy Mason adopted a hard line security policy, involving use of the SAS, with shoot-to-kill incidents and illegal police interrogation methods condemned by international Human Rights agencies. Tough security was accompanied by concessions to unionism, with an increase in the North's representation at Westminster from 12 to 17 MPs. Callaghan paid the price when the Northern nationalist MP, Gerry Fitt abstained on a no confidence motion and Labour fell by one vote in 1979.

Ironically it was under a Conservative and British nationalist government that political initiatives began to overtake security clampdowns. After the 1981 hunger strikes Sinn Fein started to make gains electorally; to counter this development, the Thatcher government gave Dublin an institutionalised consultative input into the North's affairs. Subsequently it was the Major administration that signed the 1993 Downing Street Declaration and the 1995 Joint Frameworks Document. It also facilitated the 1994 IRA and Loyalist ceasefires, although the IRA cessation collapsed when all-party talks floundered on the Tory-unionist preconditions.

In opposition Labour rejected British withdrawal but did adopt a new policy of pursuing Irish unity by consent, and Kevin McNamara, known for his pro united Ireland outlook was appointed shadow Northern Ireland Spokesperson. Labour manifestos supported Irish unity and indeed Labour conference policy in the late 1980s and early 1990s reflected progressive policies designed to secure Irish unity. However, in 1994 Tony Blair became Leader and replaced Kevin McNamara with Mo Mowlam. Ignoring party policy, Blair's draft 1996 Labour Manifesto dropped 'unity by consent' for the 'unity of the peoples of Ireland', while the 1997 Labour Manifesto stressed reconciliation and consent in Northern Ireland. The stage was set for a new Labour government and a return to Labour partitionism.

Labour Obstacles

Obstacles to conflict resolution presented by the Labour government are highlighted by two events in 1997: Tony Blair's Belfast speech of 16 May just after his election victory, and Labour's response to events at Drumcree in July. In May Blair called for 'a settlement which can command the support of Nationalists and Unionists', and supported the 'principle of consent', but narrowly defined this principle as meaning that 'there can be no possibility of a change in the status of Northern Ireland without the consent of a majority of the people of Northern Ireland'. In policy terms the speech continued to drift away from any visionary or balanced approach as he stated, 'I value the Union. My agenda is not a united Ireland. The Government will not be persuaders for unity. None of us in this hall today, even the youngest, is likely to see Northern Ireland as anything but a part of the United Kingdom.' With regard to relationships within the island of Ireland there could be 'sensible arrangements for co-operation with the Republic of Ireland. If such arrangements were really threatening to Unionists, we would not negotiate them. Any fears would be much reduced if the Irish Constitution were changed to reflect the consent principle. That must be a part of a settlement and would be a helpful confidence-building step in advance of it.' There was no mention of parallel changes in Northern Ireland's constitutional status, contradicting the Joint Frameworks Document's proposition that a settlement required a comprehensive agreement, including constitutional change North and South.

In fairness, Blair's speech opened the door to talks with Sinn Fein and led to the removal of the decommissioning obstacle to their involvement in all-party talks, precipitating the 1997 IRA ceasefire. However, in policy terms the speech *reaffirmed a unionist veto* on constitutional change; it rejected the possibility of a united Ireland and belittled the vital all-Ireland dimension. It was a deeply conservative, flawed and timid performance. Tony Blair did not speak as a neutral, contradicting his own requirement that in all-party talks, 'all parties are treated equally, with a comprehensive agenda and no predetermined outcome'.

Worse was to follow during the Orange Order 'marching season' in July. In 1996 Orange Lodge marchers were prevented from marching through a largely nationalist area at Drumcree; unionists mounted a lengthy and violent confrontation with the security forces that spread across Northern Ireland, with Loyalist

blockades on many streets and widespread intimidation of nationalists. The Conservative government capitulated and permitted
the Orange march; with the new Labour administration there
were great expectations of a change in policy. But, as Mo
Mowlam told the Garvaghy Road residents, as far as she was
concerned Drumcree was a 'black and white issue'; a contradictory negotiating style that was underlined when residents were
battered out of the way to force the march through. As Labour's
leaked 'gameplan' revealed, the least worst outcome was 'getting
some Orange feet on the Garvaghy Road'.

What Drumcree Three revealed was once again the fundamental and iniquitous contradiction in the British Government's
position. It had again allowed the threat by Loyalists of disruption, violence and the boycotting of talks to prevail. A similar
threat by Nationalists would have been faced down. A British
Government, no matter how well meaning will never win
Nationalist trust until it resolves contradiction. It was an example
of might triumphing over right and it represented a failure of
Labour's political will and judgement.

There is no doubting the sincerity and commitment of Mo
Mowlam; she has achieved what clearly seemed beyond the capa-
bilities or perhaps wishes of previous Secretaries of State who
were given the same task; and she clearly has more understanding
of the obstacles to peace than has Tony Blair. However, her
understanding is predicated on a very specific British mindset,
namely that the British and the Secretary of State are not part of
the problem in Ireland but are there to hold the ring between 'two
warring tribes', neutral between unionists and nationalists and
facilitators for agreement between the traditions. In negotiations
they pose, not as participants, but more as disinterested overseers
of local agreement. They even believe that their disinterested and
impartial attitude contrasts with the partial and interfering
attitude of the Dublin government.

This twin mindset is captured in a quote by Mo Mowlam after
Fianna Fáil won the 1997 Irish General Election: 'Fianna Fáil
have a Nationalist electorate. I don't have a Northern Ireland
electorate here but what I do have is a job to try and hold both
sides in.' The reality is that Britain currently exercises jurisdiction
over Northern Ireland, but even here the distancing and denials
highlight the contradictory mindset. At Drumcree the person in
charge of Northern Ireland engaged in shuttle diplomacy to try
and get local accommodation; when it failed, she washed her
hands of it and, blaming intransigence on both sides, defended

the Chief Constable of the RUC's decision to force the march down the Garvaghy Road.

Positive Factors and Opportunities

Despite the abysmal Labour record there are positive factors and political opportunities on offer to remove the Labour obstacles to conflict resolution. Labour's shameful record does not mean that circumstances and attitudes cannot change in the future. This requires rejection of deterministic interpretations in favour of more dialectical perspectives.

On the positive side, Tony Blair has a large majority in Westminster; unlike John Major, he is not dependent on Unionist MPs. A second term is quite possible, with a stable Labour government in office until 2007. Furthermore, Tony Blair has genuinely prioritised Northern Ireland; the conflict is offensive to his political instincts and, more important, is an international political embarrassment. Tony Blair wants a settlement and his ally Mo Mowlam is putting her political future on the line to secure it. Although his administration is imbued with British nationalism, it is of a more flexible and 'weaker' variety than the strident nationalism espoused by leading lights in the previous Tory government (see Chapter 6).

As for the Irish government, in the crucial 'Agreement' period at least, it is led by Fianna Fáil which, because of its Republican history, can deliver on balanced constitutional change. In the White House, President Clinton and the US political establishment are committed to exercising constructive pressure to deliver a settlement. Constitutional nationalists across Ireland and the Republican movement are committed to change based upon democratic accommodation and political compromise. Within unionism attitudes are also changing; unionist business interests want a settlement and it is the Loyalist parties, the PUP and the UDP, who most clearly articulate a desire to be involved in inclusive talks and in securing agreement. Key elements of unionism are abandoning political intransigence; equally important are the attitudes of the trade union movement, women's organisations and the community and voluntary sector, all of which are mobilising opinion and demanding political agreement.

The changing attitudes of the British ruling class, as represented in the British state and in its business and financial establishment, also provide opportunities for change. British

policy towards Northern Ireland was always based upon the principle of 'insulation', of keeping the whole problem at arm's length
from British politics. Post-Partition Northern Ireland affairs were
not to be discussed at Westminster and this was observed in a
bipartisan manner. By giving unionists their own Stormont parliament, Irish affairs were distanced from British politics. But British
indifference had the opposite effect as it allowed unionists to
mismanage things so badly that the 'Irish problem' thrust itself
back on to the British agenda. Through the ensuing 30 years of
war and conflict an underlying political pattern of disengagement
became apparent. It was no accident that Conservative governments negotiated the 1985 Anglo–Irish Agreement, the 1993
Downing Street Declaration and the seminal 1995 Joint
Frameworks Document. There is no longer any room for indifference; today the British Foreign Office want an end to the
international embarrassment that is Northern Ireland; the
Treasury want an end to the £3 billion plus drain that Northern
Ireland represents.

Tony Blair's Labour government has inherited these
favourable circumstances and brings its own limited experience
and political personalities to the problem. The learning curve is
replicated with their current attempts to apply the old managerial
pacification policies to Northern Ireland, while timidly ducking
the key constitutional issues. However, a rethink can and will
occur; it can occur if constructive pressures are applied on the
Labour leadership, and will occur because the old outdated
policies cannot deliver a lasting settlement.

The Labour government is already subject to external and
internal pressures to re-examine its Irish policy. British aspirations are limited to retention of the Union, to power-sharing
devolved government and to a few cross-border advisory bodies.
This approach will not deliver a lasting settlement. Nationalist
expectations are rising and today Northern Ireland has reached
'critical mass' where both nationalist and unionist communities
have equality of veto. Overtly unionist parties are losing their electoral majorities in every representative forum and will continue to
do so, while an undefeated IRA remains in the background and
international pressure is maintained. Historic compromise and
accommodation is the only option, a reality that necessitates the
creation of a new British polity.

Internal pressure on the Labour leadership will also intensify.
Labour backbenchers and Labour conference will demand
greater influence over Irish policy and the sleeping giant of the

British trade union movement will cautiously support this development. The Irish community in Britain which votes Labour will also exert pressure for a rethink while British business interests which are now represented at the heart of Blair's government will counsel that a new strategic approach is required.

Other pressures arise out of the wider debate on constitutional change, for example arising out of the election of the Scottish Parliament and the referendum on PR. Through these and other issues, Tony Blair will be intellectually challenged on fundamental constitutional issues and indeed he could change his opinions. To dismiss this possibility is politically defeatist; Blair says he is a British patriot but hold up the intellectual mirror and ask why Irish nationalists should not be permitted constitutional expression of their allegiances, to encompass dual and mutual recognition of the two national allegiances on the island of Ireland. Think the unthinkable. Policies can and will change.

Labour Hopes

A New Labour Policy?
Politics is about principle, persuasion and power. It is possible for British Labour to progressively resolve a conflict at the heart of Britain's future. There is one vision of Britain that is inflexible, politically over-centralised, militantly majoritarian, intolerant of real diversity and actively hostile to a culture of political compromise and accommodation. Or there is another which gives way to a new appreciation of the cultural and political diversity of nations and regions on the two islands, to a new tolerance of political difference and to a new culture of consensus-building through mutual recognition, compromise and accommodation.

It is possible for Britain to adopt a new internationalist and democratic set of principles with regard to Ireland based upon mutual recognition and accommodation of different national allegiances. The application of these principles requires the exercise of persuasion and power by those primarily responsible for the conflict and for Northern Ireland – namely, the British government.

What needs to change in the first instance is Labour's definition of consent and its related understanding of sovereignty, jurisdiction and self-determination. A guiding principle laid out in the Joint Frameworks Document is that 'the consent of the governed is an essential ingredient for stability'. Here consent clearly means the consent of both unionists and nationalists, not just the consent of the unionist majority. Mowlam's narrower policy view contradicts this interpretation, for her 'consent is an inviolable principle. There isn't going to be any change in Northern Ireland's constitutional status unless a majority here want it.'

Labour has to recognise the key concept and principle of *mutual consent* which requires agreement between and from nationalists as well as unionists. The existing status of Northern Ireland does not command the consent of nationalists. The reason is simple; nearly 80 years ago Partition was imposed in the face of a majority verdict for Irish Independence at the all Ireland 1918 election. Imperial Britain had its own strategic interests at the time and also it was threatened with armed rebellion by unionists. The point is that Partition was imposed without the consent of nationalist Ireland and this guaranteed its instability. The maintenance of this *status quo* is not an option and an internal settlement in Northern Ireland will not work. Equally, coercion of unionists into a united Ireland is not an option. What is required is a new agreement based upon political compromise and democratic accommodation, where the key inviolable principle of mutual consent is applied.

The imperative for Labour is to address the accommodation of Irish and British national allegiances on the island of Ireland. A new and creative understanding of sovereignty, jurisdiction and self-determination is required. National sovereignty defined in traditional territorial terms must be replaced by a new constitutional dispensation that embraces a sharing of sovereignty and jurisdiction, and facilitates the exercise of Irish self-determination. Such a transnational bridging concept would transcend the exclusive sovereignty claims that are at the heart of the conflict. In principle, the British government must state its intention to withdraw its claim of sovereignty over Ireland or part thereof and must recognise the existing birthright of everyone born on the island of Ireland to be part of the Irish nation as a right. This would be an act of a modern post-imperial Britain coming to terms with its colonial legacy and would establish a level playing field for negotiations with all the parties on the island of Ireland, on the terms of an Agreed Ireland. These negotiations would have to take account of the need for accommodation of Irish and British national allegiances, with Britain facilitating agreement and implementing the terms of a settlement.

The key element in this approach is a recognition that it is for the people of Ireland alone to exercise their right to self-determination. This involves the recognition that there is one Irish nation on the island of Ireland, irrespective of how jurisdiction is exercised or what form of mutually agreed political linkages or unions are established. In essence, Labour would be divesting Britain of its colonial legacy and transferring sovereignty to the people of Ireland. It is the responsibility of the Irish people alone to exercise this right of self-determination as sovereignty is vested in its people and not in the 'Crown' at Westminster. In exercising this right an accommodation has to be secured between Irish and British allegiances, including recognition that Partition exists, albeit imposed, and that change requires mutual consent. British Labour are obliged to take account of the unionist desire to retain a connection with Britain, and not to be forced into a united Ireland. An agreed Ireland is the shared inheritance of all the people of Ireland and the requirement of mutual consent, at this historical conjunction, points to a combination of one nation with two jurisdictions. The terms of the jurisdiction in what currently constitutes Northern Ireland must be determined by agreement between the nationalists and unionists who reside there and that agreement must be endorsed by the Irish people as a whole. At the same time, there must be an agreed mechanism that facilitates the possibility of establishing a unitary jurisdiction on the island of Ireland. This would represent a new act of self-determination for the island as a whole: a new determination covering the totality of relationships with particular emphasis on relations within the island as the key relationship for a settlement.

There are other areas that require the development of a new Labour Irish policy. For example, Britain should adopt a proactive harmonisation agenda with the Irish Republic to prepare the ground for agreed North–South institutions; and as Britain currently exercises jurisdiction over Northern Ireland it has the immediate responsibility of delivering equality of treatment and associated confidence-building measures. There needs to be equality of treatment in all sectors of society relating to social, economic, cultural, justice, democratic and national rights issues. These issues do not require negotiation. They can be acted upon as basic civil and human rights and can be addressed progressively now. The European Convention on Human Rights needs to be incorporated into law immediately and the independent Parades Commission should have effective powers. The Orange right to march should be subject to nationalist consent in terms of routes through nationalist areas. More generally the British can provide for confidence-building through demilitarisation, with fundamental structural change in policing and a humane regime for prisoners pending release programme agreements, and a public apology following the independent inquiry into the events of Bloody Sunday.

British Labour's attitude has to change. They are not a referee or moderator between the two 'Irish tribes', but bear a great deal of the responsibility for the conflict. They also bear responsibility for a successful resolution of the conflict.

The Terms of a Settlement

If the new Labour Irish policy outlined above is adopted, then the outline terms of a settlement become more possible to foresee. Britain withdrawing the claim to exclusive sovereignty in Northern Ireland would open the door to the concept of *shared* sovereignty and transnational bridging in terms of the all-Ireland dimension. The vesting of sovereignty in the people of Ireland clearly entails the end of British Direct Rule, as the right to jurisdiction in matters of self-government is transferred to the people of Northern Ireland. The fact of Partition requires mutual consent and the accommodation of British national allegiances held by unionists and Irish national allegiances held by nationalists. It is obviously a matter for the parties to settle on new political arrangements by mutual consent. But clearly this would entail renegotiation of Northern Ireland's constitutional status and would necessitate, because of unionists' allegiances, a continuing British connection of some description.

These and related changes would establish Northern Ireland as a self-governing, democratic region that is the shared national territory of the island of Ireland and the United Kingdom. Its sovereignty is vested in its peoples, and its citizens are entitled to full citizenship rights of either the Republic of Ireland or the United Kingdom, or both. Its government is organised according to cooperative principles which guarantee the rights and fundamental freedoms of its peoples in all their diverse identities, allegiances and traditions. It ensures proportional representation of its constituent communities in public institutions and protects their equality of treatment and security. Its institutions include a North–South Ministerial Council charged with catering adequately for present and future political, social and economic interconnections on the island of Ireland, enabling North and South to enter agreed dynamic cooperative and constructive relationships. Its institutions include provision for participation in an Intergovernmental Council to deal with the totality of relationships, to include representatives of the British and Irish governments, the Northern Ireland Assembly, the Scottish Parliament and the Welsh Assembly. Its government accepts that it is for the people of the island of Ireland alone, by agreement between the people in both of the jurisdictions which exist within that territory, to exercise their right of self-determination, on the basis of consent, freely and concurrently given, to bring about a united Ireland.

To ensure that there is no possibility of a return to the old Stormont, the self-government arrangements would have to reflect cooperative principles. These would include the creation of a responsibility-sharing Executive, and a Northern Ireland Assembly, with elections by proportional representation (PR). To ensure democratic clarity and accountability to all communities, a directly elected 12-person Executive, using PR and the whole of the six counties as the electoral unit, should be established. At the same time a 108-person Northern Ireland Assembly should be elected, also by PR. Appropriate democratic balances and checks both within the Executive and the Assembly and between them, should be agreed to ensure mutual accommodation and agreement. In addition, there would be agreed representation in Westminster, the European Parliament and North–South institutions. As part of the all-Ireland framework, people in Northern Ireland should be granted direct representation to the Dublin Oireachtas, in the first instance to the Seanad Eireann (Senate). Finally, Northern Ireland must have an autonomous legal personality to assist the process of radical reform of the judiciary, of the whole justice system and of internal security arrangements. A Charter of Rights, North and South, must be entrenched to protect individual and collective human rights subject to the European Convention on Human Rights.

Conclusions – 'Hope and History Rhyme'

The record of the British Labour Party demonstrates that its attitudes and relationships towards Ireland have been neither honourable, internationalist nor socialist. In some respects it even compares unfavourably with the Tories' attempts to manage this and other national or colonial conflicts. It is also true that Blair's initial Belfast speech in 1997 signalled his constitutional timidity and suggested a throw-back to Partitionist 'internal' solutions and a denial of the vital importance of the all-Ireland dimension. Not surprisingly, there is a mechanical school of thought that believes that Labour cannot change and will never deliver on Ireland.

Against that, however, the Labour government is inheriting extraordinarily favourable circumstances for a settlement. There are constructive internal and external pressures on Labour that combine to compel a rethink of its still traditional and limited approach. Most importantly, nationalist and Republican parties are committed to democratic accommodation and compromise. The people of Ireland thirst for settlement. The organisations of civil society are mobilising; the Churches and the business community historically associated with unionism are clamouring for a lasting peace.

The Loyalist parties, the PUP and the UDP, display a willingness to negotiate an accommodation. Indeed in the context of a balanced constitutional settlement there is the real possibility of working-class alliances between loyalism and republicanism. Unemployment, social deprivation and a lack of educational opportunity directly affect both working-class unionist and nationalist communities. The socialist-inclined Billy Hutchinson is not alone in worrying that Labour's social policies will benefit mobile middle-class constituents to the detriment of working-class communities steeped in endemic unemployment and deprivation. The common material interest of the working class could lead to joint campaigns by Loyalist parties and Sinn Fein around, for instance, demands for investment, jobs and the development of the 'shared' university campus in Springvale. Such developments could combine to transform the political landscape.

As for British Labour, there is democratic dignity in explicitly adopting the concept of shared sovereignty with transnational bridging on an island-wide basis. This would in effect be the restoration of sovereignty and jurisdiction, not to London and Dublin, but to a self-governing Northern Ireland with a responsibility-sharing Assembly and Executive, linked to the Irish Republic by a dynamic North–South Ministerial Council and other bodies which developed all-Ireland democracy. The British Labour government is the most powerful player in the settlement process, and if it advanced this new Labour Irish policy in a determined and flexible manner it could create the conditions for a genuine lasting settlement – an 'Agreed Ireland'.

The choice is simple and stark. Northern Ireland emerged as the result of a great fudge by the greatest fudger of them all, David Lloyd George. No new fudge by Tony Blair will bring enduring peace, any more than did the 1920 Government of

Ireland Act. He needs to do more than implement the Tory policy which the Tories themselves failed to deliver. Going beyond the Belfast 'Agreement', it's time to 'think the unthinkable': Labour could deliver on Ireland.

8   Women, the Peace Makers?

Rosemary Sales

Women in Northern Ireland are frequently described, both by men and by women themselves, as the 'backbone of the community', as the people who have kept their communities together during the years of violence, and fought to improve the conditions of daily life. Women have been able to leave their differences aside and work together on issues of common concern. Yet the very concerns on which women have found common cause – from the need to improve childcare to action against domestic violence – have been ignored in the current negotiations in Northern Ireland. Public debate has been conducted almost entirely by men, and has centred on relations between the two communities. Women, celebrated as the peacemakers, have been largely excluded from the 'peace process'.

That women have been very active in peace and reconciliation work throughout the 'Troubles', and do often claim to be better than men at talking to people from 'the other' community, was confirmed by a series of in-depth interviews conducted with women's organisations and individual women from both 'sides' of the sectarian divide. A women's group in Protestant East Belfast suggested that 'women on both sides of the political and religious divide were more compassionate and tolerant than men and more ready to try to understand different points of view'. Joyce McCartan of the Ormeau Road Women's Centre put it succinctly: 'Women talk more sense. Men just say no.' The best known peace movement has been the Peace People, which for a short time during the 1970s enjoyed mass support. The energy and commitment soon dissipated, however, as traditional political divisions reappeared. The recent growth of community activity and cross-community networks has produced a more solid basis of trust and support across the sectarian divide. Many women would like to see this development reflected in any negotiations about Ireland's future. The hastily formed Women's Coalition, which won nearly 2 per cent of the vote in the election to the

Forum in May 1996, was a reflection of the desire of many women to bury their differences and 'get on with it'.

But women cannot speak with one voice. The conflict, and therefore the peace, has had different meanings for different women. While women from the two communities can agree on a range of important social and economic issues, they remain divided on the constitutional questions which are central to politics in Northern Ireland. The separation of 'women's issues' from the mainstream constitutional issues has allowed women to unite around some limited common goals. But it also risks marginalising women's voices and concerns in the discussions about Ireland's future.

This chapter begins by discussing the meaning of the religious divide in Northern Ireland, and particularly its gendered dimensions, and the impact of the conflict on women from the two communities. The period of conflict has witnessed a substantial shift for women into the public sphere, and women's involvement in employment and in politics is discussed in the following sections. The final section discusses women's responses to the ceasefires and the 'peace process', and argues that women's issues need to be made central to the mainstream political agenda.

The chapter is based on a range of published sources, including official publications, and reports produced by women's and community groups. It also includes material obtained through interviews carried out over a period of four years with women engaged in formal and informal politics, which were carried out for a larger project (Sales, 1997a). Where the views of interviewees are well known within the public domain, I have referred to them by name. In view of the sensitivity of the issues discussed, it has been necessary in many cases to disguise the identity of interviewees.

The Meanings of the Sectarian Divide in Northern Ireland

Divisions between Protestant and Catholic dominate virtually every aspect of life in Northern Ireland. Residential segregation, widespread segregation in the workplace and strong discouragement of 'mixed' marriages, all make it possible for Protestants and Catholics to live their lives largely in isolation from each other. Segregation provides the basis for the promotion of a common set of values and beliefs. The school system is almost entirely separated on religious lines (Murray, 1985 and 1995) so that many children grow up with no social contact with people from the other community.

Separation is most intense within urban working-class ghettos, where mass unemployment further restricts the range of social contact (Dunn, 1995, p. 5). People in work, particularly those in middle-class occupations, tend to have wider social networks, and are more likely to live in mixed areas. The wealthy constituency of North Down, however, has such a solidly Protestant population that no nationalist party thought it worthwhile to put up a candidate in the by-election in June 1995. Even in mixed areas, social networks remain largely separate, and are often focused around the church or other institutions (such as Orange Lodges or Gaelic clubs) which would tend to exclude the other community.

Segregation affects women and men differentially. Women are generally less mobile, since caring and domestic responsibilities tie them more closely to the home. They are also more likely to be out of employment, and if in paid work, to work part time and to travel shorter distances. They have less access to cars, and less money to spend. Many young people in both communities rarely leave their own area. Single parents often have the most difficulties. A study of childcare needs in the Protestant Shankill area of Belfast found that few had access to any form of regular childcare; this meant severely restricted social lives, with few able to work (Taillon et al., 1992, pp. 2–3).

Religion is not an immediately visible identity: social interaction in mixed settings therefore depends on 'telling', the '[s]yndrome of signs by which Catholics and Protestants arrive at religious ascription in their every day interaction' (Howe, 1990, p. 13). The 'signs' used by the Fair Employment Commission (formerly the Fair Employment Agency) include 'the forenames and surnames, the schools attended, the subjects studied, the leisure interests, the employment histories and the persons named as referees on application forms' (FEA, 1986, p. 3). This list illustrates the depth of divisions between the lives of Protestants and Catholics.

Although religious divisions are deeply embedded in the structures of economic, social and political life, they are rarely discussed openly. As Bruce put it, 'there are two languages spoken. There is what you say in public and in "mixed" company and there is what you say in private, among your own people' (Bruce, 1994, p. vii). Contact between Protestant and Catholic is characterised by 'avoidance' (McAuley, 1994, p. 56). Avoidance extends into the workplace, constraining debate on any topic likely to be deemed sensitive. As one health service trade union official put it: 'Religion doesn't matter here. We never discuss politics in the union.' The religious divide is increasingly described, both by academics and those working in the 'community relations' field, in terms of 'ethnic' divisions (Howe, 1990; Bruce, 1994; McAuley, 1994). Much of the debate, particularly that sponsored by the official Community Relations Council, focuses on difference, and recognition of 'cultural traditions'. The concept of ethnicity is, however, centrally concerned with power. Ethnic relations encompass relations of dominance and subordination, and exclusionary and inclusionary practices (Anthias and Yuval Davis, 1983, p. 67). In Northern Ireland these practices have been reinforced through the privileged access of Protestants to the state, and the exclusion of Catholics from full citizenship. Sectarian divisions pre-dated the partition of Ireland, but they became more firmly entrenched with the creation of the Northern Ireland state. Protestant ethnic identity became tied to economic and political power over Catholics, reproduced through unionist rule at Stormont. Class differences and struggles, though never absent, were accommodated within the wider political divide which centred on the national question.

The use of religion as a 'boundary marker' for ethnic divisions (Shirlow and McGovern, 1995) does not mean that the differences are primarily about religion. Sectarianism is not merely individual prejudice against people with different beliefs, nor is it about disagreement over religious observance: sectarian (or ethnic) divisions are embodied in the concrete political process. The identification of Protestants with unionism and Catholics with nationalism, though by no means complete, is nevertheless strong.

Gendered ideologies have been prominent in the construction of the two communities. Nationalist mythology uses images of woman's eternal suffering, 'Mother Ireland' and 'dark Rosaleen', as a metaphor for Ireland's oppression. The Virgin Mary, watching over the dying prisoners, featured prominently in the murals which decorated the walls of nationalist areas during the hunger strikes of the 1980s. Within loyalist or unionist communities there is no equivalent symbolic role for women (McWilliams, 1991, p. 86). Its predominant imagery is masculine, most notably bowler-hatted Orangemen celebrating Protestantism's triumph at the Battle of the Boyne; and the harsh fundamentalist rhetoric of Ian Paisley.

These gendered stereotypes are reflected in the labour market. Catholics are disproportionately represented in traditionally female occupations. There are more Catholic men than Protestant men in the 'caring' profession of nursing for example. This reflects the exclusion of Catholics from higher status occupations, particularly from skilled craft occupations which have been monopolised by Protestant men. The loss of these traditional 'labour aristocracy' jobs has been a major source of Protestant insecurity in recent years.

Although the meanings attached to a person's identification with a community have little to do with religious belief, the churches play a powerful role in cementing community identity. Church attendance is high, particularly among women (Morgan, 1992). Even for non Church-goers, 'the language of religious identity is not very distant' (Morrow *et al.*, 1994, p. 6) and the churches provide a major focus for social and community life. They promote and reinforce notions of deference and obedience, and conformity to a rigid code of sexual behaviour. The sexual division of labour, with male clergy and a predominantly female membership who carry out the servicing and housekeeping tasks, exemplifies gender relations in the wider society.

Churches have been influential in shaping state policy. Northern Ireland under Stormont had, in the words of its first Prime Minister, Lord Craigavon, 'a Protestant parliament and a Protestant state' (quoted in Farrell, 1980). Catholics were excluded from state power and a 'Catholic/Protestant "apartheid"' in welfare services developed (O'Dowd, 1981, p. 16), with religious organisations playing a prominent role (Morrow *et al.*, 1994). State schools became effectively Protestant schools, while the overwhelming majority of Catholic children attended schools controlled by the Catholic Church (Murray, 1985).

Both Protestant and Catholic churches have promoted conservative views on social issues, particularly in relation to the family and sexuality. Opposition to abortion and gay rights has been one of the few areas of agreement between politicians and clergy from both sides. Abortion remains illegal in most circumstances, while the law on homosexuality was brought into line with British law only following a ruling by the European Court. Ian Paisley, leader of the Democratic Unionist Party, organised 'Ulster Against Sodomy' in protest at this decision. Church leaders and unionist politicians have united in a campaign against the Brooke Clinic in Belfast, which provides sex education and advice to young people.

The role of religion in cementing political allegiances means that politicians have been reluctant to challenge the churches' teaching on these issues. Feminists in Northern Ireland have had to confront the ideological dominance of church doctrine, and the idea that to challenge the prevailing politics of their community is 'disloyal'.

The Impact of Conflict

National conflicts present contradictory possibilities for women (Ridd, 1986). In Northern Ireland, the conflict has brought widening economic, social and political opportunities, but also pressures to conform to traditional values (Morgan and Fraser, 1994, pp. 3–4). Inevitably, due to the contested nature of society, these possibilities have been very different for Protestant and Catholic women.

For Protestants, the experience of the past two decades has been largely of alienation and loss (Dunn and Morgan, 1994). Politics under Stormont was constructed as a zero-sum game, with unionists viewing any advance by Catholics as being necessarily at the expense of Protestants. Although Stormont was overthrown 25 years ago, this view of politics remains. There has been more space for radical ideas within nationalism, and women have been more visible in politics, both as spokespeople for their community (Edgerton, 1986, p. 70) and in the armed struggle (Morgan and Fraser, 1995, p. 89). In contrast, for many unionists, feminism is 'conflated with socialism and nationalism, even republicanism, and thus regarded as an object of suspicion' (Morgan and Fraser, 1994, p. 5).

The use of violence against the 'other side' has been sanctioned, or at least tolerated, by large sections of the population. Republican violence has generally been aimed at what it defines as 'legitimate targets', those with some connection with the security forces. There have been phases when a more indiscriminate policy towards civilian areas has operated, for example in the 1990s with the bombs in Warrington, Canary Wharf and Manchester. Loyalists have more often, and explicitly, engaged in purely sectarian killing (McGarry and O'Leary, 1995).

The sanctioning of violence has also extended to those who do not conform to the codes of behaviour within their own community. Evason suggests that paramilitary weapons have been used to increase control over women in the home, 'adding an extra dimension to all the means men normally have for oppressing women' (Evason, 1982). Women experiencing domestic violence may be inhibited from calling the police when they are attacked, since this may be viewed as 'squealing' and be unacceptable within the community (McWilliams and McKiernan, 1993). Violence against women who transgress community norms by having sexual relationships with men from 'the other side' has also been common (Fairweather *et al.*, 1984).

Some women have themselves become involved in military activity. There have been a significant number of Republican woman prisoners for many years. A pamphlet produced by Sinn Fein Women's Department, *Women in Struggle* (1994), celebrates women's involvement in all aspects of the Republican movement, including as 'volunteers'. Some of these – Mairead Farrell, the Price sisters, Maire Drumm – became well-known names throughout Ireland and elsewhere. Less is known about Loyalist women paramilitaries who appear to have had less autonomy within the movement (Morgan and Fraser, 1995). The women's UDA was disbanded in 1974 after a group of its members killed Ann Ogilby, a married Protestant woman who had made visits to an unmarried prisoner. Her murder provoked revulsion even among UDA prisoners (Fairweather *et al.*, 1984, p. 283).

Women in the two communities responded very differently to the presence of security forces on the streets. For nationalist women, particularly those living in strongly nationalist working-class areas, the British army is an alien force, provoking hostility or indifference. The banging of dustbin lids to warn of the army's approach was one of the most potent symbols of women's resistance in the early days of the 'Troubles'. This experience helped politicise many nationalist women and brought many into community activity. Republican women have also highlighted specific ways in which women have been intimidated by the security forces, for example through strip searching and sexual assault.

The response of Protestant women has been more ambivalent. The army, and even more the police force, is seen as theirs. The Royal Ulster Constabulary (RUC) and the Ulster Defence Regiment (UDR) are both over 90 per cent Protestant. When in recent years, there has been conflict between the police and Loyalist or unionist communities, the security forces are seen as 'betraying their own'. Protestants did not develop the experience of resistance which provided nationalists with such a powerful basis for community activism, but many Protestants are now keen to emulate Catholic expertise.

The period of conflict has produced major changes for women. They have increasingly moved from the private domain of the home into the public sphere, as a result not only of the conflict, but of the social and economic restructuring which has taken place. Women are participating more in both the labour market and in political activity. Although women's political involvement has often begun through organising support for male relatives (for example around the issue of prisoners) women are now becoming increasingly active in community and women's organisations on their own behalf.

Women's Employment

Women's employment has increased dramatically in the past 20 years, with 58 per cent of women of working age now in the labour force (EOCNI, 1995, p. 11). Female participation rates increased by more than ten percentage points between 1971 and 1991, while men's declined by almost the same amount (EOCNI, 1993). The labour market continues, however, to be structured by religion and gender in terms of access to employment and occupational specialisation. Catholic women are doubly disadvantaged, experiencing inequalities based on both religion and gender. A recent report for the Northern Ireland Equal Opportunities Commission concluded that Catholic women faced deeper disadvantages than those faced by Protestant women (Davies *et al.*, 1995, p. 46).

The overriding concern of policy makers and researchers has been male employment, particularly the religious differential in male unemployment rates. Preoccupation with male employment is a result not only of greater differentials in official figures than for women; it also reflects society's undervaluation of women's work. In spite of the growing importance of women's paid labour, it is still considered secondary. As in Britain, the ideology of the 'male bread-winner' continues to permeate thinking and policy making in relation to the labour market.

Catholic men are less able than Protestants to be 'bread-winners'. According to official figures for 1991, only 60.8 per cent of Catholic men of working age were in work, compared to 79.2 per cent of Protestants (Sales, 1993). The difference was due mainly to the higher unemployment of Catholic men. This also had implications for Catholic women's employment. Labour market activity among women is now greatest among single

women or women married to men in full-time jobs. Women are
most likely to be out of the labour force if they have an unemployed husband (McLaughlin, 1986). The benefit system creates
a disincentive for the wives of unemployed men to enter the
labour force, since their partner would lose benefits as a result.
This is particularly important for part-time work, where potential
earnings are unlikely to compensate for the loss of benefits and
the other expenses incurred in employment (McWilliams, 1991).

Women therefore experience different relations to the labour
market through their partners. Women married to Catholic men
are less likely to be in work than those married to Protestants. The
high rate of endogamy (marriage within the community) means
that Catholic men are likely to be married to Catholic women.
Religious inequality therefore reinforces economic dependence
for Catholic women. Inequalities are compounded, with growing
disparities between 'work poor' and 'work rich' households.

For those in work, gender and religion also structure access to
particular sectors and occupations. The Eastern Health and
Social Services Board, noting the under-representation of
Catholics in maintenance, professional, technical and medical
occupations among its employees, commented that this reflected

> ... the trend within society in Northern Ireland – a strong emphasis
> within the Protestant community in science and engineering and a
> corresponding emphasis within the Roman Catholic community in
> the 'caring services' such as nursing and community work. (EHSS,
> 1991, p. 3)

This observation appears to require no further investigation by
the Board, even though it is drawn from its Equal Opportunities
Monitoring Report. The concentration of Catholics in 'caring
professions' does not stem, however, from any innate quality in
Catholics, but from the exclusion of Catholics from many high
status occupations, both in public and private sectors. The occupational structure also reflects a wider 'social apartheid' in which
each community largely services its own needs, most notably
through the segregated schooling system.

The workplace remains highly segregated on religious and
gender lines (FEC, 1995; McLaughlin and Ingram, 1991), and
women are more likely than men to be in religiously segregated
employment. Residential segregation has increased since the
'Troubles', and difficulties in travelling to work are exacerbated
by the problem of crossing 'hostile territory'. This has increased

the likelihood of women working with women from the same community. Women travel shorter distances to work, and are more likely to be in part-time work. Segregation reduces opportunities for women to work together on issues of common concern. It has also helped perpetuate uninformed stereotypes of the other community, making common activities more difficult.

The extension of the welfare state widened the circle of Catholics who benefited directly from state spending, through services and increased access to employment. The reforms carried out under Direct Rule have produced a greatly expanded Catholic middle class with a more direct stake in the state apparatus. But deregulation and casualisation have created a mass of unemployed and part-time and casualised workers. While this group remains disproportionately Catholic, an increasing number of Protestants are facing unemployment and economic deprivation as the traditional sources of, predominantly male, employment disappear. Protestant areas are becoming more prominent among the most deprived wards in Belfast, although Catholic areas continue to dominate (Northern Ireland Council for Voluntary Action, 1993).

Women and Political Organisation

'We don't talk about politics here. We only talk about women's issues.' This comment, from the administrator of a local women's centre, expresses the politics of avoidance which dominates many organisations in Northern Ireland, organisations which in other contexts would be considered unambiguously political. It represents an accommodation to the sectarian divide, a way of allowing women to work together on issues where they have a common interest. With 'politics' in Northern Ireland identified with the constitutional issue, women have often had to separate themselves from the formal political process in order to gain a voice for their concerns.

This search for a neutral or non-sectarian space is not confined to people working on 'women's issues'. Trade unionists often use similar terms to distance themselves from anything connected with the conflict. Trade unionism is thereby seen as self-evidently non-sectarian. This response to the conflict has allowed organisations and campaigns to be built which cross the divide. The politics of 'avoidance', however, makes it easier to marginalise feminist, and trade union, issues from mainstream political debate.

The vibrant women's movement which developed during the years of the conflict has challenged women's traditional roles. The history of the women's movement has shown, however, that unity built around women's demands is always fragile, and in danger of fracturing, as campaigns have forced women to take a position on the constitutional issue.

Women and Mainstream Politics

The formal political process has been dominated by the constitutional issue, with voters overwhelmingly giving allegiance to parties from their 'own side'. The construction of politics around community loyalties has given little space for movements which challenge other forms of inequality, and it is the constitutional issues which dominate political debates and political programmes. Northern Ireland's current constitutional status has created a political vacuum, in which local people have little political influence or control. Decisions on the major policy issues affecting people's lives in Northern Ireland are made by civil servants or by politicians at Westminster. District councils, the only elected bodies with local responsibilities, have few functions, their powers largely restricted to being 'in charge of "bins and burials"' (Rooney and Woods, 1995, p. 17).

Women are largely excluded even from this limited space for formal politics. There are no women MPs from Northern Ireland at Westminster, and only three have ever been elected. The last was Bernadette Devlin (now McAliskey) who represented Mid Ulster as a nationalist Unity candidate from 1969 until 1974. Several women candidates stood for major political parties in the 1992 general election, but none in a winnable seat, and no woman has been elected to Northern Ireland's three European Parliament seats.

There are now 582 local council seats across Northern Ireland. In the 1993 local elections, 67 women were elected, 11.5 per cent of the total (Lucey, 1994, p. 171). Subsequent by-elections have increased their number to 71 (12.2 per cent). Women are under-represented in all parties, but particularly in unionist parties. In the elections to the Forum in June 1996, women won 17 seats out of a total of 111 (15 per cent): five were for unionist parties (8 per cent); three were for the SDLP (14 per cent); one for the Alliance (14 per cent); and one for Labour (50 per cent). Sinn Fein was the party with the largest number of women elected with five (30 per cent).

The Women's Coalition won two seats. Its vote was between 1 and 2 per cent across Northern Ireland, but significantly lower in the Sinn Fein stronghold of West Belfast than elsewhere.

All major Northern Ireland political parties now have policy statements on women's issues, and claim they encourage women to become involved in party structures. These statements are often fairly limited. The main area of change has been in relation to employment, where all express support for the principle of equal opportunity. Launching the Ulster Unionist Party's statement on Women's Issues in 1992, the Reverend Martin Smyth declared that social attitudes 'must adapt to allow women scope to make their own decisions as the balance between family and work ambitions, in an atmosphere of support and encouragement'.

Although not a very radical statement, this represents a substantial shift from the attitudes prevailing in the 1970s. Structural changes in the labour market which have brought the erosion of traditional male 'bread-winner' jobs, and the increase in women's employment have forced politicians to confront the realities of changing gender roles. Legislation on sex discrimination has been in force since the 1970s, and a more pervasive culture of equal opportunities has developed. The development of party policies on women's issues also reflects the campaigning work done by women both within political parties and outside the formal political party structure. The more progressive policies in relation to employment have not extended to sexual politics. All the main parties remain either hostile or at best ambivalent in relation to abortion for example, and no party has been prepared to risk an open debate on the subject.

The Feminist Movement

In the 1970s, feminist campaigns emerged which challenged conventional views of women's role in the family and society in Northern Ireland, particularly in relation to the control of sexuality and fertility. The links between the main churches and the state have sustained a strongly conservative family ideology, which is underpinned by some of the most restrictive legislation in Europe. In addition feminists face problems of conflicting loyalties in relation to their own communities. Many Republicans oppose in principle any campaign which demands reform by Westminster. For unionists, any challenge to the *status quo* is seen as dangerous, and as 'rocking the boat' (Gordon, 1990).

The Northern Ireland women's movement, like all feminist movements, has split on grounds of ideology and tactics, but the sectarian divide has often been at the root of these divisions, and has proved the most intractable (Roulston, 1989). The Northern Ireland Women's Rights Movement, founded in 1975, has played a major role in feminist campaigning. It attempted to avoid taking a position on the political situation, but this proved difficult to sustain since its priorities suggested by implication that 'progress could be made within the existing political framework' (Roulston, 1989, p. 227). Divisions intensified during the hunger strikes of the 1980s, when the issue of whether to support women Republican prisoners 'became a metaphor for everything that has kept Irish women divided from each other' (Ward, 1991, p. 156).

'Julie' was involved in the feminist movements in the 1980s. She now works as a community worker in Protestant West Belfast and has become active in one of the new parties associated with the Loyalist paramilitaries. She recalled her experience of the women's movement at this time.

> Nationalists were more politicised than the Protestants then. Their awareness of oppression of Catholics made them more aware of their oppression as women. This didn't happen so much in the Protestant community and this set the tone for the women's movement.

Her feeling of difference was based on an identification with Protestant culture and politics, rather than religious affiliation. She was brought up in a strongly segregated Protestant community of East Belfast.

> I went to a Protestant church school, I was brought up with that culture. Our perceptions were different. In the women's movement it was not possible to express it. The only experience that was valued was of the down-trodden Catholic woman.

'Mary' was also active in the feminist movement at the time, but her political development has taken her in a different direction and she is now active in the nationalist grouping Clár na mBan:

> In the late 1970s I thought women could come together and make their own demands. But with the debates around strip searching and whether or not it is a 'feminist issue', I realised it was not possible to ignore the issues which divide us. I have gone right round over a twenty year period to believing in United Ireland as a priority.

Community Politics

By the early 1980s, feminists, frustrated at the obstacles to developing a programme which could avoid sectarian splits, began to devote their energies to more practical issues (Ward, 1991). Local women's centres were established, providing advice and support for women, and the base for a range of activities, including education and research about women's lives. While explicitly feminist groups had involved a relatively small number of women, a much wider spectrum of women has become active in community politics. May Blood, from the Shankill Women's Forum, was a member of a delegation of women's groups to an international women's conference in the United States. She recalled: 'The other delegates were surprised that the women from Northern Ireland were mainly working class. All the other delegations – including the one from the south of Ireland – were middle class.' Community activity, which is not quite part of the formal public sphere, has traditionally been a 'safe' area for women's political activity. Community groups also provide space for more radical groups and individuals for whom the concerns and practices of the formal political parties hold no attraction (Nelson, 1984). Protestant women were slower than their Catholic counterparts to become involved in community organisations. There remain deep-seated beliefs in the Protestant community that resources should be theirs by right and they should not have to campaign for them. Although this ideology has been undermined in recent years, Catholics still dominate the 'community development' field. A substantial network of community and women's centres has, however, developed in Protestant areas.

Most centres are in either Protestant or Catholic areas and tend to serve one community or the other. An exception is the Downtown Centre in the 'neutral territory' of Belfast's city centre. It is also the most explicitly feminist. For others based within tightly-knit, mainly working-class communities, raising contentious issues such as abortion or lesbian rights can be problematic, since these centres depend on local support. Even raising 'women's issues' can be dangerous. One woman involved in a project to investigate women's needs was threatened by people claiming to speak for Loyalist paramilitaries in the area. Soon afterwards, the slogan 'watch your back fenian lover' appeared on a wall near the women's centre.

In spite of being focused on separate communities, women's organisations have been at the forefront of developing cross-community links. The Women's Information Group brings together women's groups across Northern Ireland, and organises monthly meetings in women's centres, alternating between Protestant and Catholic areas. Another notable example of co-operation was the joint approach by the Falls and the Shankill Women's Centres (based in Catholic and Protestant areas respectively) to Belfast City Hall when the council cut off funding for the Falls Centre. This precipitated the foundation of the Women's Support Network to campaign on issues of mutual interest.

The centres have now become more established with paid staff, but this development has been double-edged. They are increasingly dependent on funding sources, and funding bodies often attempt to impose an agenda which may not be appropriate to the work involved. The channelling of funding through church organisations, for example, can create tensions, as many of the issues of concern to women's groups, particularly domestic violence and sexuality, are those which the churches have attempted to deny.

There has recently been an insistence on a 'community relations' element as a condition for official funding. Some activists have suggested that this emphasis can be 'to the detriment of important issue-based activity for women' (Taillon, 1992, p. 7). Dependence on funders can also make it more difficult for women to confront issues of state violence and breaches of human rights.

While British government policy has promoted reconciliation, this has not necessarily been the case for councils under local political control. In 1996, the unionist-controlled Belfast City Council suspended funding to two of Belfast's most active women's centres – the Shankill and the Downtown Women's Centres. This move exposed the fragility of the relationship between women's organisations and official bodies, particularly when their work begins to conflict with traditional attitudes. No reasons were given for the withdrawal of grants, but many women suspect that the Shankill Centre was considered too 'soft on nationalism'. The Downtown Centre, with its more overtly feminist stance, has also generated opposition from unionists on the City Council. The impact of the loss of funding has been especially severe, leading to the closure of its advice service.

Women and the 'Peace Process'

Reaction to the Republican and Loyalist ceasefires in 1994 was very different amongst women in the two communities. In both

there was overwhelming relief that the violence which had dominated their lives appeared to be at an end. As 'Jane', a
professional community development worker put it:

> We dealt with the Troubles by not dealing with it. You don't notice
> normality. I have always gone everywhere in Belfast, but now I
> notice I don't worry, the tension has gone that I did not realise was
> there.

There was an initial euphoria in the nationalist community which
was not echoed in Protestant areas. The excitement in nationalist
areas sprung partly from the anticipation that some concessions
must have been won to encourage the IRA to lay down its arms.
To the Protestant community any such deal was anathema, and
suspicion and caution prevailed.

For nationalist women, the ceasefires appeared to open up the
possibility of developing a new, more inclusive agenda. A broad
nationalist grouping, Clár na mBan (Women's Agenda) had
already started to discuss 'the future of women in the context of
Irish national unity' (Clár na mBan, 1994, p. 3). A conference in
1994 brought together women from across Ireland, representing
a wide spectrum of nationalist opinion, with the aim of ensuring
that women had a voice in discussions about future political
structures and policies.

Opening the conference, Oonagh Marron of the Falls
Women's Centre criticised the terms of the debate, which was
dominated at that time by the Hume–Adams talks:

> The danger is that once again we are going to be asked to bury our
> demands, this time in the common purpose of achieving peace. I think
> it is time to send a message to those negotiating on our behalf that this
> time around our support will not be unconditional. (Clár na mBan,
> 1994, p. 9)

In a similar vein, Bernadette McAliskey criticised the limited way
in which the issue of violence was being discussed:

> When the government says they are talking about guaranteeing an end
> to violence, they are talking about the IRA handing over the weapons.
> They are not talking about an end to the Prevention of Terrorism Act.
> ... They are not talking about making it a criminal offence for a man
> to beat his wife. (Clár na mBan, 1994, p. 15)

The cessation of violence allowed women to talk about alternatives with greater confidence and security. The optimism was,
however, gradually lost in the long months of prevarication which
followed. As 'Sheila', a Clár na mBan activist put it:

> After the ceasefires there was a terrific lot of talking, but there has
> been a dissipation of all this. The key issue is being defined by nation-
> alists as all party talks, and the intransigence of the British, and the
> women's agenda is being left outside.

'Mary' was also disappointed with the response of people in the
South to the possibilities opened up by the ceasefires: 'Southern
feminists have not taken up the opportunity to fight for a new
Ireland. They should be arguing the need for a new type of
Ireland.' The debate in Southern Ireland around the peace
process has been limited. The ceasefires allowed the development
of more cross-border links between women's groups, but this has
not led to a wider debate about the politics of the peace process,
which might have influenced the discussion in the North. Before
the ceasefires, many people in the South, including the feminist
movement, were reluctant to get involved in discussing the situation in the North. The ceasefires made it less dangerous, but this
has not led to any wider re-evaluation of the possibilities for transforming Irish society.

The response from Protestant women to the ceasefires was
initially more uncertain. The years of the 'Troubles' have created
a sense of loss and alienation in the Protestant community. For
the majority, their British identity is extremely important, but
they feel that the British government has let them down. Many
Protestants expressed ambivalence about the future. On the one
hand, they are determined to hang on to their Britishness; but on
the other, there is for some a resignation in the face of what they
see as the inevitability of a united Ireland. As 'Joan' put it:

> Protestants feel that there will be a United Ireland, that Britain will
> pull out. That sentence in the Downing Street Declaration, that
> Britain has no strategic interest in Northern Ireland. When I read that
> I realised that Britain will pull out eventually.

This sense of betrayal extends to the British people who, it is felt,
do not recognise the Britishness of Northern Ireland Protestants.
'Tracey' is a feminist and an advice worker in the Shankill

Women's Centre. She was invited to speak at a conference organised by women in England.

> The meeting was on the changing relations between Britain and Ireland. The English women there talked about us from the North as if we were Irish. I felt my Britishness was being denied. Ireland North and South are two different countries.

Loyalist women, however, like nationalists, are also concerned at the dangers of male control over the negotiations. 'Julie' expressed this fear:

> I am worried that we were at war on the say so of paramilitaries, and the peace is also at their say so. This is a threatening situation, and indicates the fight women have for the future.

'Joan' expressed other worries about women's position within the loyalist communities as the peace process developed:

> Men have always praised women's role in the community, but are we going to be ousted when the men come out of jail?

There is no Protestant equivalent organisation to Clár na mBan, and a less confident assertion of future agendas. The Protestant Women's group which began meeting in 1995 to explore alternative identities for Protestant women has remained small. The group includes women with a range of views, from those who are committed Loyalists, to those who have rejected unionism and want to develop a role for Protestant women within an all-Ireland framework. The political realities make it extremely difficult to construct any common Protestant feminist agenda. One member, 'Sarah', expressed frustration with the group's limited agenda. A major priority for her is to campaign against the continuing hold of religious conservatism over the communities:

> I would like the group to take a more activist role in the community, to attack fundamentalism more energetically. But the group is more of a discussion group.

As both Protestant and Catholic feminists recognise, unionism has seen feminism as alien and viewed it with suspicion. The ties of unionism to Protestant privilege have traditionally placed it on the side of the *status quo*. There have been attempts to find more progressive forms of unionism, in civic unionism, and in socialist or social democratic versions as well as feminist ones. The Northern Ireland state has, however, been inescapably linked to exclusion and inequality, both in relation to religion and gender. For many feminists, the contradictions have been resolvable only through a renunciation of unionism, or through 'avoidance' of broader political questions.

Many Protestants have lost their trust in traditional leaders, and are consciously learning from the experience of Catholics in organising around community politics. The ceasefires opened up the space for more progressive politics, but the long delay in moving towards negotiations led to a vacuum, and increasing cynicism. As 'Siobhan' from Clár na mBan put it: 'There was initial enthusiasm about discussion change, but now the focus is on getting a share of the money that is going around.'

The resumption of IRA violence in 1996, together with the emergence of breakaway Loyalist paramilitaries, brought a hardening of sectarian attitudes. Even during the ceasefires, 'punishment shootings' were continuing. Some women reported an increase in violence, particularly against women. As 'Joan' explained, 'There has been no demilitarisation and these men have their own arms. They have been encouraged to feel violent, to hate the enemy, and now there is no outlet for violence.'

Against this background, the Women's Coalition attempted to build a common agenda in which women could bury their differences. The coalition brought together community activists, trade unionists and academics to promote a women's platform in the elections for the 1996 Forum, the gateway to all-party negotiations. Recognising that they had differences over the constitutional issue, they agreed to work together in areas where there was agreement, such as childcare and employment opportunities. Although the group won nearly 2 per cent of the total vote in the election to the Northern Ireland Forum, and two seats, support for the coalition has not been universal among feminists. As Sheila from Clár na mBan said, 'they do not speak for me'. Many fear that the unity of the group can only be maintained so long as the peace process remains stalled. If serious progress were made in discussing future constitutional arrangements, differences would inevitably surface.

For nationalist women, the key question remains the integration of women's issues with the constitutional debate. Many women believe that maintaining unity around 'women's issues' must not be at the expense of ignoring injustice and inequality. As

'Siobhan' put it: 'In order to develop a women's agenda we need to grasp the nettle of taking a position on the national question.'

Conclusion

Women have made substantial moves into the public sphere, both in employment and in the largely informal politics of community groups. The women's centres, and the many groups which campaign around women's issues and provide mutual support for women, have made a real difference to women's lives, and are starting to have some influence on policy at local level. The early 1990s witnessed a tremendous upsurge of energy and creativity by women in Northern Ireland. The range of groups and organisations established included large numbers of women, many of whom became involved for the first time with 'women's issues'. The ceasefires provided an impetus for this movement, opening up possibilities of fundamental change in Northern Ireland. In developing cross-community work, some women were starting to move from the politics of 'avoidance'.

Formal politics in Northern Ireland, however, remains dominated by men. The absence of women's voices and women's concerns was particulary marked in negotiations and debates around the 'peace process'. Men are able to acclaim women as 'the backbone of the community' as long at they remain excluded from the real power and decision-making. The separation of women's issues from the mainstream agenda of politics remains firmly entrenched. It is ironic that women are prominent as 'peace makers' but have been allowed little role in making the peace.

The structures of Northern Ireland were built on the denial of rights to Catholics. This exclusion, by constructing a politics around community loyalties, helped sustain the patriarchal structures which have oppressed all women. The programme put forward by groups such as the Women's Coalition challenges the traditional values in Northern Ireland society. But unless women are involved with politics as it is traditionally defined in Northern Ireland, their influence is likely to remain marginal. If women are to reconstruct the meaning of politics in Northern Ireland, they face the even more difficult task of engaging with the issues which divide them.

The opening up in Northern Ireland society after the ceasefires, particularly among women, was in marked contrast to the attitude of the British government. The narrow and grudging response to the ceasefires, and the painfully slow progress towards talks, gradually turned that optimism to frustration and despair. The opportunities opened up by the peace process for a serious examination of Britain's policy were not seized. Feminists in Britain have a role to play in helping to ensure that women's concerns are placed at the centre of future discussions of Northern Ireland. This must involve confronting the politics of Britain's involvement in Ireland, and working to redefine the relations between Britain and Ireland on the basis of equality.

9   The Human Rights Deficit

Conor Foley

'We have had our Weetabix. We shall not be moved', sang the
crowd, as the riot police edged closer. 'We have had our
Weetabix ... '

August 1996 – but it could have been any August in recent
years. It was an incongruous sight. Sitting in the middle of the main
road of the small village of Bellaghy in south Derry were about 150
local residents, ranging from teenagers to grandparents.
Surrounding them were two lines of at least 500 officers of the
Royal Ulster Constabulary (RUC), in full riot gear, equipped with
plastic bullet guns and backed by 25 armour-plated Land Rovers,
with engines revving. At the other end of the village were about 50
members of the Royal Black Preceptory, dressed in collarettes and
bowler hats and accompanied by an accordian band.

Between the RUC and the residents was a small group of self-
styled international peace monitors consisting of American
pacifists and a delegation from a European network of aid organisations, including myself. The night before, the RUC had
batoned residents off the road to make way for an Orange march
and we were there in fearful anticipation of a re-run.

Whether it was us or the mass media presence who averted the
confrontation is debatable, but the RUC chose not to force the
march through this time. After an all-night vigil by the residents
and negotiations involving Northern Ireland's most senior police
officers, a compromise was hammered out whereby the
Orangemen extended the length of their march by approximately
six yards but were denied the opportunity to parade through an
overwhelmingly Catholic village. As one of the observers noted,
the confrontation had similarities with some battles of the First
World War.

Our delegation had gone to Northern Ireland to observe the
Apprentice Boys Parades which converge in Derry City in mid-
August every year. The parades commemorate the start of the
siege of Derry in 1688 when 13 young apprentice boys defied the

city Governor, William Lundy, and closed the gates against the advancing army of King James II. The heroism and sacrifice of the city's residents helped to secure the eventual victory of King William of Orange and the triumph of the 'Glorious Revolution', securing the system of parliamentary democracy which the United Kingdom currently enjoys.

For Northern Ireland's Protestant, unionist community the annual parades are a source of pride and hope that the cry of 'No Surrender' will forever deliver them from their ancient foe. But for Catholics the Orange marching season is a sectarian display of triumphalist bigotry which annually reminds them of their second class citizenship in the state in which they live.

Orange marches have always been a source of tension in Ireland since the Orange Order was founded in 1795, in opposition to the nationalist and secular society of United Irishmen. Catholics resent the fact that some marches are held near to their areas, which they see as provocative. Rioting after one Orange parade in Belfast in the 1930s left 13 people dead, and it was a confrontation during the Apprentice Boys Parade in 1969 which sparked the Battle of the Bogside, the redeployment of British troops and over 25 years of bloody conflict.

More recently, disputes have centred around the particular routes of parades. In part this is because demographic changes have transformed some routes from staunchly Protestant areas into mixed or predominantly Catholic neighbourhoods. Territory and identity are fiercely guarded in Northern Ireland, and religion, politics and symbolism often intertwine over disputes about the respective validity of the two cultural traditions. Demands for marches to be re-routed are seen as an attack on the Protestant unionist tradition just as the early civil rights agitation was seen as an attempt to subvert the Protestant state. The fact that some areas where Orange parades have traditionally taken place are now Catholic-dominated reinforces the Protestant self-image of a community under siege. Lundy's spectre looms large over possible compromises on the issue.

When the IRA declared their ceasefire in August 1994, Sinn Fein's president, Gerry Adams, spoke of the need for a settlement which guaranteed equal rights and 'parity of esteem' between the two traditions. The failure of the British government to lock the parties into negotiations after the ceasefire or to extend the process of demilitarisation beyond token gestures allowed the peace process to stagnate. There were clashes during the marching season in the summer of 1995, and in February 1996 the IRA formally ended its ceasefire with bombs in London which killed two people.

An uneasy truce was maintained in Northern Ireland itself until the week of 12 July 1996 when the province lurched back to the brink of full-scale conflict over a disputed parade through Drumcree, near Portadown. Unionist leaders, side by side with some hardline loyalist paramilitaries, were held back by the RUC for several days. Finally, under overwhelming pressure the RUC caved in and batoned their way through the residents to allow the parade to take place. Six thousand plastic bullets were fired in a week; about four hundred of them at Loyalists in Drumcree, the rest at protesting nationalists across Northern Ireland – four thousand over a weekend in a single street in Derry.

The partisan brutality of the police outraged nationalist Ireland. The IRA issued a statement that they would not allow Catholic areas to remain unprotected. There were boycotts of some Protestant businesses in rural areas. The world's attention turned to Derry and the forthcoming Apprentice Boys Parades. In the event it was the RUC who contained the situation, re-routing the Apprentice Boys from the walls of Derry City overlooking the Catholic Bogside and banning feeder marches which were deemed provocative. The Orangemen grudgingly accepted these conditions and, more significantly, in some areas agreed to open discussions with local residents groups about future marches. The peaceful end to the Bellaghy stand-off brought a collective sigh of relief in Ireland and a realisation that something fairly fundamental might have changed.

The Security State and Emergency Powers

The relationships between the British state, Irish Catholics and Protestants in Ireland have been described as 'the fateful triangle of the modern history of Ireland' (O'Leary and McGarry, 1993, p. 65). That history has also been characterised by an inability of the British rulers to view agitation for equal treatment or full political rights for the Catholic majority as anything other than a cloak for subversion. For rulers and rebels alike, the distinction between reform and revolution has always been blurred.

Ireland's first nationalist Republican movement, the United Irishmen, was founded mainly by Presbyterians but advocated equal rights for Catholics and aimed to replace the sectarian political labels Catholic, Protestant and Dissenter with a common

THE HUMAN RIGHTS DEFICIT

Irish label. In the aftermath of their failed uprising of 1798 a British parliamentary committee was established to consider the causes of the revolt and to make recommendations for future policy. Its report stated:

> ... the rebellion originated in a system, framed not with a view of obtaining either Catholic emancipation, or any reform compatible with the existence of the constitution, but for the purpose of subverting the government, separating Ireland from Great Britain and forming a democratic republic, founded on the destruction of all Church establishment, the abolition of ranks, and the confiscation of property. ... [T]he vigilance of the executive government, in detecting and arresting many of the principal conspirators in the very act of concerting their plans of insurrection, the convictions which have ensued, and the still more complete development of the treason by the confession of some of its most active and efficient conductors, have not only essentially contributed to the defeat of the rebellion, but by enabling the Committee to disclose the views and machinations of the conspirators, may suggest means for securing the future tranquillity of the country.[1]

Between the Act of Union of 1800 and the Anglo–Irish Treaty of 1921 Ireland was governed directly from Westminster.[2] During this time 105 separate coercion acts were introduced which kept the country in an almost permanent state of emergency (Townshend, 1983). A military police force, the Royal Irish Constabulary (RIC), was established which became a model for other colonial forces. Ireland also became a useful testing ground for counter-insurgency tactics, leading Karl Marx to make his famous warning to the emerging English social revolutionary movement that 'a people which enslaves another people forges its own chains' .[3]

In 1883 the Metropolitan Police formed a Special Irish Branch to combat the activities of the Irish Republican Brotherhood, the Fenians, who were then engaged in a bombing campaign in British cities. In 1887 the Special Branch broadened its scope to deal with other forms of subversion and serious crime (Allason, 1983, pp. 1–16). The Special Branch today has an extremely wide range of responsibilities and although staffed by police officers, in many respects operates like a security service and has strong links with MI5.

After Partition, responsibility for policing Northern Ireland rested with the unionist-dominated government at Stormont. The

principal piece of legislation by which the authorities exercised
emergency powers was the Civil Authorities (Special Powers) Act
1922 which re-enacted much of the previous British coercion
legislation (Hogan and Walker, 1989, p. 14). Initially designed to
be temporary, it was renewed annually until 1933 when it was
made permanent.

The Special Powers Act provided for arrest without warrant or
charge and detention for 48 hours, indefinite internment without
trial, house raids without warrant, flogging and execution, depor-
tation, the destruction or requisition of property, the blocking of
roads, curfews, the prohibition of inquests and the banning of
organisations, meetings and publications.[4] The Home Secretary
was also empowered to introduce additional regulations, by
decree, if the government considered them necessary for the
preservation of law and order.[5] What is striking about this list is
not only that virtually all of these measures breach internationally
accepted human rights standards but that the Stormont government found it necessary to maintain them despite the fact that the
IRA was largely inactive for most of the period, and that most of
these practices, in modified form, have been re-enacted by the
British government during the period of Direct Rule that began in
1972.

The two main pieces of legislation which have sanctioned the
use of special emergency powers and practices since the introduction of Direct Rule are the Northern Ireland (Emergency
Provisions) Act (EPA) and the Prevention of Terrorism
(Temporary Provisions) Act (PTA). Other issues, such as the role
and functions of inquests, the treatment of prisoners or the use of
plastic bullets are dealt with under secondary legislation, rules
and guidelines.

The EPA retains the power to order internment without trial,
which is a clear violation of the European Convention on Human
Rights (ECHR),[6] although its use was gradually phased out in
1975 as the authorities made increasing use of other powers. The
EPA re-enacted other provisions contained in the Special Powers
Act giving the security forces extended powers to stop, search,
question, arrest and detain people, and to block roads,[7] and it
gives the Secretary of State for Northern Ireland the power to ban
organisations.[8]

The EPA also creates a separate legal regime for people
arrested on suspicion of committing what are known as 'scheduled offences' – principally crimes of violence, attacks on
property, explosives and firearms offences, theft, intimidation,

blackmail and membership of a proscribed organisation. Those arrested under this regime face special provisions governing notification of arrest and access to solicitors and, if charged, are tried in special 'Diplock Courts' which sit without juries where there are special rules governing the admissibility of evidence and where, in some cases, the burden of proof rests with the defendant not with the prosecution.[9]

Most significantly, the EPA lowers standards on the admissibility of confessions which may have been obtained through improper means. While under ordinary law confessions must automatically be excluded if they have been obtained through any breaches of the Criminal Evidence (Northern Ireland) Order, under the EPA they may remain admissible provided they have not been obtained through torture or inhuman or degrading treatment or through any violence or threat of violence.[10]

In 1974, the year after the passage of the EPA, the government enacted the Prevention of Terrorism (Temporary Provisions) Act (PTA). It was tabled in Parliament four days after the Birmingham pub bombings killed 21 people. The Home Secretary at the time acknowledged the Act's powers were so draconian as to be 'unprecedented in peacetime' and during the debate it was estimated that the Act would only be in force for about six months.[11] It passed in 42 hours virtually without amendment or dissent.

Over 20 years later the Act is still on the statute book, having been re-enacted in 1979 and 1984, and then in 1989 made into a permanent law. While some of its provisions have been modified its basic powers remain largely unchanged. The most significant modification was in 1984, when its scope was widened to include 'international terrorism'. This had the *de facto* effect of making it a permanent piece of legislation as it is difficult to envisage circumstances where there will never be a threat of terrorism from somewhere in the world.

People detained under the PTA can be held for 24 hours in solitary confinement and for up to seven days without access to a court, although the Home Secretary must authorise the extension of a detention beyond the first 48 hours. Detained individuals can be held incommunicado during the first 48 hours of their detention, they can be denied access to a solicitor and may be questioned in the absence of one. A 1993 study by the Home Office into PTA detentions in Britain found that access to legal advice was delayed in over a quarter of all cases where detainees asked for it and that in a substantial minority of cases no grounds were given for this delay.[12] Only 19 per cent of foreign nationals were informed of their right to communicate with their embassy and Irish nationals were even less likely to be informed of this right. The PTA enables the police to use 'reasonable force' to photograph and fingerprint detainees without a court order and without consent. Files on detainees can be kept even if they are released without charge.[13]

The PTA also enables the Secretary of State to proscribe organisations without needing to refer the matter to Parliament, and to exclude people from Britain or Northern Ireland on suspicion of their involvement in 'the commission, preparation or instigation of acts of terrorism to which this Part of the Act applies'. The terms of the Act allow an exclusion to be made if the individual may have been involved in terrorism in the past or could harbour some intention to involve themselves in terrorism in the future. It is a criminal offence, punishable by up to six months' imprisonment, to break an Exclusion Order.[14] These provisions effectively created a system of internal exile.

Exclusion Orders are entirely at the discretion of the Secretary of State, who acts on the advice of the police. The Order gives no explanation as to why it is being served. The person subject to exclusion has no right to know the evidence supporting it, to cross-examine that evidence, to offer a defence or to have the case heard in public. A person subject to an Order may appeal by requesting an oral hearing before a government-appointed adviser, but the individual being excluded has no right to legal representation or to be given any information about the reason for the exclusion. The Secretary of State has a duty to take into account these representations, but has no obligation to state why the appeal was successful or unsuccessful.

Much of this emergency legislation is contrary to international human rights standards. Seven day detentions are in breach of Article 5 of the ECHR and the British government has been forced to derogate from this Article.[15] This derogation was upheld in May 1993, on the grounds that an emergency existed in Northern Ireland which was sufficiently serious to justify the denial of these rights.[16]

Britain also cannot ratify protocol 4 of the ECHR, providing for freedom of movement and settlement within one's own country. Indeed, Britain is the only country in Europe to have a system of imposing internal exile on its own citizens (Sieghart, 1983, p. 464). After the 1994 ceasefires were declared a number of exclusion orders which were being challenged in the courts were dropped. The London-based civil rights group Liberty won a reference to the European Court over the exclusion of Gerry Adams from Britain and was still pursuing this case in 1996, although the order against him was revoked some months after the IRA ceasefire.

Concern about the treatment of suspects in interrogation centres has been a recurring feature of the Northern Ireland conflict. Britain has been found guilty before the European Court of Human Rights of using inhuman and degrading treatment,[17] and of carrying out arbitrary arrests.[18] In 1979, following damning complaints from human rights organisations, the government's own Bennett Report concluded that detainees were suffering injuries whilst in custody which could not have been self-inflicted. After 1979 the numbers of complaints about ill-treatment dropped rapidly, although they were to rise again at the end of the 1980s and the start of the 1990s. In 1991 the United Nations Committee on Torture expressed concern about the regimes operating in Northern Ireland's interrogation centres[19] and in 1994 the Strasbourg-based Committee for the Prevention of Torture accused the British government of permitting psychological and physical ill-treatment of detainees during police questioning, including assaults and death threats.[20]

Since 1988 judges in Diplock Courts in Northern Ireland have been instructed to 'draw adverse inferences' if a defendant has failed at the earliest possible moment to mention facts which are material to their defence while under police questioning, or have failed to account for anything else which might connect them with a crime.[21] It also requires courts to call on defendants to give evidence at trials and gives them power to draw adverse inferences from their failure to do so. Silence may also be treated as corroborative evidence against the accused.

Abolition of the right of silence has greatly increased concern about the risk of wrongful convictions in Northern Ireland.[22] This is of particular concern given the existing denial of rights under the legal regime governing the arrest, detention, interrogation and trial of people accused of scheduled offences in Northern Ireland. A person arrested in connection with a scheduled offence in Northern Ireland may be denied access to their legal representative for 48 hours. Solicitors cannot sit in on interviews and these are not tape-recorded. The courts have ruled that adverse inferences can be drawn from the failure of a suspect to answer questions even if they have requested legal advice before making a statement.[23]

The Belfast-based Committee on the Administration of Justice (CAJ) has documented a number of cases in Northern Ireland where it believes the safety of convictions to be in doubt, and where either adverse inferences were drawn from the silence of the defendant, or the defendants may have been induced to make false confessions for fear that their refusal to answer police questions would be held against them at their trial.[24] There is concern that the new caution, given when charged, is little understood and widely misinterpreted and has placed undue pressure on suspects to speak and that at the same time, the standard of proof has been lowered and burden of proof shifted to the defence.

A study carried out by CAJ in 1994 confirmed these concerns while highlighting that the abolition of the right of silence had not reduced crime nor improved charging or conviction rates (Weaver, 1994). Clear-up rates (where someone is charged with an offence) peaked at a record high of 45 per cent in 1988, but fell in each successive year after the abolition of the right of silence and were 11 per cent lower in 1992 than they had been in 1988.[25] Conviction rates had also dropped on average 3–4 per cent lower in the four years after the abolition of the right of silence. The study noted that judges had initially shown considerable caution in giving weight to the fact that a defendant had chosen to remain silent at some point while in police custody or during the trial. However, it noted a 'real and pronounced' shift in the burden of proof required by judges when applying the Criminal Evidence Order 1988 'which almost takes silence as presumptive of guilt'. It concluded that the Order 'offends the principles of self-incrimination and presumption of innocence' and 'raises serious considerations on whether the provisions of the Order can be compatible with the right to a fair trial enshrined in Article 6 of the European Convention of Human Rights'. It further concluded that 'as a weapon in the fight against crime, the abolition of the right of silence is of little use'.

Despite the experiences of Northern Ireland, and in the teeth of opposition from most of the British legal establishment, in November 1994 the government pressed ahead with the abolition of the right to silence in the Criminal Justice and Public Order Act. The Act also increased the powers of the police in a variety of situations, reduced the rights of defendants and created a number of new criminal offences through amendments to the Prevention of Terrorism Act.

The Act conferred stop and detention powers on the British police similar to those that the RUC and Army possessed under the Northern Ireland (Emergency Provisions) Act 1991. A police officer of commander rank can authorise the stopping and searching of people in a particular location for a period of up to 28 days 'where it appears' to them 'that it is expedient to do so in order to prevent acts of terrorism'. The police are empowered to stop any vehicle and search it as well as its driver or passengers, and stop and search any pedestrian for 'articles of a kind which could be used for a purpose connected with the commission, preparation or instigation of acts of terrorism'.[26] The Act specifies that: 'A constable may, in the exercise of those powers, stop any vehicle or person and make any search he thinks fit whether or not he has any grounds for suspecting that the vehicle or person is carrying articles of that kind.'[27] Furthermore it became a criminal offence to refuse to cooperate with a stop and search.

Prior to the passage of the Act the City of London police had established roadblocks around the centre of London, in July 1993, and were carrying out random checks on motorists, claiming to be acting under powers contained within the Road Traffic Act. Liberty received a number of complaints from people who objected to being stopped, and gathered anecdotal evidence that some people were being arrested for technical motoring offences and that black people were frequently being detained. In response to one complaint about this from a member of the public, the Acting Commander of the City of London wrote that:

> I note your comments about black people being stopped. Many members of the public who are stopped may not necessarily fit the current profile of a terrorist, however, terrorist tactics are constantly changing and we must be alert to all possibilities.[28]

In November 1994 the police issued statistics for the number of stops of vehicles where details were recorded (significantly less than the total number of vehicles being stopped).[29] The figures show that while the overall number of stops fell, the proportion of black people being stopped rocketed. Between 1 July 1993 and 31 December 1993, 1.7 per cent of those stopped were black. By October 1994 this figure had risen to 10.8 per cent.

The Act also made it an offence for a person to have in their possession any article 'in circumstances giving rise to a reasonable suspicion' that it is intended 'for a purpose connected with the commission, instigation or preparation of acts of terrorism'.[30] A person is also guilty of an offence if they are found to be collecting or possessing, without authorisation, 'any information which is of such a nature that it is likely to be useful to terrorists'.[31] There is no requirement for the material to be possessed with the intention of using it for terrorist purposes. In theory, someone could be prosecuted for holding a list of the private addresses of government ministers, as this information is not publicly available. The creation of this new offence is likely to be of particular concern to campaigners, journalists and other researchers, who might in certain circumstances have to prove that information they were collecting about government ministers, for example, *could not* be of use to terrorists. The reversal of the onus of proof means that a person charged with this offence will be forced to answer questions and give evidence in court.

Journalists attempting to report about the Northern Ireland conflict have already fallen foul of Section 18 of the Prevention of Terrorism Act 1989 which makes it an offence to fail to disclose information that a person knows or believes might be of assistance in preventing terrorist acts, or in arresting or convicting terrorists. In 1992 Channel Four and Box Productions were convicted under this section of the Act and fined £75,000 for broadcasting a documentary concerning alleged links between the security forces and Loyalist paramilitaries.[32]

Indeed, overt censorship and the 'chill' factor had made truth an early casualty of the conflict. Despite the government's adamant denials of a shoot-to-kill policy or high level military–Loyalist collusion, the security forces are widely believed to have targeted Republican activists for assassination. The security forces killed over 300 people during the conflict,[33] of whom only about a half had paramilitary connections.[34] In September 1995 the European Court of Human Rights ruled that the British government had violated the right to life of three unarmed members of the IRA killed by the Special Air Services (SAS) in Gibraltar in 1988. There have been numerous other incidents in which it is claimed people have been killed when they could have been arrested or have been 'finished off' after initially being wounded.[35]

The inadequacy of the inquest system in determining the causes of deaths, the inability of the police complaints mechanisms to redress grievances and the fact that only four soldiers have ever been convicted of murder while on duty in Northern Ireland have reinforced the impression that the security forces are beyond accountability. Even in the cases of the four soldiers who received mandatory sentences of life imprisonment, two were released, after serving two and a half and four years respectively, and both were readmitted into the British Army.[36]

Another worrying aspect of the conflict was the growth of unaccountable counter-terrorist organisations. There were indications that sections of the security and intelligence services, which were previously able to rely on the Cold War and the Northern Ireland conflict to justify their existence, may now be seeking a new rationale. In 1992 MI5 was given primary responsibility for Northern Ireland counter-terrorism within Britain which had previously, and historically, been the preserve of the Special Branch. Following the 1994 ceasefire Stella Rimmington, the head of MI5, said that the organisation would be taking an increasingly active role in criminal prosecutions and would be focusing attention 'on the potential for integrating secret intelligence into the judicial process. ... The question now arises about what role the Security Service should play in the prosecution of such crimes.'[37]

In 1994 MI5 changed the criteria of its information gathering activities, adding 'for the purpose of any criminal proceedings' to purposes of 'national security'. In October 1994 it was reported that MI5 had taken control of all investigations into computer hacking and abuse in Whitehall.[38] This action, which was made without reference to Parliament, gives the security service formal access to all Whitehall computers, including the Police National Computer, and personal information about millions of people.

The security services are not accountable to Parliament or to the public. A Commissioner reviews their operations and reports their activities, but parts of this report are never made public. A tribunal can hear individual complaints but it has never upheld a single one. It can never give reasons about its decisions or reveal anything to the complainant about their case. The Intelligence Services Act 1994 creates, for the first time, a parliamentary committee with limited scrutiny powers over the operations of MI5, MI6 and General Communication Headquarters (GCHQ). However this cannot examine operations, can be denied access to 'sensitive' material and reports to the Prime Minister rather than to Parliament. Also its members are appointed and can be dismissed by the Prime Minister.[39]

Conclusions

During the history of Britain's involvement in Ireland temporary measures have been entrenched, exceptional powers have been normalised and secret service agencies have been created that are beyond the reach of formal democracy. In several cases these have subsequently been applied in Britain and elsewhere. This shows that policing in the absence of consent and without mechanisms for effective accountability has dangerous implications for democracy.

The 'Glorious Revolution' of 1688 occurred before notions of citizenship, consent and universal human rights had gained common currency. The Westminster system of government, built on that system and imposed on Northern Ireland in 1922, consequently contained few checks on majoritarianism or safeguards for the protection of minorities. The Northern Ireland conflict has highlighted how vulnerable human rights are at moments of crisis, and demonstrates that the British doctrine of parliamentary sovereignty is incapable of defending them.

In this context, the marching season of the summer of 1996 marked a potential watershed. Despite subsequent 'Drumcrees' and continuing opposition from the Orange Order and other unionists, the idea that one community in Northern Ireland should be required to seek the consent of another before taking a particular course of action is beginning to take root and has potentially far-reaching implications. It requires recognition that sometimes rights must be balanced and traditions accommodated. It also requires dialogue and discussion with people who you disagree with but who you must work with to secure common goals.

Notes

1. *Report from the committee of secrecy of the House of Commons in Ireland as reported by the right honourable Lord Viscount Castlereagh,* August 21, 1798, Debrett, J. No. 179, and Wright, J. No. 169 Picadilly, 1798, pp. 24–5.
2. For details see Kee, 1982; Lyons, 1979; Martin and Moody, 1967.
3. Quoted in Beresford Ellis, 1985, p. 147.
4. Civil Authorities (Special Powers) Act, 1922 section 5, Schedule 1-5 Regulations 7a, 18a, 22a, 23a, 24a. Also Regulations 18c (1923), 26a (1930), 8a (1931), 4 (1933), 22b (1933), 24c (1933).
5. Civil Authorities (Special Powers) Act, 1922, s1(3).
6. *Lawless* v. *Ireland* Appl. No. 332/56, (1961) 1 EHRR 15; and *Ireland* v. *United Kingdom*, (1978) 2 EHRR 25.
7. s16-26 Northern Ireland (Emergency Provisions) Act, 1991.
8. s28 Northern Ireland (Emergency Provisions) Act, 1991.
9. s10(1) and s12 Northern Ireland (Emergency Provisions) Act, 1991.
10. s11(2)(b) Northern Ireland (Emergency Provisions) Act, 1991.

11. *Hansard,* 25 November 1974, col. 35.
12. David Brown, *Detention under the Prevention of Terrorism (Temporary Provisions) Act 1989: Access to Legal Advice and Outside Contact,* Home Office Research and Planning Unit, paper 75, 1993, pp. 8–23.
13. s15(9) Prevention of Terrorism (Temporary Provisions) Act, 1989.
14. s8 Prevention of Terrorism (Temporary Provisions) Act, 1989.
15. *Brogan* v. *United Kingdom,* Series A, No. 145B, (1988).
16. *Brannigan and MacBride* v. *United Kingdom,* 26 May 1993, No. 14552/89.
17. *Ireland* v. *UK* (1978) Case No. 5310/71.
18. *Fox, Campbell & Hartley* v. *UK* (1990) Case Nos 1224/86 and 12383/86.
19. Summary Record of 92nd Meeting of UN Committee on Torture, November 1991.
20. *Independent,* 'RUC accused of ill-treating detainees', 18 November 1994.
21. Articles 3 and 4 Criminal Evidence (Northern Ireland) Order, 1988.
22. For details see *Fair Trial Concerns in Northern Ireland: The Right of Silence,* Amnesty International, 1992.
23. *Murray* v. *United Kingdom,* App No. 18731/91, 27 June 1994.
24. For details see *A Major Miscarriage of Justice,* Committee on the Administration of Justice, undated.
25. *Commentary on the Northern Ireland Criminal Statistics,* Northern Ireland Office, 1993, p. 15.
26. s76(1) Criminal Justice and Public Order Act, 1994.
27. 42. s76(4) Criminal Justice and Public Order Act, 1994.
28. Letter from the City of London Police, 10 January,, 1994, forwarded to Liberty's legal office.
29. *Home Office Statistical Bulletin,* 'Operation of Certain Police Powers Under PACE, England and Wales 1993' (Issue 15/94 Table 1). See also bulletins for 14/91, 15/92 and 21/93.
30. s82 Criminal Justice and Public Order Act, 1994.
31. s82 Criminal Justice and Public Order Act, 1994.
32. *The Times,* Law Report, 1 September 1992.
33. *Observer,* 'Irish special', 11 July 1993.
34. For details see Kader Asmal (Chairman) *Shoot to Kill? International Lawyers' Inquiry into the Use of Firearms by the Security Forces in Northern Ireland,* Mercier Press, London.
35. For details see Murray, 1990.
36. Amnesty International, Annual Report 1996, p. 311.
37. Stella Rimmington, James Smart Lecture, 3 November 1994.
38. *Guardian,* 'MI5 hacks way into privacy row', 19 October 1994.
39. s10(1) Intelligence Services Act 1994.

10 Irish Republicanism: A New Beginning?

Ronnie Munck

In the shocked aftermath of the IRA's first ceasefire in August 1994, many commentators realised how little they really knew about Irish republicanism. Beyond the cliches about 'doves' and 'hawks', 'militarists' and 'politicos', there was a real vacuum of political analysis. Over the years, there have been a number of sociological or anthropological studies (Burton, 1978; Feldman, 1991; White, 1994) which have contributed considerably to our understanding of the Irish Republican community and movement. From political scientists, there have been some critical approaches to Republican politics (Goldring, 1982; Patterson, 1989; O'Malley, 1990) but, on the whole, the field is dominated by the narrative history (Boyer-Bell, 1979; Coogan, 1980; Bishop and Mallie, 1987) which probably obscures as much as it illuminates. My purpose here is to contribute to a better understanding of the Republican movement and its contemporary discourse(s), but first it is necessary to sketch a brief account of the recent Republican struggle from the late 1960s up to that first historic ceasefire of 1994.

Towards a Stalemate

Since 1969, the conflict between the Irish Republican movement and the British state has seen clearly defined phases and shifts in the balance of forces. An early phase of Republican ascendancy catching the state unaware was followed by a concerted, and largely successful, state effort to contain republicanism. The by-now familiar strategies of 'Ulsterisation' and 'criminalisation' took the Republican movement to the brink of defeat in the mid-1970s. The reorganisation of the IRA in the late 1970s and the dramatic hunger strikes of the early 1980s put republicanism back in the running. However, breaking out of containment did not lead to a new Republican ascendancy but, rather, to a political and military stalemate with the British state, albeit with fluctuations. It is this objective process, which we shall now examine, which sets the parameters for the gradual emergence of what one can call a 'realist' Republican tendency, beginning to break with the more 'theological' aspects of Irish Republican doctrine.

The hunger strike and the subsequent rise of Sinn Fein as an independent political force (see Clarke, 1987) signalled the defeat of the British state's attempted containment of republicanism. But the reality was that since Sinn Fein entered the electoral arena in 1981, its share of the nationalist vote had been steadily declining. From early expectations that it might actually surpass the Social Democratic and Labour Party (SDLP), it saw its share of the nationalist vote decline from a peak of 43 per cent in 1983 to around 33 per cent in the early 1990s. A symbolic, but also real, mark of the limits of Sinn Fein's electoral turn was the loss of the West Belfast Westminster seat held by Gerry Adams in 1992. The Republican movement's turn towards electoralism in the 1980s must be seen in the context of the 'long war' strategy then being developed. In retrospect, the notion of a 'long war' seems less of a new strategy than an attempt to explain away the failure of the oft predicted 'victory' of the early 1970s to materialise. The implicit notion of an integrated politico-military strategy as advocated in international guerilla strategy did not really come to fruition. If anything, the concept of a long war tended to marginalise the role of Sinn Fein within the overall Republican strategy. That is because the electoral turn was still conceived within a world-view which was profoundly militaristic. Thus, Sinn Fein signally failed to develop realistic and relevant social and economic policies beyond pious platitudes. This was due not only to militarism but the nationalist optic which united 'left' and 'right' Republicans. In a rapidly integrating world, clinging to the narrow boundaries of the nation state was a major stumbling block to the development of radical democratic politics. It is in the South of Ireland where this failure was most manifest, with Sinn Fein failing abysmally to capitalise on the social contradictions engendered by dependent capitalist development. In the North, the political limitations of Sinn Fein were masked by the adoption of a 'gas and water' type socialism embraced enthusiastically by the new generation of Sinn Fein councillors.

When the 'Troubles' began in 1968–69 the international context had considerable bearing on the local Northern Irish situation. In 1988–89, the emerging realisation that the war had to end was, equally, influenced by the new international context. A key factor, of course, was the collapse of the Soviet Union and the associated discrediting of the non-capitalist development path. The new post-Cold War era became manifest with the Gulf War of 1991. Not only was the military might of Western imperialism clear for all to see but it also achieved a certain moral regeneration. The whole concept of national liberation began to seem a quaint anachronism to many one-time progressives. In Ireland, Republican eyes turned towards the incipient demilitarisation of struggles in South Africa, Palestine and El Salvador. Pragmatism was boosted by changing international realities. By late 1993, the Republican press was noting how 'All across the world, direct and indirect dialogue is used as a means to end seemingly intractable conflicts. ... Conflict areas throughout the world are being transformed from theatres of war into political arenas' (*An Phoblackt/Republican News*, 11 November 1993).

What had emerged by the early 1990s was a particular type of stalemate between Irish Republicans and the British state. During the 1980s, the IRA had clawed back from a bleak defensive period in the 1970s. The determination was to wage a more selective 'political' war rather than the total onslaught of an earlier era. There were spectacular successes, particularly in Britain, and war material had become sophisticated and sufficient for its purposes. Yet, through all its multifaceted arenas, from 'shoot to kill' to draconian legal measures, the British state hit back. By the early 1990s there was undoubtedly a certain war weariness if not amongst hardened volunteers, certainly in their surrounding community support. That is where the political stalemate comes in, because for all its political advances Sinn Fein could not unblock the political situation. A new initiative was called for. From the socialist camp there was nothing new on offer, so clearly the dominant discourse would be the familiar territory of Irish nationalism. Given the new international dispensation and traditional Republican alliances, the role of the United States was to be crucial.

In the long, often hesitant, movement towards a historical settlement, the Irish Republican movement played a key role. For a long time this movement seemed locked in an historical vice and the seemingly inevitable dynamic of 'war', with all its rhetoric and denial of reality. The failure to devise a strategy to move beyond this situation cannot be blamed purely on the Republicans. It is, however, extremely interesting to see how a movement can move beyond its history and actually make history.

Of Fundis *and* Realos

I wish here to develop, by analogy with the German Green movement, a distinction between a fundamentalist *(fundis)* and a realist *(realos)* current within Irish republicanism. It has been commonplace to draw distinctions between 'doves' and 'hawks' within the Republican movement. While plausible at a significant level it misses the fundamental point that divisions occur over the *politics* of the armed struggle. So, just as one cannot have a purely political reading of republicanism, nor can one focus purely on the military aspect (see Smith, 1995) as though that existed in isolation from politics. The distinction between Republican 'hawks' and 'doves' sees the first as hard, uncompromising supporters of physical force and the latter as the (relatively) more reasonable and flexible advocates of a (more) political approach. However, these categories are simply inadequate to convey the complexity, and often contradictory, elements of the Republican discourse. A 'left' versus 'right' wing distinction would be equally simplistic and of dubious applicability to republicanism beyond a crude measure of political utterances. To distinguish between Sinn Fein 'politicos' and IRA 'militarists' is equally of limited interest beyond the obvious, and often does not apply in practice.

In the 'theological' republicanism of the *fundis* there can be no dilution of 'principles' such as abstentionism or the armed struggle. We can recall Max Weber's notion of the ethic of ultimate ends *(Gesinnungsethik)* in which all pragmatic considerations are suspended in the face of a single and absolute imperative. For the Irish Republican 'fundis' this absolute end is, of course 'the republic' as defined in the movement's theology and reproduced in practice and discourse. The means – in this case physical force – can also, of course, be perceived as absolutes. The 1986 Sinn Fein Ard Fheis debate on whether to drop the traditional abstentionist policy in Southern elections illustrates this mindset well. For one delegate, going into Leinster House amounted to betraying the republic; another argued that it meant 'forgetting everything the men of 1922 died for' (Sinn Fein, 1986, p. 24). The Irish *fundi* discourse is all about 'inalienable' principles, ill-defined or theological at best, which cannot be 'betrayed'. In a very literal sense this becomes a faith, which further confirms the epithet of theological. The *fundi* discourse, which cannot pass a basic 'falsifiability' test, may be well suited for defence but its limitations are clear.

For the new breed of Republican *realos* of the 1980s, practice imposed its demands over 'principles'. Abstention from the political processes established by partition began to be seen by this current as a tactic and not a principle. For the *realos*, in whatever opposition movement, change is possible, if perhaps not on an 'all or nothing' basis. By pursuing the impossible, the *fundis* are seen to be turning their backs on real possible gains. One is reminded of George Orwell's somewhat overstated comment that 'behind every revolutionary idea lies the secret expectation that nothing can be changed'. In the new realist mood of the 1980s Republicans would take a stand on issues on a pragmatic basis. The primacy of rhetoric began to give way to a *realpolitik* where issues were considered on their merits. This shift was far from consistent, there was much backtracking, and often a *fundi* discourse lurked in the background. The main point, however, is that a political current emerged within republicanism, committed to realisable goals, which become hegemonic within all structures of the movement, especially after the breakaway of Republican Sinn Fein in 1986.

The contradictory, and sometimes incomplete, turn towards realism could be seen in the developing Republican position towards the British role in Ireland. This was a key issue given the far-reaching, if contested, claim by the British government in 1990 that it had no 'selfish, strategic or economic interest in Northern Ireland'. An early Republican response (McThomas, 1992, p. 10) was a restatement of past positions: Britain has an economic motive (not perhaps direct), a strategic motive (the 'laboratory of repression' argument) and political motives (two conservative statelets in Ireland compared to the negative 'demonstration effect' of withdrawal). However, a more realistic analysis was developed in the same journal issue in which the above analysis was contained. According to that position (McClelland and Dowd, 1992, p. 13) Republicans 'should consider whether Britain's interests might be more contradictory and ad-hoc than this'. Calling for Republican analysis to be more fluid and less 'necessitarian', the article argued that Britain's claim to not having 'selfish' interests in Ireland could not be countered by an outdated analysis (capitalism today does not require physical occupation of a territory to dominate it) and a lack of proportion (no state would maintain a war that long to test its weaponry).

Another debate where the *fundi v. realos* strands of republicanism clashed was over attitudes towards the European Community. The *fundi* line was manifest in Sinn Fein's 1989 European Parliament Election Manifesto – 'For a Free Ireland in a Free Europe' – which referred to how 'a nation like Ireland, on the fringes of the market ... will increasingly become not just a dependent colony but part of NATO territory'. Republicans saw themselves holding high the flame of 'neutrality' even when the actually existing Republic's government had long since reduced this to a token policy. This essentially theological approach contrasted with a contribution from Republican prisoners (where critical thinking had emerged in the past) which said that a 'yes' vote for Maastricht would present 'a political reality which we would have to come to terms with' (Campbell, 1992, p. 24). In the ensuing debate a far more nuanced view of Europe developed, including the possibility of democratic alliances rather than a simple nationalist stance. As the peace process unfolded in the early 1990s, the European arena was recognised as vital by Irish Republicans and many of the old shibolleths were quietly shelved especially when Sinn Fein opened a European desk.

There is, of course, a certain level at which *fundis* and *realos* agree on basics. It is not just Ruari O Brádaigh and the 1986 break-away Republican Sinn Fein who believe that 'The Republic' is somehow above politics, even a negation of politics. It is this world-view as Roy Foster notes which 'is one of the factors which conditions the Republican mind against political negotiation and compromise' (Foster, 1993, p. 36). The view of politics as corrupt and corrupting has, of course, a basis in reality for Republicans. O Brádaigh can, from his viewpoint quite understandably, see Gerry Adams today as but the latest Republican leader, such as De Valera, who slipped down the slopes of constitutionalism to compromise and, ultimately, the abandonment of Republican principles. Yet in Gerry Adams we find his most considered polit-ical statement *Free Ireland: Towards a Lasting Peace* (Adams, 1995) ending with an appeal to the Easter Proclamation of the Irish Republic in 1916. To base the politics of a movement for political change in the late twentieth century on a hastily written leaflet of 80 years ago is a measure of its limitations. Of course, lacking a strategy for real social and political change does not stop the movement engaging in power politics, after all power does come out of the barrel of a gun to some extent.

Towards a Settlement

This is not the place to rehearse the full history of the so-called peace process (see Mallie and McKitrick, 1996; O'Brien, 1993).

Our purpose is the more limited one of seeing how the early signs of a 'new departure' in Irish republicanism in the mid-1980s came to fruition in the 'peace process' of the 1990s. The Republican discourse took a distinctive turn between the 1987 document *Scenario for Peace* and the 1992 document *Towards a Lasting Peace*. For many commentators on the Left, the shift from a language of 'victory' to one of 'democratic compromise' masks a simple 'drift towards respectability' and provides an opportunity to lecture Republicans on 'the dangers of opportunism' (Ryan, 1994, p. 74). From this perspective, Gerry Adams is simply the latest in a long list of Republicans who have eventually succumbed to the discrete charms of constitutional nationalism. Maybe from the future that may appear to be the case. However, there are sound arguments to see in the 'new departure' of the 1990s a decisive shift towards a realism which is more likely to have a fundamental impact on Irish politics.

The 1992 Sinn Fein Ard Fheis adopted a document entitled *Towards a Lasting Peace in Ireland* which appeared to mark a break, albeit partial, with the earlier 'theological' discourse of the party. Previous programmes tended towards an 'absolutist' and rhetorical argument about self-determination and national 'rights'. It was hard, in previous formulations, to find a coherent statement on how a British withdrawal might actually be timetabled and achieved. They were totally superficial on the post-withdrawal scenario and left their own supporters quite unable to deal with the 'power vacuum' or 'bloodbath' scenarios. The watchwords of the 1992 document were those of pragmatism and flexibility. Certainly the traditional themes of self-determination and Irish national sovereignty are rehearsed but we also see here a move towards a new realist terrain.

Towards a Lasting Peace recognised implicitly that Irish republicanism might come to play only a catalyst role in the conflict over the North. It had become clear to many Republican realists that it would not be them who would reap the fruits of 'victory', the meaning of which was becoming quite fuzzy. The document calls on the British and Irish governments to initiate a peace process, possibly under the auspices of the European Union or with United Nations mediation. The traditional nationalist discourse of Irish republicanism is, at least in part, contested or not replaced by a new democratic discourse. For example, the once cavalier attitude towards the Northern Protestant minority was replaced by a clear recognition that: 'peace in Ireland requires a settlement of the long-standing conflict between Irish

Nationalism and Irish Unionism. We would like to see this conflict, often bloody, replaced by a process of national reconciliation, a constructive dialogue and debate' (Sinn Fein, 1992, p. 3). In terms of the broader principles of how politics is/should be conducted the document argues, 'it is necessary to break out of the present conception of politics in Ireland, where one person's gain is conceived automatically as another person's loss' (Sinn Fein, 1992, p. 14). It is a far call from the ultimatist arguments of *fundi* Republicans to recognise that all lose from a continuation of the conflict and all might gain from its resolution.

As an 'all or nothing' conception of struggle began to cede way to a terrain of democratic compromise, so the question of methods of struggle began to be reconsidered. In 1992, it was already stated that 'the development of ... an alternative [to the armed struggle] would be welcomed by Sinn Fein' (Sinn Fein, 1992, p. 10). Towards the end of 1993, Gerry Adams concluded talks with the SDLP's John Hume aimed at establishing a nationalist consensus. At first reactions were sceptical about the prospects for the Hume–Adams proposals bringing about peace. However, Hume successfully put the proposals on the agenda of the Dublin government. In bilateral negotiation with the British government a commitment to Irish national self-determination was obtained. Furthermore, it was established that a termination of the IRA campaign would allow Sinn Fein to attend the negotiating table. The result was the Downing Street Declaration which Sinn Fein did not reject outright but sought a process of 'clarification' in relation to its more ambiguous formulations.

Into 1994, negotiations continued and 'clarifications' were obtained all round. After what appeared like a setback at Sinn Fein's conference in Letterkenny in June when the Declaration was still not accepted, the IRA made an historic announcement at the end of August that it was ceasing hostilities. The 'long war' was replaced by an era of 'long negotiations'. More would be gained from unarmed than from armed struggle. The unilateral and complete cessation of Republican military operations was called on the basis of the 'potential of the current situation and in order to enhance the democratic peace process'. Republicans felt that the forces of Irish nationalism both at home and abroad could create the conditions for a lasting settlement. That this might not mean a united Ireland in the short or medium term was also accepted. It would seem that 25 years of armed struggle had 'won a draw': Britain recognised the validity of Irish nationalist aspirations and Irish Republicans accepted that there was no 'quick fix' to resolve the pro-British sentiment of a minority of the Irish people.

Reflecting back on developments since the first IRA ceasefire of 1994, we can now assess whether there has been a victory for realism or simply a retreat by Irish republicanism. The IRA's own assessment was a balanced and sober one. Basically it was argued that 'Republicans at this time and on their own do not have the strength to achieve the end goal' [a united 32 County Democratic Socialist Republic] ('The IRA Peace Document', *Sunday Tribune,* 23 April 1995). Furthermore, with the SDLP, the Dublin government and the Irish-American lobby 'rowing in behind' basic Republican principles, it was possible to now adopt the oddly labelled 'TUAS' option, widely interpreted as meaning 'Total Un-Armed Struggle, but in fact meaning (only) 'Tactical Use of Armed Struggle'. While seen as a risky strategy, it was felt that presently favourable circumstances (and presumably 'balance of forces') were 'unlikely to gel again in the foreseeable future', and that the success or otherwise of the new turn depended on maintaining commitment: 'It is vital that activists realise that the struggle is *not* over' ('The IRA Peace Document'). The statement of the Republican leadership reflected the realism which had been gaining ground in its ranks over previous years.

Bernadette McAliskey has for her part, however, articulated a pessimism about the peace process which is shared by many grassroots Republicans. It is her contention that the Republican leadership has been sucked into a process in which the SDLP and the Dublin government are motivated by a desire to end all forms of struggle, violent or otherwise. This is seen as an historical mistake on a par with 1875 and 1922. More specifically: 'I see this present road as something like a funnel, the further they go down it, the narrower it gets. There is a point down this road that is a trap, where there is no way back for them.' Peace, a concept everyone is now in favour of, may from this perspective be a front for the conservative British and Irish states to stifle dissent for a whole new historical period.

It is the political weakness of republicanism which is now becoming apparent. As a delegate to the 1995 Ard Fheis put it: 'We are floundering out of our depth in territory controlled by the enemy' (*Irish Times,* 27 February 1995). At most, the Republican leadership admit to problems in communication with grassroots in the process leading up to the ceasefire. The problems go deeper than that though. For a movement largely geared towards an armed struggle, the new political terrain is, indeed, daunting. Much larger political questions have to be addressed than those which faced Sinn Fein's early councillors. In 'coming in from the cold' Sinn Fein is, indeed, operating 'in territory controlled by the enemy'. The nationalist optic which guided the struggle and the peace process will not easily lead to a rounded radical democratic politics. Certainly the Republican base will be expecting results in traditional terms – a British declaration of intent to withdraw – before these are likely to be achieved.

Given the weaknesses of republicanism, and in particular its left wing, it seems premature to advance the view, as did Mitchel McLaughlin, that 'there will be a very dramatic evolution of politics on this island' after a settlement, and that 'what will emerge is a very clear debate between right and left' (*Belfast Telegraph*, 18 January 1995). This view was once prevalent and possibly is even correct in a broad historical sense. However, it now seems rather anachronistic, since 'right and left' do not have the clear meanings and affiliations they once had. In a post-Cold War, 'post-nationalist' era these traditional divisions have lost some of their relevance as political bearings. Furthermore, the Republican movement is ill-equipped and lacks the tradition to articulate radical democratic politics, having been submerged in nationalist militarism for so long. On reaching the 'negotiating table' Republicans find that with their main asset (force) set aside, they lack the political experience and imagination to adequately deal with their opponents.

Given the international and domestic situation, it seems that, as Gerry Adams feared, circumstances are forcing Republicans 'to lower nationalist expectations and dilute nationalist aspirations' (*Irish Times*, 27 January 1995). Previous promises to 'end the nationalist nightmare' have come to nothing. Certainly the British state is now bound, given the international pressure, to deliver something more substantial than in the past. Republicans for their part have accepted that 'an agreed Ireland needs the allegiance of varied traditions to be viable' ('The IRA Peace Document'). This is a long way from traditional Republican discourse. The challenge now for Republicans will be to find ways to move beyond the zero-sum conception of politics in practice and not just in declarations. It may actually be necessary to dilute the nationalist position in order to strengthen democratic politics in Ireland, if the radical democratic roots of republicanism are to be renewed in a new phase of the conflict.

Results and Prospects

After three decades of intense and bitter struggle what have Republicans achieved? They have not been defeated by a powerful enemy. They have placed the 'national question' firmly on the political agenda. They have made it impossible for Northern Ireland to return to the sectarian statelet it was under one-party unionist domination. However, the breaking of cease-fires since 1994, the Canary Wharf bombing, the unionist triumphalism at Drumcree, and continuing unionist opposition to an agreement all indicate how little some things have changed. The British stalling on negotiations led republicanism to the tried and tested 'message in a lorry' at Canary Wharf. Unionist fears of a British 'sell-out' led to the most aggressive Orange 'parading' for many years, including murder, church burnings and mass intimidation. Eamonn McCann (1995) understandably feels that the peace process has not faltered but failed due to its being based on, and thus entrenching, sectarian divisions. As McCann wrote: 'Far from being designed to loosen the grip of sectarianism on the minds of men and women, the process accepts sectarianism as a natural, central, permanent fact of Northern Irish life' (McCann, 1995, p. 22).

If we examine Irish republicanism structurally as it were, rather than in terms of its own stated aims and aspirations, we can see that not only is it 'locked into' Ulster unionism but it has also been, to a large extent, a response to British state policy. Anthony McIntyre (1995, p. 98) argues persuasively that: 'The modern Republican movement has persistently been the product of British state strategies rather than a body which has existed for the sole purpose of completing the "unfinished business" of uniting Ireland.' Indeed, many of the turns in Republican politics, as argued above, have resulted from a need to escape the British grip on the situation. One example would be the largely unsuccessful move to win increased support in the South to relieve the belea-guered Northern Republican community in the 1980s. The Republican movement has taken strategic decisions at various points but these have been carried out in conditions not of their own making. One conclusion to be drawn from this line of thought is that modern Irish republicanism owes its existence more to discrimination and repression in the North than to the 'unfinished' national question.

Republicanism is now out in the open politically. Bereft of 'armed struggle', its political weaknesses are glaring. As Ryan puts it: 'Sinn Fein's curious synthesis of traditional republicanism, old-style state socialism and Catholic pietism has little popular appeal, especially among the young people who are Ireland's future' (Ryan, 1994, p. 77). Of course, the absence of a credible economic programme, for example, may matter little in the sectarian cockpit of Belfast. Yet even supporters of the movement were complaining how since the ceasefire Sinn Fein had turned inwards, ignoring the positive lessons of the hunger strike period. Instead of building outwards into civil society, broadening the links with community groups, the women's movement or the trade unions, Sinn Fein 'has retreated away from open, broad front politics towards the narrow elitism that characterized the movement in the early 1970s' (RP, 1996) according to one sympathetic observer. For someone brought up in a militarist tradition, going into politics usually means the 'straight' politics of parties, leaders, secret talks and backdoor deals. For a democratic compromise to be possible democratic politics must prevail and all issues – not just national boundaries – need to be out in the open.

For Irish Republicans, as Gerry Adams admitted, 'The road to peace was always going to be difficult. What we are attempting to do is very ambitious, as well as risky and dangerous' (*Irish Times*, 20 June 1996). One risk is that the Republican movement could be effectively sidelined now that its most manifest expression – IRA actions – has been largely muzzled. Going back to the old *status quo* – a bloody stalemate – seems hardly possible given the dramatic change in political alignments. Clearly a return to previous practice by Republicans would represent a major obstacle to the historic compromise(s) involved in 'dis/agreeing Ireland'. Conversely, the huge leap taken by republicanism over the last decade, as explored in the pages above, places the movement in the 'hopes' column of that historic project. A more decisive move on to the democratic terrain – and this should not be reduced to the constitutional – reclaiming the original Republican project, would place the contemporary Republican movement in a pivotal political role. The poverty of political thought, induced by centuries of colonialism, the disaster of Partition, and the heavy blanket of nationalism, leaves the terrain open for a fresh and bold approach.

When the IRA ceasefire broke down with the bomb explosion in the London Docklands in February 1996 it represented for many the collapse of the 'peace process'. For 17 months the British state had stalled on the question of inclusive political dialogue. It even looked as if the delay was consciously designed to exacerbate tensions within the Republican ranks. Certainly, much of the political rationale behind the calling of a ceasefire had become null and void. The putative 'pan-nationalist front', if it ever was real, had collapsed as Bruton replaced Reynolds as Taoiseach in the South. The whole notion of relying on others to deliver the political goods looked decisively threadbare. As for Britain's protestations of neutrality from Brooke's landmark speech of 1990 onwards, this was never meant to indicate neutrality on the question of 'giving in to terrorism'. So lacking in imagination and bravery was the British government reaction after mid-1994 that the *fundi* world-view appeared to be vindicated. The flurry of political activity by the British and Irish governments following the Docklands bomb seemed to confirm the old Republican adage that Britain only hears bombs on its own streets.

Yet none of the above meant that the Republican movement could return to the *status quo ante* – politics is not like that. A full recommencement of hostilities would not only have faced huge subjective problems – a support base now well used to the idea of peace – but the objective constraints imposed by the two governments concerned which would have the support of international political opinion. It seems there was and is no turning back from the road of pragmatism and compromise. The impressive electoral success of Sinn Fein (15.5 per cent of votes) in the 1996 'talks forum' elections, called by the British government seemingly to isolate republicanism, pointed towards the potential gains of an unarmed political strategy. This vote would hardly be repeated if militarism returned to dominance and the shutters came down again with state and Loyalist violence reaching a new pitch. Whatever attraction simplistic *fundi* themes might have at times, there is in reality no turning back from the realistic assessment of the balance of forces which culminated in the IRA cessation of August 1994. Whether Sinn Fein is able to develop the rounded politics necessary to deal with the new situation is still an open question.

End-game?

Nearly three years after the original 1994 announcement of a 'complete cessation of military operations', the leadership of the IRA declared another ceasefire on 20 July 1997. There was little euphoria this time round, only a weary expectancy. The context

was more favourable in terms of a new, more nationalist government in the Republic and, of course, the new 'New Labour'
government in Britain. Yet weeks before the ceasefire the British
concessions to the Orange Order at Drumcree had practically
ignited the whole situation all over again. Nor did the admission
of Sinn Fein to the peace talks at Stormont, following the IRA
ceasefire, usher in a new era of reasonableness amongst unionists.
Indeed, the IRA ceasefire was again denounced as 'phoney' and
the provocative issue of arms decommissioning was again raised
as a precondition for a peace settlement, instead of being seen as
one of its desirable outcomes. But the 'peace process' or 'train'
(to use Tony Blair's metaphor) was moving again. The two new
Sinn Fein Westminster MPs, Gerry Adams and Martin
McGuinness, backed by a record vote for Sinn Fein, were to be
key players in that process.

Towards the end of 1997, the Loyalist breakaway LVF
(Loyalist Volunteer Force) began a systematic campaign of assassination of ordinary Catholics. At the start of 1998, Sinn Fein was
briefly expelled from the peace talks process, following some
minor IRA activity. Then the 'Continuity IRA' (which supports
Republican Sinn Fein) began a series of not very effective
bombings. When Sinn Fein returned to the peace talks it seemed
that the process was under way again. The Irish and British
governments (with considerable support from the US government) had set the parameters of a potential agreement which
included, predictably, a power-sharing Northern assembly and
cross-border bodies linking North and South. With Paisley's
Democratic Unionists now out in the cold (and endorsed by if not
endorsing the LVF) and Republican 'rejectionists' containable, a
central issue became the need for some semblance of a dialogue
between the Ulster Unionist Party and Sinn Fein. The so-called
'pan-nationalist front' between Sinn Fein, the SDLP and the Irish
government was showing cracks but any plausible peace settlement would have to meet Sinn Fein's minimum demands, now
scaled down from 'a united Ireland or else' to 'agreement between
the people of Ireland as a whole or else'. Referendums North and
South would freely consent, or not, to the settlement agreed.

The notion of a 'peace process' or 'train' raises the possibility
that politics in the North of Ireland might move beyond the 'zero-
sum political game'. The turn towards peace may come from war
weariness (undoubtedly a factor), or a fear of losing all if hostilities continue (a factor in some quarters), or, more positively,
from a conviction that an agreement now can eventually deliver a

viable and honourable historic compromise in Ireland. If we broaden out our analysis we could consider how societies can develop once the fear at the root of their difficulties is removed. In relation to the new democracies of Latin America and its long night of authoritarian military regimes, Norbert Lechner points that while 'we might exclude subjectivity as a private affair ... sooner or later it will reappear in the political arena as rank irrationality. The subjectivity we repress returns to haunt us' (Lechner, 1992, p. 34). The doorstep murders, the torture, the car bombs and the plastic bullets leave traces which do not disappear overnight. (Ir)rational fears of what our enemies might do if we lay down our arms have powerful political effects. Negotiations entail trust and this was hardly a characteristic of the war years. Certainly there is nothing pointing towards a smooth and peaceful transition beyond armed conflict. As Corradi puts it: 'The deconstruction of cultures of fear is a long, fragile and incomplete process' (Corradi, 1992, p. 285). It is, of course, possible and the example of South Africa's slow but steady exorcising of the past and its construction of a new democratic order shows what can be done. One precondition is to take seriously the political aspirations of the insurgent movement.

Peace is more than just the absence of war; it entails an active process of construction in the discursive and extra-discursive domains (see the case studies in Munck and De Silva, 1998). If we can learn nothing else from a critical reading of the counter-insurgency or 'terrorism' literature it is that nothing can be gained from labelling insurgents as criminals, psychopaths or murderers – at least in the long term (because some short-term or opportunistic political advantages may be gained by a regime or opposing parties). However, in the longer term it is clear that a regime which refuses to recognise a legitimate interlocutor may only postpone the inevitable. The accumulated years of bitterness and distrust make a democratic settlement that much more difficult and fragile. Within the insurgent movement, conversely, we have seen a rise of a new realism and a foresaking of absolutism. Politics as the art of the possible is understood and democratic compromise is not automatically translated as cowardly betrayal. The democratic terrain, procedures and discourse are the privileged planes for the full settlement, including the subjective aspects, to remedy the situations which gave rise to nationalist insurgency in the first place.

After a decade of developing a viable 'peace strategy', the Republican movement faced up to the political 'end-game' in

1998. Before that the end-game envisaged by republicanism included, at its core, a British withdrawal and a re-united Ireland. Now it seemed to accept the principle of 'consent', meaning perhaps that while today the unionists do not want a united Ireland, tomorrow a nationalist majority in both South and North might deliver one. The 1998 Agreement was seen as delivering, at best, only 'transitional arrangements' towards the ultimate goal. The Irish Foreign Secretary, David Andrews, has spoken of the need for 'parity of pain' to match the 'parity of gain' in any agreement, and most Republicans have certainly adjusted their sights. In return they are becoming key players in a new political dispensation, with greater freedom to develop a more democratic and rounded politics capable of responding to the 'normal' issues of a society no longer 'at war'. The conflict between Irish nationalism and pro-British unionism will continue, but hopefully military force will no longer be the primary mechanism for both sides.

While for some unionists the 1998 Agreement meant that Republicans now accepted the continued British presence in Northern Ireland, for mainstream Irish republicanism it opened a 'transition phase' towards Irish unity. In fact, what was put together by the two governments, with American and European backing, was a hybrid political being. For the future of Northern Ireland to be decided by its inhabitants was a fluid, unstable and indeed 'provisional' status for a regional or provincial territory, a status quite in keeping with the postmodern era. It is now the political process or, to be precise, struggle which will decide the future of the North and the extent to which all-Ireland dimensions will develop. A new horizon of possibilities opens up with demilitarisation possible though by no means guaranteed. After the Agreement, the proponents of war (offensive or defensive) were a small minority, but a genuine political solution is still a long way off.

Sinn Fein did have reservations about supporting changes to the (in)famous Articles 2 and 3 in the Constitution which lay claim to the whole island of Ireland. In fact, the amended articles are a far better expression of the democratic nationalist aspiration to Irish unity as they are couched in the language of citizenship and not as a territorial imperative. And now Irish republicanism faces the challenge of reconstituting itself as a radical opposition within the broad nationalist consensus. The traditional Republican agenda (like that of unionism) is at a crossroads: the political clock cannot be turned back to before the Agreement, but the future can only be uncertain. The undoubted commitment and enthusiasm of those at the historic Sinn Fein Ard Fheis which accepted the provisional settlement just might get translated into a new radical democratic discourse, a discourse more in keeping with Wolfe Tone's tradition than the Provisionals' of 30 years ago.

11 A Process of Surrender? Loyalist Perceptions of a Settlement

James White McAuley

A process of surrender has been under way since the ceasefire began. (Ian Paisley, *Belfast Telegraph*, 19 December 1994)

To blame the troubles on a small minority within each community is sheer stupidity. The IRA/INLA and the UDA/UFF are simply products of the sectarian attitudes widely held and deeply rooted in both communities. Terrorists were not imported. For twenty-five years our communities bred and raised them – thousands of men and women took up the gun because they were encouraged to do so by communities fearful of the 'others'. (Peter McGuire, ex-Loyalist prisoner, 1996)

The naked face of Loyalist resistance has been clear for the world to see in the July Orange confrontations at Drumcree near Portadown, Co. Armagh. In 1996, for instance, Northern Ireland erupted into widespread disorder during and following an aborted police attempt to stop the annual Orange march going through a Catholic area. For Bob McCartney, the UK Unionist Party MP, Drumcree was symbolic of a people who have said, 'enough is enough'. Certainly, these actions marked a unity of thought and behaviour, not seen for many months, perhaps years, within unionism. But what was it that the 'unionist people' had had enough of? The DUP leader, the Rev. Ian Paisley, claimed that those present were 'not here to play a game but to save the country'. It was, of course, a typically Paisleyite expression of the times. Yet, as so often before, he seemed to have judged admirably the mood of many Loyalists and unionists in Northern Ireland. Paisley was articulating the widespread apprehension, confusion and fear felt by many Loyalists, surrounding the contemporary 'peace process'.[1]

Against this background the chapter seeks to outline and analyse the politics and ideology of contemporary loyalism. It considers Loyalist reactions to the 'peace process', particularly as they developed through the key period of the paramilitary cease-fires of 1994, the publication of the 'Framework Documents' in February 1995, and the events surrounding the Forum elections and the Orange Order marches in the summer of 1996 – the prelude to unionism's very divided responses to the 1998 'Agreement'. The chapter examines the different positions of the main representatives of working-class loyalism – the Democratic Unionist Party (DUP), the Ulster Democratic Party (UDP) and the Progressive Unionist Party (PUP). It then deliberates upon the direct responses of the Protestant working class and the contemporary roles and political directions of Loyalist paramilitaries. Finally, the chapter outlines some major considerations for the Left in relation to contemporary events in Northern Ireland.

The 'Ceasefires' and the 'Peace Process'

It is important to outline the initial Loyalist response to the 'peace process' to understand the events that followed. Behind populist euphoria at the thought of long-term 'peace', many Loyalists also expressed distrust, anxiety for their future and clear notions of 'betrayal'. Loyalist suspicion remained widespread that the real process was clandestine – that a surreptitious 'deal' had been struck between the British government and the Republican movement, in order to bring the IRA military campaign to a halt.

This position was and still is most clearly presented by the Democratic Unionists. They were loquacious in their opposition, echoing past calls to arms, and issuing a promise to lead a vigorous campaign against any 'deal'. For the DUP, the 'peace process' was part of a grand plan to move Northern Ireland out of the United Kingdom; more steps along a 'one-way road to Dublin'. Partly for this reason, the DUP almost immediately dismissed the IRA ceasefire as a 'peace of surrender', no more than a simple 'tactical manoeuvre', the sole aim of which was to wring further concessions to republicanism from the British government, which clearly could no longer be trusted to secure the Union (see 'The Framework of Shame and Sham: Yes the Framework Document is a One Way Road to Dublin', DUP, 1995; Campbell, no date; Robinson, 1995).

Both the major Loyalist paramilitary groupings, the Ulster Defence Association (UDA) and the Ulster Volunteer Force (UVF), were militarily active in the weeks following the IRA ceasefire. Behind the scenes, however, the leaderships of both organisations were synthesising a political response to the growing pressure from their own members, and the wider Protestant working class. As the IRA ceasefire held, detailed consultations were undertaken with 'Loyalist prisoners'. This culminated, six weeks and one day after the IRA ceasefire, in the Combined Loyalist Military Command (CLMC) announcing that they too would halt their campaign. Further, they claimed their ceasefire would be permanent unless Republican paramilitaries were to resume violence.[2]

The main party political representatives of the Protestant working class also played a central role. The DUP has always claimed to be the essence of political loyalism, yet in the period immediately following the ceasefire declarations they were, at most, tangential to the pivotal voices speaking for working-class loyalism. Instead, politicised representatives of the Loyalist para-militaries took up the mantle. This precipitated the elevation to increased eminence of the representatives of the Ulster Democratic Party and the Progressive Unionist Party.

That the DUP could no longer claim to be the sole, legitimate political representative of the Protestant working class, at least at this time, was evidenced by the defection of several DUP local councillors to the UDP. It was claimed this was largely because they believed the DUP had 'misread' the real feelings of many Loyalists. This notion was reflected in a statement from Gary McMichael of the UDP, at the time of the 1996 Forum election:

> Since the Loyalist ceasefire the UDP has given the Loyalist community real leadership in this peace process, the kind of leader-ship they were denied by others. ... We will give a voice to those who have been without a voice for the past 25 years. For too long our people have suffered ineffective leadership. Our community has been plagued with political leaders who refuse to lead. (*Irish Times*, 18 May 1996)

The ideological and pragmatic conflicts between the DUP and the two groupings representing the paramilitaries has continued throughout the 'peace process'. Ian Paisley, for example, referred to both the PUP and UDP as agents of the Northern Ireland Office, and as groupings operating without any real political mandate. Later, from 1996, there were acrimonious exchanges between the DUP and the fringe Loyalist parties at the Northern Ireland Forum. The acrimony was especially clear following death threats issued by the Combined Loyalist Military Command against two dissident Loyalists. The DUP pressure on Progressive Unionist and Ulster Democratic parties, to condemn the threat, appeared to have at least as much to do with undermining the political credentials of the UDP and the PUP, as with any concern for the individuals involved.

In trying to dismiss these groups, Paisley and the DUP were seeking to project themselves, yet again, as the Union's true defenders. For the DUP, any form of negotiation with the Republican movement, the Irish government, or even with an ambiguous UK government, simply represents 'surrender'. The implications of this position are clear. No one other than the DUP, including the politicised paramilitaries, can be faithful to the defence of Northern Ireland's constitutional position (see Robinson, 1995; Campbell, no date). Indeed, this position was at the heart of DUP electioneering for the Forum. Campaigning under the slogan, 'the Unionist team you can trust', Ian Paisley made the party's position clear; that in any talks, the DUP 'will negotiate only within the parameters of the UK', adding, 'we will talk only to constitutional politicians and parties' (that is, excluding any party linked to a paramilitary grouping, whether Loyalist or Republican).

In response, the UDP and PUP remained highly critical of 'traditional' unionist political leadership. The PUP was particularly hostile to Ian Paisley, who they claimed had destroyed any sense of 'unionist unity', and was increasingly disconnected from the response of 'ordinary people' to the 'peace process'. There was also an overt articulation by PUP representatives of a belief that the DUP was unrealistic in the way it had excluded itself from any meaningful input into the 'peace process'. Both the PUP and the UDP claimed it was they that best reflected broader Loyalist views, and who could highlight working-class experiences and social priorities. Throughout the contemporary phase, it is the PUP who have expressed this position in its most consistent, coherent and intelligible form.

Locus of Resistance – Obstacles to Peace

Despite the divisions outlined above, it remains clear that there is widescale opposition within sections of loyalism to the 'peace process'. One point of convergence for this resistance was the publication of the Framework Documents in February 1995, which were designed to form the basis for all-party talks on the future of Northern Ireland. To begin with, much unionist hostility targeted on the document's reference to 'the people in the island of Ireland'. In many ways this simply reinforced the DUP's political position as the crucial focus for opposition and defence of the Union. In important ways, for many unionists, it also reinforced the DUP's ideological analysis. As Peter Robinson expressed it:

> This is not a discussion document; it is a declaration of intent – a joint government programme for Irish unity. When the verbal foliage is pruned away, only one central proposition remains and it is an entirely nationalist programme. (*Belfast Telegraph*, 22 February 1995)

The lineage of this perspective can be traced back at least to the unionist response to the Anglo–Irish Agreement of 1985. In the contemporary period, it was, for Loyalists, made transparent by the 1993 Downing Street Declaration and particularly the statement that Britain had 'no selfish, strategic or economic interest in Northern Ireland'. For many unionists and Loyalists this, at best, represented the British government distancing itself from the Union. At worst, it meant that they had put in place a dynamic, the result of which would be an all-Ireland state. Much of this fits with the broad DUP 'world-view', and their dissection of events to reveal an untrustworthy British government that has been steadily seduced by a 'pan-nationalist set agenda', and the threat of a continued, or resumed, IRA ceasefire.

This thinking was entirely apparent in the following statement by Peter Robinson in March 1996, when, referring to the structure of any future talks, he said:

> This is an obvious attempt to buy a further IRA cease-fire. The content of the proposals is so self-evidently unacceptable to unionists that nobody in the government would have been unaware of the reaction to it by the unionist leadership. ... In one move the government has managed to show the IRA that murder succeeds and tell unionists that constitutional democratic parties are dispensable and irrelevant. (*DUP Press Release*, 13 March 1996)

Clearly one of the greatest obstacles to the 'peace process' is the possibility of the return to a military campaign by Loyalist paramilitaries. The prospect of this increases should Republican military activity escalate to a point where Loyalist paramilitaries feel tactically obliged to react.[3] This can be seen in the message issued by the CLMC in March 1996. Part of the statement claimed:

> The IRA must come to terms with the indisputable fact that we, the unionist people, are the British presence in Northern Ireland and our democratic desire, freely and continually expressed, cannot and will not be changed, as has been clearly demonstrated over 70 years, by threats, bombs or even death itself. ... These atrocities cannot be permitted to continue without a telling response from this source. We are poised and ready to strike to effect. We will give blow for blow. As in the past, whatever the cost, we will gladly pay it. Now is the time to draw back from the brink! (*Irish Times,* 13 March 1996)

That said, there are obviously those who are actively promoting armed resistance as the only way to oppose what is seen as the undermining of Northern Ireland's constitutional position. The most public focus for this in the period discussed was the UVF in mid-Ulster and Portadown who, until their enforced dissolution, openly opposed the ceasefire and articulated what they claimed were the views of 'grassroots Loyalist discontent'.[4] It was this grouping which later formed the basis for the Loyalist Volunteer Force (LVF). This met with opposition from the more politicised members of the UVF and the PUP. From these exchanges it is apparent that any resumption of Loyalist paramilitary violence will be dependent on wider political circumstances. The 'real' obstacles that loyalism seeks to put in the path of any 'peace process' are, therefore, both political and ideological.

To fully understand this Loyalist reaction, it is necessary to broaden the perspective to consider the construction of Loyalist ideology. It is this which marks out that framework of thought in Northern Irish society, by which many Protestants make sense of and give meaning to their social and political worlds. It is these boundaries which mark out a distinct sense of 'Loyalist history' and give rise to an identifiable 'Loyalist political identity'. Such ideas are linked within a definite discursive space; and it is this which provides many members of the Protestant working class with the parameters within which to express their 'politics'.

In one important sense, the main obstacle to any solution, let alone a progressive one, is that many Loyalists perceive the whole 'peace process', the supposed concessions to the IRA and the British government's perceived duplicity, as yet further examples of a dynamic which consistently undermines their fundamental social and political identity. Central to this is the belief of many unionists that as a group their status and power have been in continual decline during the past 30 years of social and political conflict. It is this particular awareness and understanding of contemporary events that orders and structures much Loyalist consciousness. Such views dovetail with others in broad currency within the Loyalist community, to produce a meaningful way of understanding the world. The 'peace process' is thus seen as only part of a much broader set of trends, all designed to weaken unionism, the unionist position and the Union itself.[5]

This was reflected in several recent Loyalist publications. Many recent editions of the main publication of the Orange Order, the *Orange Standard*, for example, have claimed that over the preceding three decades, Protestants had been consistently driven from large areas of Northern Ireland. Further, they have spoken of the 'ethnic cleansing' of Protestants from parts of Ireland, both in the past and in the contemporary period. For them, the analysis of contemporary events was straightforward – the June 1996 edition argued that 'Ulster Protestants and Unionists have made it clear that enough is enough and they will not be surrendering any more of their territory to the enemies of Ulster.' Only in the context of such defensive social and political attitudes can the political response of loyalism be understood.[6]

The Future for Loyalism – Political Alternatives

So how have these different trends been manifested in party political terms? The sense of distrust, maybe even unfolding downfall, felt by many Loyalists has been marked by the partial concentration of unionism around calls for 'unity'. Central here is the restatement and reorganisation of traditional loyalism around the DUP, and the central figure of Ian Paisley. In doing this, the DUP were seeking to reoccupy their central hegemonic position within loyalism, lost to them in the period following the initial paramilitary ceasefires. The DUP's centrality was strengthened as the 'peace process' faltered and the IRA resumed armed conflict. Such events for the DUP highlighted the untrustworthiness of all those engaged in any negotiating process. The party was then able to argue that the contemporary phase was the ultimate and final struggle for

Ulster's destiny: in the DUP's terms, '(n)ever before has there been such a concentrated effort by republicans to destroy the very foundations of Northern Ireland' (*Election Communication*, 1996).

With such views drawing strong support within unionism, all of the unionist political parties competed with the DUP to put their credentials on the line. Much of the unionist agenda for the Forum election centred on who could best 'defend the Union', and take unionism forward 'positively' into the forthcoming talks. Here, however, I shall limit my considerations to the rivalry between the major political representatives of loyalism, the DUP, the PUP and the UDP.

The Democratic Unionist Party
For the DUP the election was significant; 'vital', because those elected would be responsible for negotiating 'the very future of Ulster'. They also emphasised that they were the only unionist team that could be trusted. They claimed full vindication of their analysis of recent events, including the 'Downing Street Declaration sell-out', the 'treacherous Framework Document' and the 'bogus IRA ceasefire'. In fact, the DUP largely campaigned on a mandate not to take part in any negotiations. They indicated that they would not sit down with Sinn Fein, even if the IRA ceasefire was restored. Indeed, part of the manifesto stated that there would be:

> No negotiation on the basis of the Downing Street Declaration and the Framework Documents. Both documents are gravely detrimental to the Union and follow the pan-nationalist agenda. They have been rejected by the people of Northern Ireland and cannot be the basis of any negotiations involving the DUP.

The DUP's manifesto also sought to form an 'unbreakable Covenant with the Ulster People', and to ensure Northern Ireland's constitutional position would be fully recognised and accepted without any ambiguity. Underpinning this was the clearly articulated belief that the Union was not safe under the terms of the Downing Street Declaration or the Framework Documents.

Much of the manifesto sought to challenge 'Dublin's illegal claim over Ulster', strongly arguing that there could be 'No role for Dublin in Ulster's affairs'. Elsewhere, they promoted the establishment of 'democratic and accountable structures of government for Ulster'; demanded that 'IRA/Sinn Fein' be made to hand over their weaponry and 'dismantle its terrorist machine', arguing that what is needed is 'the defeat of armed terrorists, not some accommodation with them'.

The Progressive Unionist Party

In their Forum election material the PUP sought to stretch the distance between themselves and the representatives of traditional unionism. They claimed, for example, that 'because of political instability in Northern Ireland the real issues had "gone by the board"'. Further, the party argued that: 'For too long your politics have been propounded by those who failed to consult and therefore misrepresented the views of the Unionist people especially in working class areas.'

Under the banner of 'a political strategy for a new beginning in Northern Ireland', the party strongly restated their commitment to Northern Ireland's position as an integral part of the United Kingdom. They did, however, defend the right of any group to seek constitutional change by 'democratic, legitimate and peaceful means', recognising the rights and aspirations of all law abiding citizens, 'regardless of religious, cultural, national or political inclinations'.

In other parts of the manifesto, they promoted a new Constitution and Bill of Rights for Northern Ireland, containing 'stringent safeguards' and 'mechanisms for protection of individuals, associations and minorities'. Unlike the DUP they specifically addressed the issue of paramilitary prisoners, calling for an amnesty; a phased release of 'all political prisoners' and a comprehensive 'social re-integration programme' for returning prisoners to the community.

These differences reflect just how important the position of Loyalist paramilitary prisoners had been to the direction of the 'peace process'. A continual refrain from this group had been their disillusionment with unionist politicians. There had been an almost constant complaint, for the best part of two decades, from within Loyalist paramilitary circles, that the political leadership which first generated the situation had subsequently washed their hands of it – and of them. The differing attitudes on this topic again mark distance between the PUP and the DUP, who have claimed that during the 'peace process' the Loyalist paramilitaries had been 'singing off the same hymn sheet as Sinn Fein/ IRA'.

The Ulster Democratic Party

The Ulster Democratic Party launched its election campaign also promising 'effective leadership' which 'others' have denied the electorate. Under the slogan, 'Look to the Future', Gary McMichael, the party leader, said the election was the designed to lead to meaningful negotiations, and the party would:

> ... argue a political settlement which puts the people back into the driving seat. We will pursue an accountable democratic framework of government for Northern Ireland, a settlement in which the rights of the people are enshrined in their own constitution. Over the past 25 years Loyalists have resisted all attempts by those who sought to force political change against the will of the people. We will not now allow them to do so by political coercion. (*Irish Times*, 26 May 1996)

The UDP also promoted the notion of a 'Council of the British Isles' to deal with the totality of relationships 'across these islands and not the narrow confines of Anglo–Irish policy'. The model proposed was that of the Nordic Council 'founded on the common values shared by the people of the region as a result of their historical, cultural and linguistic ties', a model that the UDP argued would revitalise British–Irish relations.

The 1996 Forum Elections – A Brief Analysis

The period immediately before the Forum election saw a hardening of unionist rhetoric and an intensification of the competition for the claim to the right to represent 'true unionism'. This repositioning could be seen across political unionism. The 'new' leadership of the UUP, for example, adopted a more overtly aggressive stance. Likewise, both the DUP and the United Kingdom Unionists made much of their refusal to ever discuss formally the status of the Union, or to negotiate with those who represented the paramilitaries, including the UDP and the PUP. Both also placed an emphasis on the principle of self-determination for the 'people of Northern Ireland'.

The major conflict within political unionism, of course, was the longstanding struggle between the DUP and the UUP for the majority of unionist votes. In the 1992 General Election, the UUP triumphed, gaining nearly 35 per cent of the votes cast, as against only 13 per cent for the DUP. The UUP domination continued into the 1993 local elections, where they secured 29 per cent of the vote, compared with about 17 per cent for the DUP. However, in the European election of 1994, the Rev. Ian Paisley, the only representative of his party, reversed the fortunes when he won 29.2 per cent of the votes compared with 23.8 per cent for the UUP's Jim Nicholson.[7] In the end, the Forum poll was reasonably close, with the UUP taking 41 per cent of the unionist vote and the DUP almost 32 per cent.

Table 11.1   The Forum unionist vote

Political party	No. of votes	% of the vote
Ulster Unionist Party	181, 829	41.0
Democratic Unionist Party	141, 413	31.9
Alliance	49, 176	11.1
UK Unionist Party	27, 774	6.3
Progressive Unionist Party	26, 082	5.9
The Ulster Democratic Party	16, 715	3.8
Totals	442, 989	100.00

Source: Constructed from election returns; *Belfast Telegraph*; *Irish Times*, May 1996.

This overall result was largely predictable. The 'fringe' Loyalist parties, however, did better than expected, winning a combined vote of 43,000 between them, representing almost 10 per cent of the pro-unionist vote (see Table 11.1). The DUP claimed victory, arguing that with around 32 per cent of the unionist vote, it was obvious that a sizeable percentage of the electorate wanted nothing to do with any 'peace process' that included Sinn Fein.

'New' Loyalism and the Protestant Working Class

Given the above, is it possible to consider any hope for Loyalist accommodation? Within the narrow confines of the contemporary 'peace process', both the PUP and UDP are agreed on the need for a Northern Ireland Assembly; the PUP seeks an administrative assembly, with power-sharing, while the UDP looks to a more powerful institution with 'proportionality' for elected representatives. Both are committed to a 'Bill of Rights'. Clearly, there may be some room for political movement here and some sense of political accommodation is forthcoming. A more important question, however, is whether a strengthening of the UDP and PUP marks any ideological change in loyalism.

Loyalism is, of course, bound by a set of ideas and values which give it its social functions, and centrally locates it in the day-to-day practices of Protestant workers. Sectarianism remains the most crucial form of social relationship affecting the Protestant working class as a whole. It is sectarianism that still constitutes the most meaningful political experiences for, and relationships between, both Protestant and Catholic workers.

For many Loyalists, however, their experience also needs to be seen in the context of dramatic economic decline, political disarticulation and ideological disintegration. In the political response of loyalism, sectarian consciousness has not negated other forms of consciousness, such as class, or vice versa. Rather, these co-exist within the same world-view, and within the same political parameters. What the Left needs to encourage is a process whereby the balance of those central elements that comprise Protestant working-class ideology can be altered to eradicate, or at least marginalise, sectarianism as a fundamental organising principle.

The ceasefires opened up some room for debate within Loyalist working-class communities. The spirit of these debates has been captured in several publications recording events organised by community activists in Loyalist districts (see Hall, 1994, 1995; Shankill Think Tank, 1995). These record serious and thoughtful discussions, organised at the local level, around the nature of contemporary Protestant culture, the structure of unionist politics and the future direction of unionism. This has revealed a debate and discourse that has not been seen in such communities, perhaps since the founding of the state.

The broad contours of these debates, while never really questioning the Union, have been pluralistic. This is consistent with much of the recent output from the political representatives of the paramilitaries. That is not to say that the views expressed by such community groups, or indeed by the PUP or UDP, have replaced sectarianism. Rather, as I have argued elsewhere, sectarianism and other forms of consciousness, some contradictory, co-exist within the same ideology, the same pragmatic space, the same day-to-day considerations and the same set of social relationships (McAuley, 1991 and 1994).

The 'Left', Loyalism and the 'Peace Process'

The Left, in all its forms, must harness and attempt to build upon several important portents that the 'peace process' has revealed in Loyalist community politics. Such a task will remain difficult until the Left recognises the full nature and range of Protestant working-class ideology. This is fragmentary, disparate, internally contradictory and built on the incomplete forms of thought through which ordinary people make sense of their everyday lives.

This has been seen in the segmented 'Loyalist' response to the 'peace process'. That there has been no unity of ideological thought or actions between those active in Loyalist political organisations, in part demonstrates the willingness by some sections of the Protestant working class to articulate the notion of a fluid, rather than a fixed, social and political identity. It is this response that the Left must take seriously, and seek to build upon. Perhaps, it may even represent some form of class identity, which could provide the possibility of a solution to the conflict.

These are the immediate political parameters that the Left must recognise. The views currently being expressed by the PUP and the UDP should be set against the range of opinions and options currently on offer to Protestant workers. Crucial here is the willingness, by some sections of the Protestant working class, to reassess their own position, and to challenge the authority of the established unionist political leadership. There is evidence that this process is in operation, even if only to a limited extent.[8] What is of importance is the balance of such forces at any given point. The ideological terms of reference within contemporary loyalism are multi-discursive. Ideas of 'Britishness', or a 'British way of life', for example, mobilise across a wide range of identities. They have been articulated in the unionist bloc, and have played a central role in shaping Northern Irish society.

Certain political groupings dominate particular areas of political discourse. This can be seen in the lexicon of the DUP's discourse and their constant recent refrains of 'treachery', 'duplicity', 'betrayal' and 'sell-out'. These terms identify, and are applied to, a wide range of 'opponents', from members of Loyalist paramilitary groupings, to the Irish government. The strength of this position can be seen in the broader Loyalist response to the 'peace process'. Loyalists have constantly referred to the 'peace process' as the 'first step', or the 'thin edge of the wedge' to a united Ireland. Such discourse is capable of arousing all of the different fears held by the factions of the unionist bloc.

The kernel of a serious analysis of Protestant working-class politics must involve some notion of ideological dominance and subordinance within loyalism. The hegemonic construction of a 'British' identity by Ulster loyalism not only includes, but absorbs, a multitude of other key identities, such as gender, geographical location, sexual preference, class identity, and so on. These, however, have to be organised into a collective political will. The major organisational categories of society have to be structured into the ideological order that is expressed, and understood, as loyalism.

There are several ideological positions on offer to contemporary unionists. These can be plotted across party politics and are represented in Figure 11.1. The dominant construction of a primary identity for loyalism is expressed as 'Britishness', here broadly referred to as a 'sense' of unionism. This variegation suggests this identity is not monolithic, and given the right conditions can be broken down to form a new group identity. There is no inevitable political trajectory to Northern Irish society, that of Northern Irish Protestants, or indeed of those who currently readily align themselves as 'Loyalists'.

Liberal	The Alliance Party **1** United Kingdom Unionist Party	Progressive Unionist Party **2** Ulster Democratic Party
'Sense' of unionism		
Traditional	**3** Ulster Unionist Party	**4** Democratic Unionist Party
	Middle class Proletarian **Social Base**	

Figure 11.1   Social and political locations of contemporary unionism

The reaction of large sections of loyalism to the 'peace process' was predictable. Any criticism of the unionist position, either from within or without, was condemned as apostasy, an abandonment of fundamental principles and a further move towards a united Ireland. In response, many Loyalists receded into 'time trapped' traditions, clearly manifested during the summer of 1996 at the Loyalist 'set pieces' of the Ormeau Road and 'Derry's Walls' (see Chapter 9). It is also in this context that the events at

Drumcree must be understood. The appeals to Loyalists to rally in defence of their 'heritage' (and the Union itself) activated a strong sense of Loyalist identity. As one commentator put it: 'Drumcree touches a chord with working class Protestants who feel that there has been enough appeasement of republicans in recent years and it is time that Loyalists took a stand' (Breen, S., *Belfast Telegraph*, 8 July 1996).

Such events saw wide sections of unionism and loyalism organising to resist social change, perceived or real, by means of collective action outside of established institutional mechanisms. This only highlighted once again the importance of political violence to Loyalist political culture. It remains crucial for the Left, though, to look beyond the immediate set-piece responses, and to take a critical but serious look at contemporary Loyalist culture. There is some evidence that the close weave of unionism did begin to unravel during the period of the ceasefires, and this confirms trends and tensions within loyalism going back well over a decade.

New Loyalism – Old Dangers?

At any given time, Loyalist hegemony, around its traditional constructions, may be strong and cohesive or weaker and less integrated. One of the more important outcomes of the contemporary 'peace process' has been the emergence of a secular, seemingly liberal and, no matter how crudely expressed, even class-aware voice from within the Protestant working class. Even more important, perhaps, these political groupings have been allowed room to express these perspectives. Clearly, the PUP and UDP are prepared to engage with an agenda and discourse significantly different from traditional loyalism and unionism.

The political movement known as 'new loyalism' may, of course, in the future simply reveal itself to be the old sectarian consciousness in new clothes. If this is the case it must be vehemently opposed. There still remains, however, the possibility of an alternative understanding and structure being created. Any possibility of a restructuring of Loyalist politics towards a less sectarian, community-based expression should certainly not be hindered by those of the Left. Provided they are prepared to reconstruct their sectarian past and to engage in open dialogue, the emergence of the UDP and the PUP, from within the Protestant working class, is to be welcomed. The broad reactions of loyalism to recent developments has been fragmented, and given this, there is some room for optimism about Loyalist political developments in the future. The reaction suggests increasing self-questioning of status and of identity within the Protestant Loyalist community which can only be seen as positive.

The situation is, however, perilous. There remains the distinct possibility that those who are defining the 'new loyalism' will be reabsorbed into the dominant unionist hegemony. This could happen should they perceive the peace process as further undermining their core identity, and if the pressure to counter the 'peace process' increases to the point where Loyalists feel they can no longer resist politically. It is here that the DUP will be pivotal – ideologically, in the discourse they set – and politically, in the leadership they give.

Conclusions

This story of Loyalist realignment and redefinition demonstrates both the flexibility and endurance of ideological discourse. Writers such as Chomsky (1988 and 1992), Foucault (1979 and 1985) and Said (1985 and 1997) have effectively demonstrated that language use is inseparable from power. Indeed, in their differing ways they have also shown how power operates through particular discourses, and how discourses are firmly established in power. Althusser's work also sheds light on the workings of ideological discourse (1969 and 1972); through Althusser it is possible to argue that ideology is a system of representations, of myths and concepts, which are endowed with an historical existence and perform a particular role in a given society. Ideology is thus not a question of some consciously-held set of beliefs, but rather 'systems of representations' which work in a structured manner.

In this way, Loyalist ideology can work 'unconsciously', accepting as it does certain views and values as both 'natural' and 'pre-given'. In this sense ideology provides core values and presuppositions which can help individuals to make sense of their world. These structures work internally and recruit members of the Protestant working class into accepting a distinctive world vista. To explain this, Althusser conceptualised the mechanism of recruitment as a process of 'interpellation', whereby a person is both named and positioned. Individuals recognise they are being addressed, and submit themselves to the consequences of this positioning. There are many examples of this process of 'spontaneous identification' for Loyalists, throughout the entire contemporary 'peace process', especially around the discourse of resistance.

Yet there are differing ideological perspectives, and differing discourses on offer to Loyalists – there is no single monolithic version of loyalism. Two of these can be seen in the perspectives of the PUP and the UDP, on the one hand, and the DUP, on the other. In the early stages of the 'peace process' the former, UDP and PUP versions, were gaining the initiative. Following the 1996 Forum election the DUP regained some of the lost leverage, and its discourse began, once again, to most successfully articulate the concerns, values and perceptions of Loyalists.

The tensions between these contradictory visions are, though, unlikely to fade in the foreseeable future, 'Agreement' or no 'Agreement'. Writing of the 1996 Forum election, Dick Grogan said:

> ... there is a big 'floating' unionist vote which has distaste for Dr Paisley's bombast and rhetoric, but will turn to the most militant and strong-sounding leader at times of political uncertainty and insecurity; the outcome of their struggle will depend heavily on the psychological climate in the North as we approach polling day. (*Irish Times*, 15 May 1996)

This, as a summary of contemporary Loyalist politics, has strong resonance far beyond any election. The struggle for the dominant political voice within the Protestant working class continues; and the outcome of that struggle will determine the long-term prospects for peace and political restructuring.

Notes

1. The comments from McCartney and Paisley were reported in the *Irish Times*, 9 July 1996.
2. Senior Loyalists have admitted that one of the reasons it took six weeks to call a ceasefire, after the IRA 'cessation', was that a younger grouping of militant Loyalists believed they had bombed Republicans into ending their campaign. They argued that they should continue in order to ensure complete nationalist 'surrender' of any territorial claim over Northern Ireland. Loyalist political leaders and senior paramilitary figures had difficulty in bringing these members in line, but they eventually succeeded in mid-October 1994. The Loyalist

ceasefire was only sealed with the firm statement, strongly supported by the Loyalist icon, and UVF founding member, Gusty Spence, that the Union was 'safe'.

3. With the 1996 breakdown in the IRA ceasefire, the CLMC was under pressure to follow suit; this is not to suggest that the Loyalist para-militaries have a purely reactive agenda. Indeed, I have provided evidence to the contrary elsewhere, see McAuley, 1995 and 1996.

4. Much of the popular press at the time focused on Billy Wright, a well-known Loyalist in the Portadown area. During the CLMC ceasefire, the Portadown UVF increasingly opposed the line put forward by the PUP and UDP, warning that the Irish government was too close to the views of Irish Republicans. This became the focus for several 'dissident' members and groupings within the Loyalist paramilitaries. These tensions and events, at and following Drumcree, eventually led the UVF command to disband their Mid-Ulster unit. Mr Wright and another Loyalist were ordered out of Northern Ireland by the CLMC, on penalty of death. The Loyalist Volunteer Force, then founded and led by Wright before his assassination in December 1997, has been responsible for several sectarian murders in the contemporary period.

5. This perspective was evident at several stages during the 'peace process'; it was clearly expressed, for example, by David Ervine of the PUP, when he condemned the SDLP and the Irish government for standing 'shoulder to shoulder' with the IRA, claiming that the major concern of Loyalist paramilitaries was the 'survival of the unionist population and their way of life' (*Belfast Telegraph*, 27 August 1996).

6. For a refutation of this position, and similar more mainstream inter-pretations of the 1991 census data, see Anderson and Shuttleworth, 1998.

7. Although this has been a constant feature of European Parliament elections. Proportional representation in the single, cross-Northern Ireland Euro-constituency, grants a premium to populist personality politics, especially of the Paisley variety; see Goodman, 1996.

8. This in itself is nothing new; sections of the Protestant working class have, at various times, distanced themselves from the dominant unionist political culture. In the past this has been seen in other forms of political expression, such as the Northern Ireland Labour Party, or those within the independent unionist and labour traditions.

12 Women, Equality and Political Participation

Christine Bell

One of the difficulties of addressing equality of political participation for women is imagining what it would look like. It is not as
simple as imagining women leading political parties. As Margaret
Thatcher illustrated, this might have very little to do with equality
of political participation. It is a matter of imagining new structures of participation and new definitions of politics, and perhaps
even new ideas of 'women'. Equality of political participation for
women should mean equality of respect and equality of participation in the benefits, resources and decision-making of society.

This chapter seeks to use the experience of women's political
activity in the Northern Ireland 'peace process' over the last few
years to illustrate the conceptual and practical problems with
women's equality of political participation. The problems with
imagining effective political participation for women can be illustrated by the unsatisfactory nature of the very phrase 'women and
the peace process'. It assumes a peace process and a shared
understanding of what 'peace' is. It assumes that these women are
somehow part of that peace process, or that they at least have
something specific to contribute as women. All of these assumptions are problematic. Considering why they are problematic is
not just important for women, but for all those concerned with
social progress and settlement in Ireland and beyond. Drawing on
feminist theory and focusing on recent developments in Northern
Ireland, this chapter discusses each of these assumptions in turn.

All Women Together?

Given that Northern Ireland is a religiously, ethnically and nationally divided society, Catholic and Protestant women have come
together in different fora knowing that perhaps more separates

them than unites them. Indeed, Evason in her review of the Women's Movement in Northern Ireland claims 'we have sometimes seemed oblivious of divisions elsewhere and started from the assumption that our divisions are special' (1991, p. 48). Yet, women in Northern Ireland have tried to find common ways of addressing day-to-day concerns which they face together as women. Sometimes women have tried to deal with their differences by avoiding them and sometimes by trying to recognise them and work with the resulting tensions. These two approaches indicate two different underlying conceptions of what constitutes effective 'feminist' action which come into conflict, particularly when the question of equality of political participation is considered.

The internal debates in the women's movement or movements in the North of Ireland, together with external political battles, most often revolve around how to bring about effective empowerment and change for women while dealing with the fact of women's political, religious, ethnic and national diversity. This is a debate that is paralleled throughout the world where women seek equality. In the last decade particularly, white Western feminists have been charged with 'colonialism': that they have assumed that a feminist agenda containing a core number of issues (as defined by them) could unite women across class, ethnic and national boundaries. As women of different backgrounds — women of colour, women from developing countries, working-class women, lesbian women and disabled women – have struggled for a public voice they have questioned the relevance of this feminist agenda to their concerns, and more fundamentally have challenged the exclusionary processes by which this agenda is achieved. For example, Audre Lourde, a black lesbian feminist challenging North American feminist academics asserts:

> Poor women and women of Color know there is a difference between the daily manifestations of marital slavery and prostitution because it is our daughters who line 42nd Street. If white American feminist theory need not deal with the differences between us, and the resulting difference in our oppressions, then how do you deal with the fact that the women who clean your houses and tend your children while you attend conferences on feminist theory are, for the most part, poor women and women of Color? What is the theory behind racist feminism? (1984, p. 112)

She argues that to work on women's issues by putting the issue of difference to one side is to try to dismantle the 'Master's house using the Master's tools'. Instead she suggests an alternative approach that involves 'learning how to take our differences and make them strengths' (1984, p. 112).

In Northern Ireland there are many issues where women have a relatively clear common agenda, for example as regards lack of childcare, patriarchal societal attitudes, reproductive issues, and equality in employment. In these areas it is possible to find some 'cross-community' consensus. However, many issues – particularly those connected with 'the Troubles' – do not make these connections; for example, approaches to reform/disbandment of police and army, how to achieve peace and how to negotiate peace. Further, some issues which would seem to have the potential for a shared approach may be complicated by lack of consensus between women in how to deal with conflict: domestic violence, for example, clearly implicates the policing debate. Ideas for improving the state response to domestic violence will therefore be contingent on views of the nature of the Royal Ulster Constabulary (RUC) and its susceptibility to reform. While there may be cross-community agreement on the nature of the problem, suggestions for the way forward may break down along religious lines. Most fundamentally, the question of how women should prioritise political action (in particular the trade-offs between 'constitutional' intervention and issue intervention) is complicated by this same lack of consensus around the constitutional question, with its implications for strategies for effective social change (see Chapter 8, and Sales, 1997a).

This struggle to deal with difference politically is one which is a vital source of often untapped information for students of 'peace'. Women in Northern Ireland also have a contribution to make to one of the big debates of feminist action worldwide, namely, how women can work together without resorting to colonialism and to essentialist assumptions.

Negotiating for Peace?

The language of conflict resolution in Northern Ireland is a limited one. It is one that focuses explicitly or implicitly around the presence or absence of paramilitary violence through resolution of the 'constitutional question'. This limitation has many negative consequences, but in particular it operates to exclude women. First, it excludes a wider equality agenda, which particularly affects women. Second, its processes exclude women, who must try not just to widen the agenda, but to change the very language around what constitutes 'peace' thus changing the priorities around how to achieve it. This task is further made difficult by the tensions described above, that is lack of consensus among women, and the debate over whether working towards such political consensus is a worthwhile goal.

One of the defining problems of conflict resolution in Northern Ireland has been the lack of attention given to addressing the past in order to arrive at a shared understanding of what the conflict 'is about'. Without a shared understanding of the nature of the conflict, understandings of what peace would look like are very different. Is peace simply terrorists not fighting, or does it mean a change to state structures and choices? The post-first-ceasefire discussions about what would constitute progress illustrated this, as contending demands passed each other in the night. Ostensibly the central log-jam was one of decommissioning versus all-party talks. Unionists, supported by the British government, insisted on decommissioning of paramilitary weapons (particularly those of the IRA) prior to any face-to-face talks. Nationalists and others asserted that the process of talks, if started, would lead to settlement which would provide decommissioning of 'hearts and minds' and eventually weapons. The log-jam meant that all-party talks did not take place, and resulted in the IRA abandoning its ceasefire altogether in February 1996. It can be argued that the log-jam was merely a surrogate for the traditional constitutional debate. All-party talks would require an acknowledgement that there is something to be negotiated, namely the Union, the nature of unionist power and the underwriting of the British state, a requirement that most unionist politicians are unwilling to meet. At the same time, the unionist insistence on decommissioning prior to talks required some relinquishing of IRA power, and a surrendering of some leverage on the political process. While constitutional negotiations ostensibly did not take place during the first IRA ceasefire, in effect the issues were negotiated albeit at arm's length.

While the British government position – as recently presented through the Downing Street Declaration, the 'Framework Documents' and the 'Heads of Agreement' joint government paper which set the terms for the 1998 'Agreement' – cannot be fully discussed here, it seemed to contemplate a compromise solution, presented to unionists as 'internal' and presented to nationalists as guaranteeing an increased Irish dimension and the possibility of a 'rolling United Ireland'. This is very much an approach of trying to 'split the difference' between warring factions with irreconcilable goals. However, this search for common ground between the symbolic positions of British and Irish sovereignty does not directly address many of the key questions underlying the conflict, such as various human rights issues and the absence of just structures inspiring cross-community confidence and capable of negotiating conflicting claims and identities.

Moreover, the 'split the difference' approach to negotiating conflict resolution and the constitutional question particularly excludes women, as demonstrated by the de-gendering discourse of the all-party talks log-jam. Women as women, it is assumed, have no guns to decommission and no power or political aspirations to give up. Without guns and aspirations as women, they become undifferentiated unionists, Loyalists, Republicans or nationalists. Stripped of their gender, there is little problem with men speaking for them. As Ward asked in 1995:

> Could it really be possible that a new society, constituted upon principles of social and economic equality, can emerge from the myriad elaborate constructions now being devised by civil servants and politicians, whose employment of sophisticated administrative devices has the sole aim of mollifying widely divergent aspirations? The final goal of the main players (the British and Irish governments) is the transformation of a divided society into a liberal democracy in which differences can be accommodated. But what about other divisions, whose existence has not had the same lethal consequences but which urgently require attention? (Ward, 1995a, p. 41)

As is illustrated by the frameworks established by British and Irish governments, the proposed structures are indeed limited. While forms of power-sharing and balance between Protestants and Catholics were set out, no attempt was made to design structures which would address the issue of gender equality. This could not only have been beneficial for women, but could have changed the numbers game as regards 'Catholics and Protestants', making it less predictable (Rooney, 1996). The British negotiating endgame assumed a fairly monolithic unionism and nationalism which they would attempt to reconcile in their present forms. In so doing, it failed to ask questions such as: Why do people see unionism and nationalism as protecting their interests? Are there ways to accommodate these interests to mutual advantage? To what extent can compromise mean redefinition, rather than giving up portions of aspirations? These are questions to which women could contribute as a group who have explored the margins of both unionism and nationalism, and who have begun to redefine and subvert them. While Dr Marjorie Mowlam's appointment as Secretary of State feminised the role, not just because of her gender, but because she explicitly sought to do so (a move quickly labelled as the 'touchy feely approach' in itself indicating the backlash), at a deeper level it would not seem to have affected the British approach to conflict resolution. It is likely, however, that more analysis of her role as a woman will be developed in the future.

Women and Conflict

To understand women's possible contributions to a settlement it is helpful to review their place in the conflict; this also sheds light on the conflict. Whether as perpetrators or victims of violence, the place of women in Northern Ireland has been either denied altogether or stereotyped and then marginalised. While a few female writers have challenged this, on the whole the media, mainstream sociology, law and criminology discourses have adopted this approach.

Women as Perpetrators of Violence

As perpetrators of violence women are often placed in one (or more) of three stereotypes: the woman who is more evil and deadly than the man; the woman who will commit violent acts out of love for a violent man; and the woman who is dangerous and mad (Bell and Fox, 1996). Where the media present accounts of 'terrorist' women they often use all of these stereotypes, and in popular culture several can converge in one woman, as in 'Jude' of Neil Jordan's *The Crying Game.* In the first half of the film she is presented as the blond IRA girlfriend helping out by seducing a British soldier (with a price of harassment/assault). In the second half of the film, at the expense of character continuity, she dons an auburn wig and transforms into the ultimate female psychopath, both mad and 'more deadly than the male' (see Edge, 1995).

Academic and more serious journalistic accounts of the use of violence exhibit similar stereotypes although in many, the role of women is simply ignored. In Mallie and Bishop's account of the IRA there is no gender analysis (1987); neither is there in Boyer-Bell's account (1990). Likewise women do not feature in Bruce's or Cusack and McDonald's account of Loyalist paramilitaries other than as victims (1994; 1997). Holland and McDonald's account of the INLA twice assures its reader that 'the IRSP's programme was notable for its emphasis on women's issues. The IRSP (Irish Republican Socialist Party) would remain notable for the role women would play in its history', and later that, 'women played a much more prominent role in both the INLA and the IRSP than ever was accorded to them in the other republican groups' (1994, pp. 73 and 327). Yet what this role was, what strategies were involved, how it shaped either INLA or IRSP, and how it affected the women involved, are all left unexplored. Recently an interview with the partner of a leading IRSP/INLA activist, who was herself politically active, indicates the complex weaving together of the roles of a wife meeting her husband and children's domestic needs, an ambivalence to involvement in the IRSP, an attempt to find a women's space for her politics through the organisation 'Women Against Imperialism', and a practical commitment to women in similar situations, for example by supporting prisoners' wives (Hyndman, 1996, p. 129). It is an account of a difficult life, of many layers, that is ignored in many accounts.

Where women are mentioned, the stereotypes abound. Martin Dillon's *The Dirty War* devotes a chapter to women with the title 'Honey Traps' (1991 pp. 231 *et seq.*). As in *The Crying Game*, he cannot resist using several incompatible stereotypes simultaneously. Thus women are particularly lethal:

> The role of women in the shadowy world of espionage and terror has been depicted in novels and movies as glamorous and deadly. In reality that imagery holds certain truths, but in the world of terrorism women tended to be more deadly than glamorous. (1991, p. 233)

Yet, while acknowledging the existence of military women such as Mairead Farrell and the Price sisters, he concludes that women's most successful roles 'have been luring soldiers to their deaths and in accompanying IRA operatives abroad to create an image of young couples on holiday' (Dillon, 1991, p. 246). His own account of women in the IRA deals exclusively with women who lure British soldiers to their doom, as jars of honey lure wasps, thus the term 'honey traps', which becomes sexualised through Dillon's usage.

Stevenson's *We Wrecked the Place* is based on a series of interviews with Republicans, two of whom are women, and Loyalists (all men) (1996). Despite the inclusion of Carol Cullen and Ella O'Dwyer, both of whom were IRA members and served imprisonment, Stevenson's approach fails to address the gender dimension of their participation except to sexualise their presence through descriptions of their physical appearance at the point of introduction. Thus, Cullen is 'an attractive woman, sandy-haired with a broad smile and almondine eyes. She is hospitable as well ...', although according to Stevenson she 'has been programmed into an irrational belief in the Provos' fundamental benevolence that belies her obvious intelligence' (1996, p. 123). O'Dwyer 'is a strikingly pretty woman – her lush red hair, a sprinkling of freckles, and delicate features conjure cinematic images of milkmaid "colleens"'; Stevenson records her 'blushing' as she explains her life choices (1996, p. 163).

Accounts of the RUC and UDR address the issue of women in passing, where again their role is defined along traditional patterns. In Ryder's account of the UDR, women 'Greenfinches' appear as the counterparts to Dillon's honey traps:

> In the year since Operation Motorman in July 1972, sixty-six women were charged with specific terrorist offences and three others were detained without trial. Mr Blaker [then Under-Secretary of State for the army] said that there were not enough women in the RUC or the Women's Royal Army Corps to search women suspects at checkpoints and during patrols, a situation he described as a gap in security arrangements. (1991, p. 65)

Thus women were to be used primarily against women. Greenfinches were not to be armed, but rather protected by their male colleagues.

Brewer and Magee's account of the RUC offers a less stereotyped view. They discuss the day-to-day difficulties for women, noting that the 'occupational culture of the [RUC] is heavily masculine' (1991, p. 49). They also deal with women's reactions to this treatment (1991, p. 241). They note how the issue of violence against women is seen as the main role for police women, arguing that "the marginalisation of police women's duties has divorced some policemen from the reality of sex crimes' (1991, p. 54).

Perhaps unsurprisingly this division of duties is not merely pragmatic, but has had negative effects for women in the police. In essentialising women as better suited to dealing with violence against women and children, a route for their exclusion was established. In the mid-1980s the police tried to dismiss all women police officers from its ranks because they were not allowed to carry guns, in effect defining the combination of gun and penis as essential to the performance of police duties. This was ultimately resolved after challenge in the European Court of Justice when women were permitted to stay and later were armed (*Johnson* v. *Chief Constable of the RUC*, ECR 1651, (1986); CMLR 240 1986, Case 224/84).

Several women writers have presented a different account of women's relationship to violence; several of the best have been primarily historical (Ward, 1983, 1993 and 1995a; Benton, 1995). In addition, a few women (often journalists) have given the issue contemporary treatment. Nell McCafferty's *The Armagh Women*, while dealing in detail with the gender oppression of prison and the criminal justice system generally, also addresses the relationship between women and war (1981). In *Only the Rivers Run Free*, the place of women in different spheres of life is again presented as a picture of a relationship with political struggle and violence that was very different from the relationship between men and war (Fairweather *et al.*, 1984). A television documentary entitled 'Mother Ireland' also bore testimony to this through interviews with Republicans and nationalists, notably, Mairead Farrell later killed by the SAS in Gibraltar while on active service with the IRA (Derry Film and Video Workshop, 1988–89, not shown for some time in Northern Ireland). Less notably, MacDonald's book *Shoot the Women First* (1991) included a profile of an 'IRA woman', and Belfrage's *The Crack* (1987) looked at both Republican and Loyalist women associated with paramilitary groups. While there are problems with many of these accounts, they begin to present a picture where the reasons for women's involvement in political violence are different from those of men, particularly in being seen as part of a larger battle for equality (see McDonnell, 1996).

The case of women engaged in violence does not just pose problems for mainstream media and academic discourses; it has also proved problematic for feminists themselves. If feminism seeks to challenge patriarchal processes as well as patriarchal aims, what is its relationship with war? Does this relationship depend on the nature or justification of the war in question? The use of violence sits uneasily with feminist praxis which sees violence as a primarily male way of dealing with conflict. One response to violence has been the presence of women and feminists at the forefront of anti-war and peace movements the world over. In Northern Ireland the role of women in peace movements is particularly notable, from the Peace People which had two women at its core and had a woman-centred structure, and 'Women Together' which organised large rallies as a response to the breakdown of the IRA ceasefire in 1996. In contrast to the plethora of fact, fiction and 'factional' accounts of paramilitary and security force groupings there has been no notable account of the role of such peace initiatives or the predominant role of women in them. Women's work again fails to register as relevant to the history of conflict.

However, while it is important to recognise the role of women involved in non-violent movements, going further and essentialising women as peaceful and peace-making as the true women's role is extremely problematic. It denies the diversity of women's political views and actions, including a decision to use violence as a means to a political end. Moreover, it chooses to ignore that some women see use of violence as part of an equality debate. MacKinnon has envisaged this difficult feminist/women soldier debate as two women meeting in the after-life with the feminist saying to the soldier 'We fought for your equality', to which the soldier replies 'Oh, no *we* fought for *your* equality' (1987, p. 34). This stark division between asserting use of violence simultaneously as an equality right and a tool for achieving equality on one hand, and rejecting violence as a means to this end, on the other, is indicative of the difficulty of suggesting a 'women's approach' to peace which is consistent with both notions of diversity and of equality.

Women as Victims

Women are 'victims' of the 'Troubles' in many different senses. They are direct victims of paramilitary and state violence – they are killed, maimed and psychologically damaged. They are victims as relatives of those who are hurt or killed. They are victims as those whose relatives are imprisoned. They are victims as those who are left particularly vulnerable to the policing, military and paramilitary priorities of the conflict. Politically, victimhood has been a contested concept in Northern Ireland, where the 'proper' victim is apolitical and forgiving and therefore 'innocent' and undeserving of the hurt. Victimhood is also gendered in important although often ignored ways. Where the women's victimhood fits stereotypes and essentialist assumptions her gender will be recognised, and can even become an integral part of her victimhood; thus the grieving mother is more symbolic of loss than the grieving father. Indeed, the existence of the female 'victim' has meant that the word victim itself is problematic for women, signifying passive disempowerment. In contrast, where a woman herself is a victim or casualty, her gender is more likely to be seen as coincidental or irrelevant. She was in the wrong place at the wrong time, killed or injured because she was somebody's wife or partner, or because of her religion; not because she was a woman.

Recently, Radford and Russell have sought to politicise the killing of women, arguing that in many cases it should be re-labelled 'femicide' – 'the misogynous killing of women by men', and relocated at the extreme end of a continuum of male sexual violence in patriarchal society (1992, p. 3). This relabelling seeks to expose the ways in which women are killed precisely because of their gender, challenging the idea that many victims are women only coincidentally. It is possible then, to connect femicide with the patriarchy of 'the Troubles'. As Radford and Russell document, killings of women fail to receive attention in general. This is exacerbated in a period of conflict where resources are channelled disproportionately at controlling 'terrorism'. McWilliams and McKiernan's ground breaking research on domestic violence documents many instances of women being put further at risk by the priorities of the conflict (1993; see also McWilliams, 1997).

More directly, while women have been targeted along with men, by both state and paramilitary organisations, in practice their killings have often had a gender dimension. For example, a number of Loyalist killings, such as the killings of Marie Smyth or Margaret Wright, have had strong misogynist overtones (McWilliams, 1994). Femicide raises difficult identity questions which have not been explored. If a Loyalist killing is also misogynist was the act less loyal, or what was it loyal to?

Women and Political Strategies for Change

Examination of women both as users of violence and victims of violence indicates the complex nature of conflict, the symbiosis of state and paramilitary activity in making up the reality of women's lives, and the processes of rendering women invisible, and thereby denying the gender aspects of conflict. This has implications for women in the peace process. Women come to the issues of conflict and peace with a variety of experiences as women, which must break open any essentialist understanding of a 'woman's approach' to conflict resolution.

Women concerned with political change and equality of participation have many different and contradictory fronts to address. They have to challenge male versions of unionism and nationalism, and they have to challenge the political cultures which seek to prevent this challenge. They have to widen the debate beyond the question of where the border is; while doing this they need to cherish the relationships which they have built up between themselves, dealing with the pain which forming such relationships can bring. Impossible as this seems, this is what women attempt to achieve, many women pushing on several areas at once. Below I identify and briefly discuss four strategies. These are not the only four strategies, neither is each strategy homogenous in itself but may incorporate varying approaches. Neither are the four mutually exclusive, but serve as broad categories (see Evason, 1991 and Sales, 1997a, for fuller accounts of the women's movement).

Irish Nationalism and Women
In a broadside against Irish nationalism, Edna Longley has charged nationalist women of co-opting feminism for nationalism (1990). This fails to recognise the struggle that nationalist women have had in creating space within nationalism. It oversimplifies the convergence between nationalism and feminism as a cynical poltical manipulation, and rests on an impoverished view of a monolithic feminism, that is subject to the same criticisms as Longley launches at nationalism. The convergence is due in some part to a similarity between the key struggles of nationalism and feminism: the issues of equality that have marked nationalism are similar to the struggles of women, and for Catholic women, the struggle has therefore been profound. The contribution of feminists has been to help to shift the concept of nationalism to one of inclusion of marginalised groups, rather than one of rescue by a Catholic-dominated state. This may or may not have become the present dominant conception of nationalism, but it is a significant shift all the same.

Nationalist women have found different ways to bring together a nationalist and/or Republican agenda with a feminist one. They have argued that the two are necessarily related – equality for women is an integral part of nationalist aspirations. This approach was articulated most publicly at a conference in 1994 organised by Clár na mBan (Women's Agenda) to give a space to nationalist and Republican women to discuss the developing peace process and the Downing Street Declaration (Connolly, 1995). This discussion challenged a view of Irish unity which would not respond to women's concerns. In the words of Oonagh Marron:

> As nationalist women and as feminists, we have very often given our support unconditionally to the overthrow of British colonialism in this country. We have often buried our demands for the sake of a common purpose – Brits out. In the past, that has been a way of censoring our demands. The danger is that once again we are going to be asked to bury our demands, this time in the common purpose of achieving peace. I think that it is time to send a message to those negotiating on our behalf that this time around our support will not be unconditional; never again will we collude with the exclusion of people, with the denial of their rights. (Connolly, 1995, p. 120)

In articulating a feminist vision of Ireland, nationalist women have sought to bring a different perspective to key debates, using the experience of the female body to inform issues of consent and self-determination (Hackett, 1995). In an article in *An Camcheachta* (The Starry Plough), Republican women used the concept of bodily integrity and personal self-determination over reproductive choices to explore the meaning of national self-determination (Madden, 1994). This is a creative process capable of delivering solutions which could not be imagined using a 'split the difference' approach.

However, in terms of putting this agenda on mainstream nationalist political platforms, or negotiating strategies, there is a battle still to be won. Looking merely at women's representation in the main nationalist parties, only 28 per cent of the SDLP and Sinn Fein candidates were women in the 1996 Forum and Negotiations elections. While Sinn Fein have had a stated commitment to participation of women, and were the only party with women on their negotiating team in 1997–98, apart from the Women's Coalition, as yet it is an incomplete victory for women. The women negotiators, for example, stand out for their silence in the face of cameras while the three men all have significant media profiles. Little indication is given of whether feminism plays a part in shaping negotiation strategies or demands, and again media appearances and statements would suggest not.

Unionism, Protestantism and Women
Protestant women have stood in a more ambiguous relationship to unionism and Protestantism. Women can be found organising

together in institutions such as the churches and Orange Lodges, although their role in these would seem to be one of supporting men. While these autonomous organisations empower women, it is fair to say that as yet women have not articulated a challenge to unionism comparable to that of nationalism. This reflects a problem at the root of what constitutes unionism. A male Canadian academic (originally from Northern Ireland) once asked me: Why are there no Unionist feminists? He was publishing an 'intellectual defence on the Union' and felt there were arguments to be made that the Union would help women. In Canada, he told me, there are feminists on every issue under the sun, so why no unionist feminists?

Of course, one answer is that there are indeed unionist feminists. Rhonda Paisley articulated a unionist feminism when she discussed 'Feminism, Unionism and "the Brotherhood"' (1992). She criticised the DUP in particular, and by implication the UUP, for their inability to increase the representation of women or respond to women's needs:

> There exists very little room for feminism within the ranks of Unionism. That is the black and white of it. Unionism is well set in the rut of 'reaction to' feminist issues, rather than being in the position of setting an agenda for such issues and determining to accomplish it .... The answer to this inequality of approach must have something to do with the fact that Unionism is male dominated; and it must also say a great deal about those of us who are female within the ranks of Unionism. (1992, p. 32)

However, the problems of women with unionism go deeper than merely a problem of male representation – they raise the question of whether unionist feminism is capable of a full existence at all. To give an example, several years ago at a Young Unionist conference the Fair Employment Commission and Fair Employment law was berated using misinformed notions of both discrimination and the law itself. Most of the arguments made against this institution could have been similarly applied to the Equal Opportunities Commission of Northern Ireland and sex equality legislation. That this was not mentioned indicates the sectarian nature of the debate. It also illustrates how women's interests are submerged in a narrower unionist agenda, as both Protestant and Catholic women rely on such legislation daily. The criteria of what constitutes 'sound unionist politics' have been drawn so tightly that many unionists are left outside of the fold, pre-eminently women. This goes wider than issues of discrimination, as the possible benefits for women of a union with England and Wales, such as liberality on divorce, abortion, or matters of sexuality more generally, did not apply in Northern Ireland which was specifically excepted by a unionist legislature through the Stormont parliament, prior to direct rule (McWilliams, 1993). As Sales notes, the politics of the 'Constitutional' question rob women of space from which to challenge this: '[t]he ties of Protestantism to Unionist hegemony have made it difficult for Protestant women to challenge the authority of "their" state and political leaders. Those who fight for their own interests are seen as "rocking the boat"' (1997b).

The relative silence of a specifically unionist feminism shows how unionism has reduced the constitutional issue to a symbolic rather than a substantive benefit for many of its constituents. It also of course signifies an inability of unionism to articulate a positive vision of inclusive political participation, rather than a negative agenda of what it will not accept. While marginalising women, this has much wider implications for conflict resolution. Interestingly, a spate of attempts to consider a broader political agenda for unionism, that appeared from 1996, did little to reverse this situation. 'Women' and 'gender' fail to register as a category in indexes, and indeed there is no specific contribution discussing gender implications (see e.g. English and Walker, 1996; Porter, 1996). Shirlow and McGovern's *Who are 'the People'?: Unionism, Protestantism and Loyalism in Northern Ireland*, with Sales's essay on 'Gender and Protestantism in Northern Ireland' (1997) provides a notable exception.

One of the few unionist parties to challenge the assumptions of unionism and attempt to forge a more practical definition of unionism is paradoxically that of the Progressive Unionist Party (PUP) which is associated with the Ulster Volunteer Force and Red Hand Commando. At one level, the difficulties of feminist unionism are perhaps just a different version of the difficulties of right-wing feminism. It is perhaps therefore not surprising that it is within a party which articulates a socialist unionism within working-class communities that feminist unionism has had most space. The PUP has both showed concern with women's issues, using meetings with Ministers to raise issues such as child abuse, and has encouraged the participation of women already active in their communities. However, it faces serious problems in trying to articulate its brand of unionism and also carry its constituents.

Women articulating agendas within nationalism and unionism have a vital role to play in asking the questions that expose the contradictions within both ideologies. As Connolly puts it:

> Imagine a dialogue between Catholic and Protestant women's groups on the meaning of 'democracy'. Catholic women would be justified in asking whether it includes a state which systematically discriminated against Catholics, excluding them from housing and employment, and letting an armed and sectarian police force loose on them. But would the Protestant women be justified in asking how a democratic agenda for the future can be reconciled with a Protestant unwillingness to accept Irish unity? (1995, p. 123)

Women in Coalition

Another option is for women to work in coalition to form a common agenda. This is the approach of community and women's groups who work together on many issues. These vary greatly in their approach to politics, and an exhaustive account is not possible here. The Women's Support Network (WSN), for example, is a coalition of women's groups from both Catholic and Protestant communities who came together in response to an 'increasingly hostile attitude within Urban District Councils in the Greater Belfast Area ... culminating in funding cuts on those which fell victim to the sectarian politics of influential Councillors' (Women's Support Network, 1996, p. 3). Specifically, funding for the Falls Women's Centre in West Belfast was cut and the Shankill Women's Centre responded by showing solidarity against the combined politics of mysogynism and sectarianism.

WSN provides a forum for women's groups to work together on common issues with mutual support, and has also challenged central government priorities. In 1994 WSN argued that government Community Relations policy in practice excluded many women's groups by defining Community Relations narrowly as about projects which were cross-community in content as well as in process (1996). WSN argued for an extension of the definition to include groups whose focus was community development but whose processes were cross community. Ironically the gap in Community Relations funding continues despite the fact that many women's centres find themselves under threatening local pressure due to the effectiveness of their cross-community work.

An example of a coalition approach whose focus is expressly around the religious/political division is the *Women into Politics* education programme run from Downtown Women's Centre. This seeks to provide discussion space for women to find out more about political processes and discuss political issues. This is one of the few women's groups which meet across the religious/political divide to discuss overtly party political issues, as well as issues affecting women. It defines politics broadly to include a spectrum of political activity rather than a purely party political approach, and in particular focuses on the processes and skills of political participation (or exclusion) as much as political structures.

The coalition approach goes to the heart of the debate raised at the start of this chapter, of how far women can or should try to form common agendas. This approach has been adopted with regard to the 'peace process' by the 'Women's Coalition' – a group of women who came together explicitly to fight the elections held in May 1996 for representation in the Forum (see Kilmurray and McWilliams, 1997, for an account of its beginnings). While a 'women's party' had been discussed for some time, its final formation was a pragmatic response to the Forum election, which was designed to make some provision for the smaller parties (apparently to ensure that the PUP and the UDP would be at the negotiating table). The final system guaranteed places for ten parties altogether, and given that the traditional parties and the UDP and PUP account for only eight, that left the Women's Coalition and a collection of other parties fighting for the two remaining places. With a vote of 7,731 (1.03 per cent) the Women's Coalition secured two places out of 110 seats at the Forum (where only 15 women were elected altogether) and perhaps more significantly were then able to field a team for the talks process.

The Women's Coalition was formed to raise the profile of women as representatives; indeed, it started with a concern to gender-proof the election process. It provides a working example of a coalition which seeks to go beyond the issues which women have in common, such as inadequate childcare, to articulating a women's approach to the process of negotiation itself. Thus one of its central policies has been a commitment to 'inclusion' – namely an undertaking to attend all political fora and argue that no group should be excluded and that dialogue should involve all. This is based on the idea that women too often have known what it is to be excluded and therefore should operate on a basis of inclusion. It involved them arguing against the exclusion of Sinn Fein after the breach of the IRA ceasefires, and against the exclusion of the UDP after acts of violence attributed to the UFF.

The Women's Coalition has been openly attacked in predictable ways by many of the mainstream parties. Paisley once derided that he represented more women than the Coalition. However, in this he misses the point. The mandate is not purely a numerical one, but one of a difference of approach. Although more women may have voted for Paisley and the DUP, it is possible to challenge exactly how those women are represented as women. In contrast, the Women's Coalition has always acknowledged that it could not begin to represent the diversity of women's political views, and indeed that it would be demeaning to women to suggest that any one party could, or that women should automatically support the Coalition. An assumption that any one party could represent all men is unthinkable.

From the start the Coalition generated some unease both from women who became involved in it and from those who stayed outside. The unease centred around the dilemma of how to work together without giving up strongly held political allegiances. How workable would it be to form policies as a diverse group of women? Would all policies which sought to go beyond a core agenda specifically focused on 'women's issues' simply be the lowest common denominator to which no one could wholeheartedly subscribe? From within the women's movement, the most publicly hostile reaction has been from Republican women. A group of Republican women posted an open letter to newspapers noting that the Women's Coalition did not represent them. Also, several articles focusing on the Coalition in *An Phoblacht*, and *Andersonstown News*, quoted Republican feminists as critical of the Coalition for being not feminist enough, and not centrally concerned with human rights. Underlying such criticisms was surely the Coalition's attempt to move forward on issues without taking a stance on the Constitutional issue. This presents women with a difficult choice as to whether to fight a common battle at the expense of gains within ideologies and parties. It is not suprising that the criticism was most strongly asserted by a group of women who have made some of the biggest gains in terms of their feminist agenda and their political grouping.

The difficulties for the Women's Coalition in the future are the continuing ones of how to build a common constituency which will not by degree exclude different groups of women. However, the greatest problem is perhaps one of time and resources wherein the women involved, many of whom were extremely active in women's movements before the formation of the Coalition, can stay in touch with the broader women's movement, which they cannot claim to represent, but must nonetheless be accountable to. This must be done simultaneously with trying to make an impact among the other parties in the forum and negotiations, a difficult task in itself.

Women and 'Participative Democracy'
A final strategy for women, which receives little support or public discussion, is that of affirming and building on women's participation in institutions that take on the functions of democratic government, that is, both affirming the participation of women, and further democratising the institutions themselves by pushing for broad societal participation and accountability. Livingstone and Morison have recently argued that an ongoing constitutional revolution is taking place, whereby the traditional functions of government increasingly occur at arm's length through next-step agencies and quangos that lack accountability (1996). They argue that given it is, in all likelihood, impossible to push the clock back and undo these changes, new mechanisms of democratising these institutions need to be explored.

One possible approach is to examine how effective participation takes place in, for example, community structures, and examine how such participation could be enabled in other institutions. This process of democratisation is one which can include equality of participation for women. It is a difficult and multi-faceted approach. But it has the advantage of a feminist praxis which looks to see where women are involved in politics – usually at every level except in local parties – and then seeks to affirm that participation as equally valid as party political activity. While options like the Women's Coalition provide a forum for women who feel excluded by political processes, it may be that the processes of electing majorities is difficult to reform satisfactorily in the short term and may leave many sites of power untouched. Affirmation of participative democracy (see Chapter 13) seeks to diversify the notion of democracy from elections and representation, to one which recognises the different political contributions which actually take place, while trying to reform political institutions in the broader sense, to make them more democratic.

Livingstone and Morison have argued that Northern Ireland provides some initial examples of how the institutions of government can be democratised (1996). In practical terms groups are already working to this end, ensuring that government lives up to commitments it has made. The largest union in Northern Ireland, UNISON, and recently the Women's Support Network and the

Committee on the Administration of Justice, have explored this,
most concretely through their work using government guidelines
on Policy, Appraisal and Fair Treatment, to influence decision-
making to take account of how it affects women and other
marginalised groups (see *In Re Down and Lisburn Trust* 6 June
1995, Queens Bench Division (unreported)). Also, UNISON
have used concepts of accountability under Partnerships formed
to distribute European 'peace and reconciliation' moneys (also to
operate within Policy Appraisal and Fair Treatment). The
European-driven move to formal Partnerships as fund recipients
and distributors provides potential for diversifying the make-up of
decision-makers that may not have been possible in the formal
representative system, for example through the reform of local
councils.

Conclusion

The difficulty with phrases such as 'Women and the Peace
Process' indicates deeper difficulties with notions of womanhood,
notions of peace and notions of effective political participation.
Northern Irish women are not unique in grasping this issue.
Dealing with diversity while making progress is at the centre of
women's movements in different countries, and also at the centre
of international debates on women's rights. The Fourth World
Conference on Women and Human Rights in Beijing illustrated
the diversity of different women worldwide, the diversity of their
political agendas and the friction which common action can
cause. In Northern Ireland women are committed to working
from a variety of different perspectives and strategies simultaneously, and I have sought in this chapter to give some examples.
Although there is energetic (and sometimes personalised) debate
among women as to which strategies are the most effective and
which constitute trying to 'dismantle the Master's house using the
Master's tools', there is also a core of support for the different
strategies from a broad base of women. Differences over strategy
are themselves differences which cannot be ignored.

As Audre Lourde has suggested, the strength of the women's
movement will not be found in a measure of how it can set aside
differences to better work together, but how it can harness the
energy of those differences and provide a working example of how
to deal with diversity. This can inform the present political
processes. These processes typically focus on unionism, nation-

alism and paramilitary activity, each exclusive of women in different ways. The lesson from women is that the possibility of accommodation lies not in constructing a finely split compromise between unionism and nationalism in the hope that it depletes and eliminates, or co-opts, paramilitary support. Rather it lies in exploring the margins within each to find creative re-definitions of what lies at their core. Such re-definitions may provide for mutual accommodation of interests rather than an improbable compromise between political ideologies – unionism and nationalism – whose defining essence is their mutual difference.

13   North–South Agendas for Dis/Agreeing Ireland

James Anderson and James Goodman

Unionists striving to retain an exclusively British Northern Ireland, and nationalists stuggling to create an exclusively Irish united Ireland are unlikely to achieve either outcome. The impracticalities of the nation state ideal and the failures of British and Irish nationalisms (see Chapters 1 and 2) produced a 'zero' or 'negative-sum' conflict over territorial sovereignty which cannot be resolved in nationalism's terms. Three decades of armed conflict entrenched political deadlock. With thousands killed or injured, there has been massive economic disruption, social deprivation, cultural distortion, and associated democratic and human rights 'deficits' – mainly in Northern Ireland, but also in the Republic and in Britain (Chapters 3 to 9). So the problem of reaching agreement on territorial sovereignty – the basis for an 'agreed Ireland' – needs to be re-phrased. The challenge is to find more productive forms of *dis*agreement on other issues which can be dealt with more constructively and peacefully, issues which are also perhaps more important.

An 'agreed Ireland', in the sense of a country free of all conflict, is an unrealistic, and – for those not in positions of power or dominance – an undesirable goal. Appeals for harmonious reconciliation on the national question fall on deaf ears partly because numerous other economic, social and political problems remain unresolved, even unaddressed. However, it is precisely by addressing these problems – by mobilising around and working through these other disagreements – that agreement might be reached on the all-consuming problem of sovereignty. A political settlement requires a 'decommissioning of mindsets', and the only way to change minds fixated on national sovereignty is to encourage thought and action on other matters.

But that is just what the 1998 'Agreement' emphatically did not do. Based on the idea of 'two communities' or 'two traditions' as fixed 'givens', and politics as basically the institutionalised containment of their rival differences, the 'Agreement' could reinforce *national* identities and preoccupations to the exclusion of others, the opposite of superseding national conflict. Of course, given the history of military containment taking precedence over political resolution, recent developments are a definite improvement. It would have been unrealistic to expect much more from the two governments at this early stage of what promises to be a long settlement process without any guaranteed outcome. But here it is important to emphasise two things. First, there are many other actors and potential actors involved besides the two governments, and governments can be forced to repond to pressures from civil society. Second, the 'decommissioning of mindsets' applies not only to (many people's favourite targets) Irish nationalists and unionists in the North, but also to attitudes, official and unofficial, in the South and in Britain, particularly in relation to their 'national self-determination' and sovereignty. This wider 'mental decommissioning' will only happen if there are radical structural transformations – in both the North and the South, between North and South, and between Ireland and Britain.

The conflict is a 'negative-sum game' where the great majority on all sides lose, and society as a whole is seriously disabled. But, in very general terms, as Martin Mansergh, special adviser to several Taoiseachs, has indicated, the

> ... outline of a settlement has been clear for a long time, even to unionists: partnership, parity of esteem and equality in the North; North–South institutions capable of further development; and a balanced constitutional change in both Britain and Ireland to reflect fully the principle of consent in their constitutional law. (Mansergh, 1996a, 52)

The North–South institutions envisaged in the 1998 Agreement follow directly from the governments' joint Framework Documents of 1995, and although significantly reduced in scope, they begin to offer a real alternative to the mutually exclusive and unattainable goals of traditional unionism and nationalism. If 'capable of further development' – and that is the big 'if' – they would bring mutually reinforcing economic, social, cultural and democratic advantages (outlined in Chapters 3 and 4) which would in turn bolster their potential for conflict resolution. As discussed here in Section I, the wider circumstances of the contemporary world are now more favourable for implementing

the 'Agreement's' proposals for North–South integration than
when similar attempts were made in the past.

So why the delay? Partly it is has stemmed from the inertia of
bitterness after decades of 'low intensity warfare'. But more
fundamentally (as outlined in Chapter 1), the structures of territorial sovereignty – the basically unionist *status quo* – actively
*dis*courage Northern unionists, and also unionists in Britain, from
engaging in serious negotiations with Irish nationalists, North or
South. The nationalisms in Britain and the Republic are also part
of the problem (as discussed in Chapters 5, 6 and 7), and both
governments have at times grossly mismanaged the search for a
solution. As argued in Section II, their mindsets too – and the
British in particular – have been largely stuck in the 'sovereignty
rut', making them incapable of the 'North–South' vision needed
to imagine a genuine settlement.

Sovereignty and 'national self-determination' are issues of
democracy, but democracy has in practice been lessened by the
conflict over the territorial framework in which representative
democracy is to take place. Besides, important as it is, this is only
one form of democracy, and democracy in general is more a
means to an end than an end in itself. Leaving aside the rhetoric
of nationalism and addressing these issues seriously involves
questioning the very meaning of 'democracy' in the contemporary
world. A much deeper and wider democratisation of cross-border
relations than currently proposed in the Agreement needs to be
developed: in the first instance just to see its minimal proposals
properly implemented, in spirit as well as letter; in the longer term
to provide an adequate basis for a lasting settlement. Section III
makes the case that representative democracy must be extended,
and that it needs to be substantially supplemented with cross-
border participatory democracy and *non*-nationalist politics. The
politics of class, gender and other cross-community/cross-border
concerns are what will finally bring a settlement. 'Class' and the
other concerns, however, cannot crudely be counterposed to
'nation', and relating them productively is easier said than done,
as Chapter 12 suggested in the case of 'gender'.

I Dynamics and Institutions of Cross-Border Integration

As indicated in Chapter 4, there are four related types of dynamic
for North–South integration, four types of reasons why

North–South institutions are required – 'economic', 'socio-cultural', 'national' and 'political democratic'. The 'economic' dynamic for a 'single island economy' (Quigley, 1992) is largely a product of the the Single European Market, and there is now a large and growing constituency for economic cooperation and policy coordination across the island. Here the functional and ostensibly non-political 'consensual cooperation' which has operated up to now is simply not up to the task of securing the island's economic future. Integrating the two separate economies in two different states will require proactive and concerted polit-ical management, legitimised by democratic involvement and political accountability.

The 'socio-cultural' dynamic is wider and more diffuse, involving a range of different groups and institutions, including community and campaigning organisations, the extensive volun-tary sector, and cultural and sporting bodies. They are either already organised on a cross-border or all-Ireland basis, or, for a variety of reasons – some related to the EU, some not – they see advantages in cross-border cooperation They have also begun to demand a role in the emerging North–South policy-making process. Increasingly, the counterpart of the emerging 'single island economy', is an 'all-Ireland society'.

The Irish 'national' dynamic for Ireland's reunification under-lies the official response of 'parity of esteem' for nationalists and unionists – an impossibility in the North unless North–South institutions 'balance' or counter the unionist majoritarianism built into the Northern Irish statelet. Unionist opposition to this dynamic is a major obstacle to integration, but, in general, the economic and social pressures mesh with arguments for 'parity of esteem', as all three dynamics require an island-wide institutional and political framework. They also require a democratisation of North–South relations and institutions, and this can be consid-ered a fourth, overarching 'political democratic' dynamic.

Thus border-straddling institutions would bring mutually rein-forcing economic, social, cultural and political advantages. They would give practical expression to 'parity of esteem' for Irish nationalists in Northern Ireland, facilitate the quite separate 'economic' dynamic for a single, unified economy, the wider 'socio-cultural' dynamic and the need for more democracy. On four separate but related counts, North–South institutions are 'an idea whose time has come'. Taken together, the four dynamics suggest that, contrary to the Ulster Unionist Party's immediate and partial success in curtailing the remit of cross-border bodies, particularly in economic matters, these institutions will indeed prove 'capable of further development' under the weight of changing circumstances (and not least economic circumstances).

The wider contemporary circumstances are now much more favourable for a settlement based on such institutions than in the early 1920s when 'Council of Ireland' proposals were still-born, or in 1973–74 when the similar 'Sunningdale' scheme was halted by the 'Ulster Workers' Strike'. The 1920s, following the postwar Versailles Conference, were a heyday for national sovereignty and the nation state (though not for Ireland). For many British observers the Council of Ireland was merely a transitional stage to a re-united Ireland; for Irish nationalists it conceded too much to Partition; while for unionists, resisting reunification, it was merely an 'unstable half-way house'.

But this is not necessarily the case today, contrary to the unionist recycling of 1920s arguments.[1] The 'winner-takes-all' conception of absolute sovereignty at the centre of the conflict is increasingly anachronistic where the wider context is not 'Versailles' but 'globalisation' and the European Union. The ground has been shifting under conventional politics (Anderson, 1996) and the traditional view that sovereignty is 'absolute and indivisible' within state frontiers is every day contradicted by the pooling of power and sovereignty across the EU. The EU itself now comprises a variety of well-established border-straddling political forms; and just as 'shared sovereignty' in the EU is not transitional to a single 'Euro super-state' (Anderson, 1995b; Anderson and Goodman, 1995), so North–South institutions need be neither transitional nor unstable. Closer to home, the traditional view is countered by the permeability of the Irish border, one of the most porous state frontiers in Europe; and it is even contradicted by the reality of sovereignty in the North which already departs significantly from the 'Westminster model' – an electoral majority in Northern Ireland has the right to leave the UK (a right not granted for instance to the Scots, a majority of whom might actuallly want to use it).

The original Council of Ireland and the 'Sunningdale' version failed to materialise largely because of unionist opposition and because Irish nationalists were 'lukewarm' if not outright hostile.[2] But now most nationalists see a 'sharing of sovereignty' as the way forward, and as has been clear for some years (see e.g. Wilson, 1996), an increasing number of Northern unionists are, albeit slowly and with less enthusiasm, coming to similar conclusions. They see practical advantages in North–South institutions as a means of achieving greater economic prosperity and a peaceful settlement, though the capacity for unionists to continue delaying the process remains substantial.

The 'Agreement' and North–South Institutions

That 'capacity for delay' is in fact built into the Agreement with its elaborate mechanisms to achieve 'balance' between the 'two traditions' and 'box in' potential saboteurs from either side, and of course delay is preferable to the whole scheme being wrecked. The possibilities of delay were also signalled in the widely different interpretations put on the Agreement following its endorsement, not only by rival political parties claiming 'negotiating successes', but also by independent commentators. There was much speculation about what had been won and lost in negotiations, and particularly how the suggested scope of the North–South bodies compared with previous suggestions in the Framework Documents. In fact the long and complex Agreement was objectively open to different interpretations (perhaps necessarily so to get an initial agreement), and particularly in its underdeveloped 'Strand 2' on North–South relations.

While nationalists generally 'played up' what the proposals meant for North–South bodies, unionists who supported the 'Agreement' did the reverse; and other unionists who exaggerated the Agreement's North–South implications did so from a position of total opposition. Unionists supporting the Agreement belittled the proposed 'North–South Ministerial Council', and a week after endorsing the Agreement the Ulster Unionist Party website carried a press statement from David Trimble claiming that, unlike the Framework Documents, 'no areas of economic policy are the subject of possible cooperation', only 'areas such as plant health and canals'.

This would really be 'low politics' far from 'sovereignty', and it does seem that the Ulster Unionist Party had some success in removing references to 'economic policy', 'industrial development', 'energy' and 'consumer affairs' from the list of possible functions for the new North–South Council and sectoral 'implementation bodies'. On the other hand, EU matters were explicitly mentioned as an important area for North–South cooperation, and the list included other areas with a strong 'economic' element.

Much of the speculation was just that, speculation. The political arguments were more about symbols than specific substance, important in the political competition between, and especially within, the rival nationalist camps, but not a reliable guide to the future of North–South institutions. The Framework Documents had only said that their functions 'by way of illustration' were 'intended to include' unspecified 'aspects' of listed but undefined policy areas; and likewise the Agreement said their remit 'may [not "will"] include' a list of twelve areas, including some new and again undefined ones, such as 'urban and rural development' whatever that might mean.

However, it was very clear that (yet again) 'internal power-sharing', Strand 1, had taken precedence in being much more fully developed and agreed than North–South relations, 'Strand 2', where much of the important detail had still to be decided.

What was decided included the North–South Ministerial Council, to be set up by the Dáil and the Northern Assembly, bringing together ministers from each, and with its own standing joint Secretariat. The Council was to be established during a transitional period, following June elections to the Assembly and before – and a condition for – the Assembly acquiring powers of government in the autumn. Modelled on the EU Council of Ministers, it would be accountable to the respective assemblies but it would be able to take decisions, meeting in two full plenary sessions each year and in 'regular and frequent' smaller meetings on particular policy matters. In the transitional period the new Council was to decide at least twelve policy areas for North–South cooperation and the implementation of mutually agreed policy. Council policy in at least six of these areas was to be handled by cooperation between existing bodies in each jurisdiction, and in at least another six areas, policy would be carried out by 'agreed implementation bodies on a cross-border or all-island level' (*Agreement*, 1998, p. 12). While the Council was given the explicit brief of considering the European Union dimension of policies and the implementation of EU programmes, the open-ended list of possible areas for North–South cooperation and implementation included strategic transport planning, tourism promotion and product development, environmental protection issues, and what in some cases seemed either very limited or unspecified aspects of agriculture and fishing, education, health and social security. Whatever the functions initially given to the North–South Council, its scope and powers could later be expanded, but only as agreed by the North's representatives and those from the Dáil, and likewise any diminution of its powers could only be by mutual agreement.

There were also other North–South elements beyond 'Strand 2'. These included a British–Irish Intergovernmental Conference (successor to the 1985 Anglo–Irish Agreement arrangements) for matters not devolved to the Northern Assembly (e.g. security, legal and fiscal), though now to include participation by executive members of the Assembly. There would be new matching Human Rights Commissions North and South, and a joint North–South committee; and 'structured cooperation' between the respective police forces, criminal justice systems and broadcasting organisations. There would also be a North–South element in the proposed British–Irish Council linking parliamentary assemblies in Dublin, Belfast, Edinburgh, Cardiff, the Isle of Man and the Channel Islands. Other possible cross-border developments beyond the Agreement included more formal or systematic participation by Northern representatives in the Dáil or Seanad in Dublin.

In addition to the North–South arrangements actually agreed, 'consideration' was to be given to the establishment of a parliamentary forum composed of equal numbers of Assembly and Dáil representatives; and an 'independent consultative forum ... representative of civil society, comprising the social partners and other members with expertise in social, cultural, economic and other issues' North and South (see below), though this too was only 'for consideration' (unlike the similar internal forum for the North on its own which 'will be established' not just 'considered') (*Agreement*, 1998, pp. 9 and 13).

The power-sharing Assembly and the North–South Council were to be mutually 'proofed' against sabotage. Their initial establishment and assumption of formal powers, and their continued proper functionings, were to be mutually interdependent in that if either body was rendered inoperative the other could be closed down. The implication was that nationalists would be deterred from sabotaging the Northern Assembly and unionists from sabotaging the North–South Council if the cost was the closure of the other body, together with a resumption of British Direct Rule and Southern intergovernmental consultation, much like before the 'Agreement', though with possibly stronger Dublin input than before. In addition, serving on the North–South Council was specified as a duty of Assembly ministers. However, despite these safeguards, it was clear that unionists elected to the Assembly on an anti-Agreement ticket could still cause serious upsets, largely by mobilising support on the emotive but not central issues of paramilitary prisoners being released and the 'non-decommissioning' of weapons. They might be prepared to wreck not only the Council but also the Assembly. They would have weak allegiance to this power-sharing body, and they might ignore or discount the longer-term costs to unionism of a move towards London and Dublin effectively exercising 'shared authority' (see O'Leary *et al.*, 1993) over the North, not to mention the negative implications for the North's chronically dependent economy.

Contrary to unionists' demands, the North–South Council was not to be controlled by the British–Irish Council – in fact this latter 'Council of the Isles' was the less substantial. First proposed for conflict-resolution on the rather misleading analogy of Scandinavia's Nordic Council, it had been something of a diversion from the main North–South issue and was employed as a unionist bargaining counter to the North–South Council (Anderson and Hamilton, 1998). Nevertheless, it could come to play a constructive role, perhaps enabling Northern and Southern Irish groups to make common cause with groups in the more peripheral regions of Britain.

On a literal reading, it was possible to interpret the Agreement as essentially an 'internal' settlement, though with continuing intergovernmentalism and some cross-border additions, and that could indeed be how it will eventually turn out. On the other hand, a 'literal reading' is of limited use precisely because the Agreement left much of the substance still to be decided; and quite apart from the limitations of the text, investing too much importance in textual analysis is an idealist and static approach to what is a dynamic social and political process, not a matter of legalistic semantics. Whatever the functions initially allocated to new North–South institutions, the dynamics of integration and changing circumstances should make them 'capable of further development'.

In the first instance, the Agreement could lead to very positive results in terms of replacing military with political means of addressing differences, and making room for other political issues and new forms of politics. New North–South institutions, however limited, would provide a stronger focus or frame of reference for a variety of integrative forces in civil society, and they could eventually push developments well beyond a limited Agreement scenario. In more peaceful circumstances, the business groups, trade unions, campaigning and other organisations should feel freer to lobby for the necessary cross-border institutional support. Unionists may be able to delay further but not stop the logic of transnational cross-border integration.

It is also important, however, to appreciate the extent to which some unionists have already moved from previous political positions. Unionism has been asked to give up some existing (albeit counter-productive) aspects of 'absolute sovereignty', whereas it is an aspiration to a sovereign united Ireland which nationalists must relinquish or delay. There has in fact been considerable 'political movement' on both sides in recent years (Chapters 10 and 11) – perhaps especially in Sinn Fein – which took some of the respective opponents by surprise, 'wrong-footing' them – especially unionists.[3] Unionists did not expect that Sinn Fein would endorse the Agreement, let alone support changes to the Republic's constitutional claim on the North's territory, and then, to cap it all, change its own party constitution so that it could fully participate in the 'internal' Northern Assembly, something which until recently was anathema to most Republicans.

But the obstacles to a genuine settlement are still formidable, not least the danger that the Agreement, even if properly implemented, will simply reproduce the national conflict in a more peaceful form – progress of a sort – but now with sectarianism even further institutionalised. To reverse Clausevitz's famous dictum, the Agreement could mean that 'politics is the continuation of war by other means'. This would not be a resolution of the conflict but rather the replacement of the old failed policy of mainly military containment by a new political strategy of conflict management. It reflects the 'mindsets of national sovereignty' which must be 'decommissioned' (see Section II), something which can only be achieved by developing cross-border democracy around the politics of other issues (see Section III).

II 'Decommissioning the Mindsets' of Nationalism

The pretensions of exclusive sovereignty help sustain the conflict, most obviously in the case of Northern unionists, but also Irish nationalists who learned their theory from the peculiarly archaic British example. Also, as argued in Chapter 1, in discussing the sorry saga of political mismanagement by government, it is not only Northern 'mindsets' which need 'decommissioning'. The two governments, and especially the British, have generally lacked the cross-border vision needed for a settlement primarily because they themselves have been wedded to a 'realist' and nationalist view of their own territorial sovereignty.

Nationalist thinking, Irish and British, has misled people into believing that there are really just two options 'at the end of the day': an all-Ireland republic or a British Northern Ireland. Those alternatives are still people's primary terms of reference despite –

and indeed because of – the Framework Documents and the
Agreement. For the last three decades and longer, most public
discourse, as if mesmerised by the nation state ideal, has posed
only these two choices, each totally unacceptable to adherents of
the other. Both sets of adherents collude in this 'make-believe' –
nationalists not admitting their actual goal might be rather
different from the traditional 'united Ireland', and unionists
continuing to rely on their traditional 'bogey man' of the unitary
all-Ireland socialist republic. But the reality has been rather
different for some time. Before the 1994 ceasefires, our interviews
confirmed that nationalist and Republican leaders, whatever their
public pronouncements, no longer saw a 'united Ireland' as an
immediate or realistic objective, and none of the Loyalist leaders
we interviewed seemed worried that it might be.

Yet the leaders of mainstream unionism, in contrast to some
Loyalist leaders against whom they have often been unfavourably
compared (Chapter 11), persisted in refusing to recognise the big
shift in Republican thinking (Chapter 10), seeing only
Republican 'bad faith' – a reflection of their own perhaps. On the
crucial sovereignty/democracy issue, they insisted on seeing
North–South institutions as 'undemocratic' in a wilful misrepresentation of the Framework proposals. Ulster Unionist Party
leader, David Trimble, stated: 'my nationality is a zero-sum
issue', and North–South bodies would therefore diminish his
'Britishness' and turn the North into a 'condominium' ruled from
London and Dublin (*Belfast Telegraph*, 6 October 1995). But the
North–South institutions in the Framework Documents did *not*
mean London–Dublin rule (something which had earlier been
mooted by O'Leary *et al.*, 1993) – on the contrary, they were
centrally to involve the representatives of the North itself (who
under Direct Rule from London had no executive powers, even
within Northern Ireland). Representatives from both North and
South were to gain a role in the common concerns of people in
both parts of Ireland. Rather than being a 'one-way street' of
'Dublin rule', North–South institutions were clearly intended to
express *reciprocal* linkages: they would have to address unionist as
well as nationalist concerns, and they would require changes not
only in the North but also in the South (something which
Southern politicans seem to have recognised only belatedly, an
indication of their particular nationalist blinkers).

Mainstream unionist appeals to 'democracy' and 'majority
wishes' in Northern Ireland are disingenuous when the core
problem is disagreement over Northern Ireland with its built-in

unionist majority as the only framework for democracy. The conflict cannot be solved by conventional democratic procedures precisely because it is a conflict over who should have the vote and who should organise the election in the first place. Democracy is defined not only by decision-making processes 'within' a territory, but also by whom and by what means that territory is delimited: by democratic plebiscite, for example, or by British force of arms in response to armed conflict, as in the case of Northern Ireland. Democracy, as opposed to Northern majoritarianism, could only be enhanced by having publicly accountable North–South bodies answerable both to the Dáil and a Belfast assembly – quite apart from historical arguments about Northern Ireland itself being an undemocratic gerrymander.

The unionist refrain was that nowhere else in the 'developed democratic world' have such cross-border institutions been constructed. In a sense they were right, leaving aside related but different EU arrangements (and the implication that 'undemocratic condominiums' were acceptable for Africa or Pacific islands). But it is very conservative and unimaginative to argue that because something does not exist it cannot and should not exist. Their point can easily be turned around to say that Northern Ireland has not been part of the 'democratic world' as normally understood and that most parts of the 'developed world' are not so obviously in need of cross-border democracy. Ireland, instead of being a by-word for national conflict, has the possibility of creatively pioneering a new type of transnational settlement to nationalism's all too common problems of territoriality.

Unionist attempts to treat the South as just another 'foreign' country are functionally absurd for a small and not very wealthy island on the periphery of the Single Market and an increasingly integrated EU. The belittling of the South's significant if flawed economic progress (see Chapter 3) in order to dismiss the advantages of North–South integration (e.g., Roche and Birnie, 1995; Gudgin, 1995) has an air of desperation, particularly in view of the North's own Mezzogiorno-like dependence on a massive subsidy from Britain, and the argument that this rules out integration because the Republic could not afford to pay such a subsidy (see Anderson and Hamilton, 1995). Rather than trying to make a political virtue of economic failure and assuming it to be a permanent condition, it would be more constructive to see the South and especially the North as 'dependent' economies which might escape dependency if they combined their relatively meagre resources.

Stopping or sabotaging North–South institutions would effectively mean that the growing cross-border economy would remain
outside the realm of popular democracy. Furthermore, as the
conflict is basically over exclusive sovereignty, the unionists' alternative 'internal solution' is a contradiction in terms. Confining
institutional change to Northern Ireland would simply 'bottle up'
and intensify sectarianised conflict over the entity set up by
sectarian head-count. The 'historic imperative' of maintaining a
unionist majority in an exclusively British Northern Ireland is
what gives sectarianism its continuing virulence. Local territorial
disputes, as around disputed Orange marches such as
'Drumcree', are a playing out of the conflict over the all-impor-
tant issue of national, state territory (Anderson and Shuttleworth,
1998). They are a means of reaffirming sectarian identity, and
directly encourage the 'zero-sum mindset' reflected, for instance,
in Trimble's comments.

But here territoriality is very misleading. Whereas there is a
fixed total amount of territory, and more for one side does mean
less for the other, the same zero-sum argument does *not* apply to
economic, social or cultural realities. Social life is not so simple –
economic development, cultural achievement, democratic
responsiveness and other facets of our 'quality of life' do not have
static, fixed totals. The totals to be shared can go up, and down –
and where conflicts defined in territorial terms produce political
deadlock and violence, the likely direction is 'down'. Whereas
'territorial imperatives' freeze mindsets, North–South institutions
would allow a 'thawing' and hope of a 'positive-sum game'.

Government Mindsets
Partly in deference to 'unionist sensitivities', but also informed by
their own attachment to theories that collapse concepts of sovereignty, democracy and territory, both governments have
pandered to the mistaken notion that a solution can be achieved
without impinging on traditional sovereignty. They define their
own sovereignty claims in territorial terms, with 'democracy'
narrowly conceived in that context. Whatever innovative adjustments they might be prepared to make with respect to the North,
they generally defend a more traditional 'sovereignty' for Britain
and the Republic.

This may help explain their long-running failure to construct a
settlement, and the fact that some of the reactions of the British
in particular have been imbued with the sorts of nationalist
assumptions that they decry in Irish nationalists. Most obvious in

some 'establishment' newspapers (Chapter 6), they were also evident in the mismanaged responses to the 1994 ceasefires – the failure to seize on the new optimism, the squandering of political opportunities which led to the breakdown of the ceasefires, and particularly the delaying and dishonest insistence that the paramilitaries should and would 'decommission' (hand over, surrender) their weapons. The paramilitaries clearly were not going to comply, and there was widespread pragmatic acceptance that their weapons should be left to 'rust in their arms dumps', particularly as the IRA's ceasefire had been premised on not surrendering weapons because it remained undefeated by the British Army (and 'decommissioning' was symbolic not least because the two governments did not know how many weapons there were to hand over). But it seemed that there were influential nationalists in Britain as well as in Ireland who did not want an end to war, or at least not yet. No doubt some in the British state apparatus and political 'establishment' wanted the IRA to resume full-scale war, believing that 'softened' by ceasefire and divisions over strategy it could now be decisively beaten.[4]

British nationalist assumptions were evident in the strengthening of the unionist veto, as we saw in Chapter 1. This compared unfavourably with the previously more generous British attitude as reflected in the first Council of Ireland. Not surprisingly, unionist leaders were encouraged to claim a veto over any institutional change[5] and to continue blocking the possibility of a negotiated settlement. In the Framework Documents the British government did recognise that 'the consent of the governed is an essential ingredient for stability', which clearly applies as much to Northern nationalists as to unionists. But in practice the 'consent' requirement still amounts to a unionist veto because consent has not been defined positively or inclusively as majority *and* minority consent (Todd, 1995, p. 174). The 1998 Agreement tempers the veto with a power-sharing Assembly and by making it conditional on North–South institutions, but the same consent requirement remains central and is to be demonstrated by a 'border poll' – the oldest majoritarian trick in the book.

Britain's constitutional provisions for Northern Ireland continue to be phrased in essentially negative and sovereignty-retaining terms – the unionists' guarantee that there will be 'no change in sovereignty without the consent of a majority of the North's electorate'. It would be more positive if the British along with the Irish Government explicitly recognised the limitations of traditional sovereignty and the benefits of sharing it. But there has never been any such concerted attempt to inform the public, particularly the Northern unionists. Instead, there has been evasion of the issue and a continuing predilection for the 'internal' nationalistic palliatives of 'consociationalism': for example, the choice of electoral system for the Northern Assembly favours the big battalions of nationalism and militates against smaller and cross-community groupings such as, respectively, the small Loyalist parties and the Women's Coalition (Chapters 11 and 12).

While recognising that the national dynamic and 'parity of esteem' for Northern nationalists require North–South institutions, officialdom has mainly followed the 'neo-functionalist' prescription of avoiding rather than confronting the problem of sovereignty.[6] But a lasting solution, as distinct from interim management, requires that sovereignty questions be rethought in terms of transnational democracy.

III Increasing Democracy and Transnationalism

The Agreement provisions to replace Direct Rule by a power-sharing Northern Assembly, and establish a reciprocal North–South Ministerial Council (as distinct from the 'one-way' consultative role of the South in Northern affairs, which continues for non-devolved matters), represent substantial improvements on the North's 'democratic deficit'. Other conventional improvements would include giving smaller and cross-community or non-nationalist political groupings more representation in the Assembly and its Executive. But improvements which address the core problem of sovereignty in today's world need to go beyond the conventional, and essentially national-territorial, politics of representative democracy. They need to introduce or strengthen transnational forms of representation, and transnational forms of non-territorial participatory democracy.

With intensified globalisation, democratic theorists are increasingly having to come to terms with the fact that actions within particular states have direct impacts on supposedly 'sovereign' neighbours, and that electorates are directly affected by decisions made in other jurisdictions. In consequence, various transnational mechanisms for cross-border and 'cosmopolitan democracy' are needed, as Held (1995) has persuasively argued. Others, such as Richard Falk (1995), put more faith in the participatory democracy of transnational movements 'from below', rather than simply extending liberal representative democracy beyond state borders. These two modes of transnational democracy can, however, be seen as complementary in an EU context (Goodman, 1997), and likewise both can be used to extend the democratic content of the Agreement proposals.

Thus while the island of Ireland, North and South, is the main location of the sovereignty conflict and where a solution must be found, it could be argued, on grounds both of democratic principle and pragmatic politics, that all three electorates of Ireland and Britain should have a say, though not necessarily an equal say, in deciding a settlement. This of course is something which currently is precluded by the nationalistic mindsets on both 'sides'. Unionists object that Southerners, as citizens of a 'foreign country', should have any say in the 'internal affairs' of Northern Ireland; and Irish nationalists would object to the British electorate deciding the Irish nation's future (not that Northern unionists would happily rely on UK-wide majority decisions).

But such nationalistic reasoning blithely ignores the fact that all three electorates have a democratic right to be involved because all are affected in various ways by the conflict. For instance, the biggest bombs and the worst episodes of mass slaughter have, respectively, been in Britain and the South; and the conflict has eroded the civil liberties of both these electorates, as well as costing them 'hard cash'. The unsatisfactory *status quo* has only been kept afloat by the massive subvention to the North's economy from Britain's taxpayers. They have hardly been getting 'value for money'; and the per capita costs of the conflict have been even higher for the much smaller population in the South. There is the counter-argument that these two electorates are represented already by their respective governments, but the reality is that the British electorate in particular has effectively been disenfranchised. Given the de-politicising effects of 'bipartisanship' in Westminster, where the main parties express 'national solidarity' to defend the state from a 'national aggressor', together with the generally poor and sporadic coverage of Ireland in the British media, the general population in Britain has never been properly informed about the conflict or directly involved in finding a solution. Occasional public opinion polls indicating their majority support for a British withdrawal from Ireland have had absolutely no impact on British Government policy. Persisting with the Northern Ireland electorate as the only key decision-making unit has resulted in the North's unionist 'tail wagging the dog' in Ireland and Britain. Unionist governments have been 'out of power' since the early 1970s, but if power is defined in negative terms of preventing a settlement, the unionists have not done badly for a minority of less than 2 per cent of 'these islands'.

That is one measure of the task faced in the Agreement, and a major reason for actually implementing the cross-border bodies it merely posed 'for consideration'. One is the North–South Parliamentary Forum comprising equal numbers of delegates from the parliamentary assemblies in Belfast and Dublin. The Framework Documents suggested such a forum, but it was to be only a consultative body which would enable unionists and nationalists to acknowledge 'the respective identities and requirements of the two major traditions ... [and] express and enlarge mutual acceptance of the validity of those traditions'. Perhaps the last thing needed in Ireland is yet another opportunity to express such national differences. In a forum with no real powers or responsibilities, 'expressing identities' would be as likely to institutionalise the divisions as transcend them. There would be little incentive to forge alliances of various sorts across the nationalist–unionist and North–South divides. Better, if there is to be a Parliamentary Forum, to give it some real work and develop it in the way the European Parliament has developed: moving to direct elections and making representatives answerable to the combined electorates on North–South issues; giving them responsibility for scrutinising the North–South Ministerial Council, initiating policies and so forth.

Participatory Democracy and an 'Island Social Forum'

Moving beyond such cross-border extensions of representative democracy, it is important to see decision-making in the wider terms of participatory democracy with greater emphasis on *non*-nationalist politics, though not as a separate 'stage' or alternative to dealing with the national issue. When wider public participation was officially encouraged in the North prior to the Agreement, it merely underlined the general public's exclusion from decision-making, rarely going beyond genuinely-felt but ineffectual public demonstrations of support for 'peace', with ritualistic condemnations of 'the men (*sic*) of violence'. Democracy involves more than the formalities of territorially-based voting once 'the questions' have been decided. It can also involve the prior shaping of political agendas, partly through participatory democracy; and its more flexible basis in non-territorial social and political movements is well suited to crossing territorial boundaries.

Rather than relying on party politicians elected every four or five years, participatory democracy could involve a wide variety of organisations, some of which are responsive to continuous democratic pressures and are themselves vehicles for participatory democracy, not only in Ireland but also across the EU (see Goodman, 1997). Many people, and perhaps especially women and younger people, are excluded or alienated from conventional party politics, but are nevertheless active in the 'small p politics' of civil society. On the crucial North–South axis, there are already cross-border networks of community, voluntary and campaigning organisations, as well as business groups and trade unions, and some of their spokespeople have been stressing the need for some popular participation in shaping the emerging North–South policy agenda (see Chapter 4).

Some time ago we suggested that such border-crossing groups should be given their own North–South institution with an input into North–South policy – an 'Island Social Forum'. We suggested that it might be modelled on the Republic's 'National Economic and Social Forum', a consultative body created in 1993 to give marginalised groups a say in policy formulation (Anderson and Goodman, 1996). It includes representatives of the unemployed, the disabled, women's organisations, young people, the elderly and environmental groups as well as the corporatist 'social partners' of business, trade unions and government; and it makes proposals on social and economic issues and submits them to the government for action (NESF, 1995, Annex 1-3). The idea was that a similarly constituted 'Island Social Forum' would recognise participatory organisations as legitimate expressions of popular opinion on North–South issues, and it would harness their undoubted energies to build a much more democratic and robust cross-border 'peace process'. It was to give the party politicans some much needed guidance, supplementing their formal accountability and helping to prevent further delay or sabotage of the process. The suggestion sank without trace.

A similar idea resurfaced, however, in the questions put by the two governments to the negotiating parties in January 1998: 'Might there be a role for ... an all-island consultative forum, bringing together representatives of civil society and the social partners?' (*Irish Times*, 28 January 1998). The answer in the Agreement, Strand 2, implied that at least the question had not gone away:

Consideration to be given to the establishment of an independent
consultative forum appointed by the two Administrations, representative of civil society, comprising the social partners and other members
with expertise in social, cultural, economic and other issues.
(*Agreement*, 1998, p. 13)

Strand I specifies that a similar 'Civic Forum' *will* be established
within Northern Ireland, and perhaps it could now link up with
its Southern 'model', the two together establishing appropriate
cross-border institutional arrangements for making informed
submissions to the North–South Ministerial Council.

These various cross-border vehicles for democracy are not
simply or even necessarily important in and of themselves –
indeed 'civic forums' are open to accusations of being mere
'talking shops' for the powerless and excluded. But the
North–South institutions taken together could be very important
as a focus and catalyst for the development of cross-border social
movements campaigning on a variety of issues. Crucially, this
would begin to consolidate a range of all-Ireland political
communities and create more political room for *non*-nationalist
and non-sectarianised politics based on class, gender and the
many other concerns which straddle the sectarian and territorial
divides.

Class, Gender and Nation
The politics of class are particularly important, not least because
the national conflict is often sharpest in working-class areas. On
the other hand, similarites of class identification are often more
obvious than the differences of national identity, starting with the
fact that in terms of appearance the marks of class are generally
more visible than those of nation. However, the notion that the
concerns of class, or of gender and other identities, are 'alternatives' to the national issue should be rejected.

This mistaken strategy was codified as a Stalinist 'stages
theory' and adopted by 'Official Sinn Fein' in the 1960s and
1970s. Essentially it posited two stages in temporal sequence:
'stage one' – unite nationalist and unionist workers on a purely
class basis, within and accepting existing state borders; 'stage two'
– once they were united – the national question would be raised
and dealt with from a united class position. But politics is not so
neat and simple. There is no such thing as a 'pure' class basis,
certainly not in a society riven with national conflict and religious
sectarianism. The national question cannot be 'side-stepped' or

put off to an unspecified later date. Parties in Northern Ireland attempting to do that, explicitly 'Official' Sinn Fein, implicitly the Northern Ireland Labour Party, either failed to get support or, in the case of the Labour Party, quickly lost support when the national issue came to dominate the political agenda in the late 1960s.

On similar grounds we also need to reject the mirror-image 'stages theory' – or 'stages practice' for it is not always explicitly theorised – of 'nation first, class later'. This has epitomised some of the practice if not the rhetoric of 'Provisional' Sinn Fein, to be expected in a primarily nationalist organisation with a cross-class appeal, even if it did claim to be fighting for an 'all-Ireland socialist republic'. Issues of class, or of gender, cannot be put off to the 'promised land' of a united Ireland, and attempts to do so can be guaranteed to leave many workers and feminists unimpressed.

Conversely, the national problem cannot be solved by simply concentrating on it to the exclusion of other major sources of identity and material interest. These other social forces could help to solve the problem, even if – or because – they do not directly address it or use the language of nationalism. There are real grounds for the different 'identities' making common cause. As Chapters 8 and 12 suggested, the interests of trade unionists and women tend to be marginalised by the 'unfinished business' of national conflict, so they have an interest in seeing that it is 'finished'. But as those chapters also suggested, 'making common cause' is often difficult in practice.

We need, for instance, to beware the rhetoric of 'class' masking the priority of 'nation', whether it is the 'working-class nationalism' of Republicans or Loyalists. For instance, the Loyalist parties, particularly the Progressive Unionist Party (PUP), have talked of class issues perhaps more than the avowedly 'socialist' Sinn Fein, and apparently without much reciprocal response. However, there are doubts about whether they can break with the sectarian politics of unionism (see Chapter 10). Talk of 'class' which gets beyond terms such as 'working-class Loyalist' or 'working-class Republican' is certainly a start, but it is only when Republican and Loyalist workers unite on a class basis to tackle their common problems (as they did all too briefly around unemployment in the 1930s) that their nationalist rivalries will begin to fade.

The development of more widely defined politics will be greatly helped by border-crossing institutional frameworks which can articulate representative and participatory forms of democracy. Working-class and other movements usually have to operate within state-provided frameworks, and in that sense political movements are not alternatives to political institutions but depend on them. In the longer term, cross-border/cross-community developments would stimulate various realignments of politics around other criss-crossing conflicts and disagreements – instead of nationalist versus unionist there would be workers v. employers, or 'west v. east' (perhaps against the east coast Dublin–Belfast 'corridor'), or 'liberals v. conservatives' on 'moral' or religious issues. We can already begin to see the growth of various new cross-border alliances and partnerships, building on the existing linkages that bridge North and South. Trade unionists, for instance, have long had a formal all-Ireland institution, the Irish Congress of Trade Unions, though business has done more in recent years to forge North–South partnerships, and such alliances are being built across a widening range of other issues. The border-straddling development of *non*-nationalist and *non*-unionist politics will aid the escape from the 'dead-end' issue of national sovereignty.

Conclusions

Tensions will always exist between the different bases for political mobilisation, such as class, nation or gender. There will always be problems about the relative weighting to be given to each in particular circumstances. But these are tactical difficulties, not grounds for adopting a general strategy which fixes on any one concern to the exclusion of the others. In national struggles, whatever the leadership, it is usually working-class people, and often working-class women, who bear the brunt of the conflict, a fact well appreciated by United Irishwomen like Mary Ann McCracken (McNeill, 1988). As her brother, the United Irish leader Henry Joy, put it, 'the rich always betray the poor', though he and his sister were 'exceptions which prove the rule'. Present-day Irish people looking for inspiration on issues of nation, class and gender could well start with the Belfast McCrackens. As Protestant Republicans their memory still echoes on both sides of the religious divide despite two centuries of sectarianism.

Today, however, unlike the 1790s, it is now clear that the flaws and failures of nationalism produced a conflict over territorial sovereignty and self-determination which cannot be resolved in terms of the competing nationalisms. These are problems of democracy, and democracy needs to be re-thought.

The preoccupation with majorities within fixed territories, ignoring causes and effects which straddle national and state borders, *is* the problem. In Ireland it can only be resolved by transnational agendas which cross-cut and undercut the nationalistic divides, primarily within the North and between North and South, but also 'east–west' – between Ireland and Britain and the world beyond. Resolving the 'unfinished business' of nationalism would allow relations between Britain and Ireland to finally escape the poisonous legacy of 'coloniser and colonised'.

There is widespread agreement that Northern mindsets must be 'decommissioned', but less awareness that the same applies elsewhere, particularly to the nationalistic 'establishment mindset' in Britain. The Labour Government needs to do more than implement inadequate Tory policies which the Tories themselves were unable or unwilling to carry out. Its constitutional basis for British rule in Northern Ireland, still a simple majority 'no' vote against Irish re-unification, is negative, majoritarian and simplistic. Its implication that when the 'no' vote drops to '50 per cent minus one' all would change – from unionist 'victory' to nationalist 'victory' – is implausable and offers only two choices. It embodies a conception of democracy which is threadbare even in comparison to what is in the Agreement. There is an explicitly territorial claim to 'Northern Ireland in its entirety' (*Agreement*, Annex A), but in Britain's own territorial terms more than half the area actually has nationalist majorities. Labour assumes the same self-serving posture of 'neutrality' while the British state remains the main military force in the territory, and it otherwise avoids or plays down the central issue of redefining sovereignty. This continues to 'bottle-up' if not intensify the conflict within Northern Ireland. It remains a powerful *dis*incentive to genuine settlement negotiations.

Labour should now abandon the 'neutral' posture and negative 'territorialism'. Instead, it should positively match the Republic's new constitutional committment 'to unite all the people who share the territory of the island of Ireland, in all the diversity of their identities and traditions' (*Agreement*, Article 3, Annex B). It should say loud and clear that national sovereignty is the problem not the solution; honestly explain that sovereignty has already seen significant changes; and vigorously continue the changes to their logical conclusion. It needs to demonstrate positive political support for shared sovereignty between North and South across the island.

Irish unionists need to be persuaded that their 'winner-takes-all' form of national sovereignty was a pyrrhic victory in which

they themselves were mostly losers rather than winners. By the
same token, Irish nationalists, who learned their sovereignty
above all from the British, must realise that 'mirror-imaging' your
opponent is not the only or best route to liberation. Battering
away with the frontal assaults of nationalism is very predictable,
and, just as predictably, it simply generates nationalistic opposition which is well practised in rebuffing such assaults.

   With 'globalisation' and transnational integration in the EU,
the time is ripe for non-national realignments. There is a strong
basis for them, and for the necessary North–South bodies, in the
'economic', 'socio-cultural' and 'political democratic' dynamics
of North–South integration. The North–South bodies have
mainly been promoted to give institutional expression to 'parity of
esteem' for Northern nationalists, but they also have other important, independent objectives: countering economic dependency
and the threat of peripheralisation in the Single Market; facilitating the cross-border links of social, cultural and campaigning
groups; and democratising the growing connections between the
two parts of the island. These various forms of North–South integration could marginalise sectarianism and national division by
promoting alignments, alliances and disagreements which have
little or nothing to do with nationalism versus unionism, or North
versus South. To realise this potential, the North–South institutions need substantial executive powers, direct democracy –
representative and participatory – and real engagement with
common concerns. Otherwise, they could simply become new
sites for the same old conflict, rather than arenas for dealing
productively with other, more important, disagreements.

   North–South agendas are starting to offer a practical alternative to the two opposing versions of the flawed nation state ideal.
Transnational politics and border-crossing democracy could
finally deliver the anti-sectarian dream of the United Irishmen.

Notes

Our thanks to Douglas Hamilton for his critical comments on earlier
drafts of this chapter and also Chapter 1.

1. In 1995 David Trimble repeated that North–South institutions
    would be a 'constitutional half-way house', which would only serve
    to encourage nationalists (*Irish Times*, 12 March 1995).
2. One of the Northern Ireland Office officials who worked on the
    North–South aspects of the Framework Documents told us in inter-

view of their surprise at the lack of preparatory work put in place before the 1973 'Sunningdale' Agreement. There had been very little investigation of the options since 1920, though this shortcoming has to some extent been rectified.

3. The main Ulster Unionist Party changed its stated position very substantially in the course of the negotiations but with little preparation of its own supporters. It divided and 'wrong-footed' itself more than its nationalist opponents. For instance, in October 1997, the UUP negotiating submission on Strands 2 and 3 had been just five lines long and simply stated that 'the British Isles are divided into two sovereign states' and that 'in international law there are and ought to be no constitutional issues between these two states' (*Irish Times*, 22 October 1997) – hardly a serious negotiating stance. One consequence of Sinn Fein's unexpected endorsement of the Agreement was that David Trimble's unionists were required to support a settlement involving Sinn Fein participation for which were they totally unprepared. Worse, all their rhetoric and ideology had been about refusing to have anything to do with Sinn Fein, and this turned out to be a preparation tailor-made for anti-Agreement unionists.

4. Support for such speculation can be found in the actions of some of John Major's colleagues during the 1994–96 ceasefire, including influential right-wing British nationalists in the Cabinet's Northern Ireland Committee, such as Michael Howard (in charge of prisons), Michael Portillo (in charge of defence forces), and Viscount Cranbourne (alleged 'leaker' of the Framework Documents to *The Times* which gave them hostile British nationalist treatment). Howard's reluctance to make any concessions to Republican and Loyalist prisoners – despite the fact that they were key players in achieving the 1994 ceasefires, and especially when contrasted with official leniency towards British soldiers convicted of murder – was seen as circumstantial evidence that some elements in the British 'establishment' and the unelected security apparatus wanted a 'final showdown' not a settlement with Irish republicanism. While there has been a change of government, the unelected state apparatus remains the same. Perhaps the first mistake in assessing British strategy is to assume that there is just one single strategy, rather than a number of different strategies which sometimes conflict with one another.

5. Ian Paisley, for instance, insisted that 'all changes in the governance of the Province', including the creation of any institutional structures, should be subject to veto by the Northern (unionist) majority (*Belfast Telegraph*, 13 September 1994). Robert McCartney argued that nationalist demands for 'parity of esteem' had already been met as nationalists had formal equality before the law (*Belfast Telegraph*, 11 May 1995).

6. The Northern Ireland Secretary of State, Sir Patrick Mayhew, in presenting the 'low-profile' Foyle Fisheries Commission as the model

for new North–South institutions, managed simultaneously to belittle such institutions; indicate that one already existed, which was news to many people; and tell unionists that they had nothing to fear from a sharing of sovereignty over narrowly delimited technical matters (*Irish Times*, 1 October 1994; and 15 May 1998). The Commission was established in 1952 by the Dublin and Belfast administrations after a long court case over fishing rights in the Foyle river system which is bisected by the border. With responsibility to protect and control fish stocks, issue fishing licences, collect fees, and prosecute violators of its regulations on both sides of the border, the Commission exercises executive powers on behalf of the two administrations. Shunning publicity, it recently attracted controversy over its undemocratic nature and lack of local accountability.

Bibliography

Adams, G. (1995) *Free Ireland: Towards a Lasting Peace*, rev. edn, first published in 1986 as 'The Politics of Irish Freedom' (Dingle: Brandon).

Agnew, J. (1994) 'The territorial trap: the geographic assumptions of international relations theory', *Review of International Political Economy*, vol. 1, no. 1.

Alcock, A. (1995–6) 'Britain, Northern Ireland and the European Union', *Ulster Review*, no. 18.

Allason, R. (1983) *The Branch, a History of the Metropolitan Police Special Branch 1883–1983* (London: Secker and Warburg).

Althusser, L. (1969) *For Marx* (Harmondsworth: Penguin).

Althusser, L. (1972) 'Ideology and the ideological state apparatus', in *Lenin and Philosophy and other Essays* (London: New Left Books).

Anderson, B. (1991) *Imagined Communities*, rev. edn, 1st edn 1983 (London: Verso).

Anderson, B. (1992) 'The new world disorder', *New Left Review*, no. 193.

Anderson, J. (1980) 'Regions and religions in Ireland: a short critique of the "Two Nations" theory', *Antipode*, vol. 12, no. 2.

Anderson, J. (1986) 'Geography and nationalism', in Anderson, J. (ed.) *The Rise of the Modern State* (Brighton: Wheatsheaf).

Anderson, J. (1989) 'Ideological variations in Ulster during Ireland's First Home Rule Crisis: an analysis of local newspapers', in Williams, C. and Kofman, E. (eds) *Community Conflict, Partition and Nationalism* (London: Routledge).

Anderson, J. (1994) 'Problems of interstate economic integration: Northern Ireland and the Irish Republic in the Single European Market', *Political Geography*, vol. 13, no. 1

Anderson, J. (1995a) 'The exaggerated death of the nation state', in Anderson J. *et al.* (eds).

Anderson, J. (1995b) 'Arrested federalization? Europe, Britain, Ireland', in Smith, G. (ed.) *Federalism: The Multiethnic Challenge* (London: Longman).

Anderson, J. (1996) 'The shifting stage of politics: new medieval and postmodern territorialities?', *Society and Space*, vol. 14, no. 2.

Anderson, J., Brook, C. and Cochrane, A. (eds) (1995) *A Global World? Re-ordering Political Space* (Oxford: Oxford University Press).

Anderson, J. and Goodman, J. (1994) 'Regionalism and nationalism in the EC: the Irish case', *European Urban and Regional Studies*, vol. 1, no. 1.

Anderson, J. and Goodman, J. (1995) 'Regions, states and the European Union: modernist reaction or postmodernist adaptation?', *Review of International Political Economy*, vol. 2, no. 4.

Anderson, J. and Goodman, J. (1996) 'Border crossings', *Fortnight*, vol. 350.

Anderson, J. and Goodman, J. (1996a) 'North–South institutions do not mean London–Dublin rule', *Belfast Telegraph*, March 4.

Anderson, J. and Goodman, J. (1997a) 'Problems of North–South economic integration in Ireland: Southern perspectives', *Irish Journal of Sociology*, vol. 7.

Anderson, J. and Goodman, J. (1997b) *North–South Integration in Ireland: The rocky road to prosperity and peace*, Submission to the Forum for Peace and Reconciliation, Dublin.

Anderson, J. and Hamilton, D. (1995) 'Why Dublin could afford unity', *Parliamentary Brief* (Spring).

Anderson, J. and Hamilton, D. (1998) 'Border crossings', *Fortnight*, vol. 369, March–April.

Anderson, J. and Shuttleworth, I. (1994) 'Sectarian readings of sectarianism: interpreting the Northern Ireland Census', *The Irish Review*, vol. 16.

Anderson, J. and Shuttleworth, I. (1998) 'Sectarian demography, territoriality and political development in Northern Ireland', *Political Geography*, vol. 17, no. 2.

Anthias, F. and Yuval Davis, N. (1983) 'Contextualizing feminism – gender, ethnic and class divisions', *Feminist Review*, vol. 15.

Anthias, F. and Yuval Davis, N. (1992) *Racialised Boundaries* (London: Routledge).

Aughey, A. (1994) 'Conservative party politics in Northern Ireland', in Barton, B. and Roche, P. (eds) *The Northern Ireland Question: Perspectives and Policies* (Aldershot: Avebury).

Aughey, A. (1995) 'The end of history, the end of the union', in Aughey A. *et al.*, *Selling Unionism* (Belfast: Ulster Young Unionist Council).

Bairoch, P. and Levy-Lebeyer, M. (eds) (1981) *Disparities in Economic Development since the Industrial Revolution* (London: Macmillan).

Balakrishnan, G. (ed.) (1996) *Mapping the Nation* (London: Verso).

Barton, B. and Roche, P. (eds) (1991) *The Northern Ireland Question: Myth and Reality* (Aldershot: Avebury).

Belfrage, S. (1987) *The Crack: A Belfast Year* (London: Grafton Books).

Bell, C. and Fox, M. (1996) 'Telling stories of women who kill', *Social and Legal Studies*, vol. 5, no. 4.

Benton, S. (1995) 'Women disarmed: the militarization of politics in Ireland 1913–23', *Feminist Review*, vol. 50.

Beresford Ellis, P. (1985) *A History of the Irish Working Class* (London: Pluto Press).

Beresford Ellis, P. (1988) *James Connolly, Selected Writings* (London: Pluto Press).

Bevins, A. (1996) 'The Lion and the Eunuch', *Observer*, 28 April.

Bew, P. (1996) 'A nation proud, free and dull', *Spectator*, 24 August.

Billig, M. (1995) *Banal Nationalism* (London: Sage).

Bishop, P. and Mallie, E. (1987) *The Provisional IRA* (London: Corgi).

Blaut, J. (1987) *The National Question*, second edition (London: Zed).

Bowman, J. (1989) *De Valera and the Ulster Question* (Oxford: Oxford University Press).

Boyce, D. (1995) *Nationalism in Ireland* (London: Routledge).

Boyer-Bell, J. (1979) *A History of the IRA 1916–1979* (Dublin: Academic Press).

Boyer-Bell, J. (1990) *The Secret Army: The IRA 1916–1979* (Dublin: Poolbeg Press).

Bradley J. (1996) *An Island Economy: Exploring the Long-term Economic and Social Consequences of Peace and Reconciliation in the Island of Ireland* (Dublin: Forum for Peace and Reconciliation).

Brady, C. and Gillespie, R. (eds) (1986) *Natives and Newcomers: Essays on the Making of Irish Colonial Society 1534–1641* (Dublin: Irish Academic Press).

Brewer, J. and Magee, K. (1991) *Inside the RUC: Routine Policing in a Divided Society* (Oxford: Clarendon Press).

Brown, C. (1992) *International Relations Theory: New Normative Approaches* (Brighton: Harvester).

Bruce, S. (1992) *The Red Hand: Protestant Paramilitaries in Northern Ireland* (Oxford: Oxford University Press).

Bruce, S. (1994) *The Edge of the Union* (Oxford: Oxford University Press).

Burnside, D. (1995) 'A positive unionism in Great Britain', in Aughey, A. *et al.*, *Selling Unionism* (Belfast: Ulster Young Unionist Council).

Burton, F. (1978) *The Politics of Legitimacy: Struggles in a Belfast Community* (London: Routledge).

Caherty, T., Storey, A., Gavin, M., Molloy, M. and Ruane, C. (eds) (1992) *Is Ireland a Third World Country?* (Belfast: Beyond the Pale).

CAJ (Committee for the Administration of Justice) (1995) *Human Rights: The Agenda for Change* (Belfast: CAJ).

CAJ (Committee for the Administration of Justice) (1996) *The Misrule of Law: A Report on the Policing of Events During the Summer of 1996 in Northern Ireland* (Belfast: CAJ).

Campbell, B. (1992), 'Voices from the edge', *An Glor Gafa*, vol. 4, no.1.

Campbell, G. (n.d.) *Ulster's Verdict on the Joint Declaration*, n.p.

Centre for Research and Documentation (1994a) *Prisoners and Prisoners' Rights*, Factsheet no.1 (Belfast: CRD).

Centre for Research and Documentation (1994b) *Emigration*, Factsheet no. 2 (Belfast: CRD).

Chomsky, N. (1988) *The Culture of Terrorism* (London: Pluto Press).

Chomsky, N. (1992) *Deterring Democracy* (London: Vintage).

Clarke, L. (1987) *Broadening the Battlefield: The H-Blocks and the Rise of Sinn Fein* (Dublin: Gill and Macmillan).

Clár na mBan (1995) *A Women's Agenda for Peace* (Belfast: Clár na mBan).

Clár Nua (1995) *A Policy Framework for Reconstruction in West Belfast* (Belfast: Clár Nua).

Clayton, P. (1996) *Enemies and Passing Friends* (London: Pluto Press).

Coakley, J. (1983) 'The European dimension of Irish public opinion 1972–83', in Coobes, D. (ed.) *Ireland and the European Communities* (Dublin: Gill and Macmillan).

Colley, L. (1992) *Britons: Forging the Nation 1707–1837* (New Haven: Yale University Press).

Connolly, C. (1995) 'Ourselves Alone? Clár na mBan Conference Report', *Feminist Review*, vol. 50.

Connolly, J. (1997) *Beyond the Politics of 'Law and Order': Towards Community Policing in Ireland* (Belfast: CRD).

Coogan, T. (1980) *The IRA* (Glasgow: Gollanz).

Coogan, T. (1993) *De Valera* (London: Hutchinson).

Coogan, T. (1995) *The Troubles: Ireland's Ordeal 1966–95 and the Search for Peace* (London: Hutchinson).

Corradi, J. (1992) 'Introduction', In Corradi, J., Fagan, P. and Garreton, M. (eds) *Fear at the Edge* (Berkely: University of California Press).

Coughlan, A. (1992) 'Northern Ireland: conflicts of sovereignty', *Studies*, vol. 81, no. 322.

Coulter, C. (1990) *Ireland between First and Third Worlds* (Dublin: Attic Press).

Coulter, C. (1994) 'The character of unionism', *Irish Political Studies*, vol. 9.

Cronin, S. (1980) *Irish Nationalism: A History of its Roots and Ideology* (Dublin: Academy Press).

Cumings, B. (1987) 'The origin and development of the northeast Asian political economy', in Deyo, F. (ed.) *The Political Economy of the New Asian Industrialism* (Ithaca: Cornell).

Curtis, L. (1991) *Nothing but the Same Old Story: The Roots of Anti-Irish Racism* (London: Information on Ireland).

Cusack, J. and McDonald, H. (1997) *UVF* (Dublin: Poolbeg Press).

Davies, C., Heaton, N., Robinson, G. and McWilliams, M. (1995) *A Matter of Small Importance? Catholic and Protestant Women in the Northern Ireland Labour Market* (Belfast: EOCNI).

Davies, N. (1996) *Europe: a History* (Oxford: Oxford University Press).

Dickson, D., Keogh, D. and Whelan, K. (eds) (1993) *The United Irishmen: Republicanism, Radicalism and Rebellion* (Dublin: Lilliput Press).

Dillon, M. (1991) *The Dirty War* (London: Arrow Books).

Donoghue, D. (1993) 'Territorial claims and Ireland in a European context', in Skar, H. and Lydersen, B. (eds) *Northern Ireland: A Crucial Test for a Europe of Peaceful Regions?* (Oslo: Norwegian Institute of International Affairs).

Douglas, N. (1998) 'The politics of accommodation: social change and conflict resolution in Northern Ireland', *Political Geography*, vol. 17, no. 2.

DSO (Dublin Stationery Office) (1992) *Ireland in Europe, A Shared Challenge, Economic Cooperation on the Island of Ireland in an Integrated Europe* (Dublin: DSO).

Dunn, S. (1995) 'The conflict as a set of problems', in Dunn, S. (ed.) *Facets of the Conflict in Northern Ireland* (London: St Martin's Press).

Dunn, S. and Morgan, V. (1994) *Protestant Alienation in Northern Ireland: A Preliminary Survey,* Centre for the Study of Conflict (Belfast: University of Ulster).

Edge, S. (1995) 'Women are trouble, did you know that Fergus?: Neil Jordan's "The Crying Game"', *Feminist Review,* vol. 50.

Edgerton, L. (1986) 'Public protest, domestic acquiescence: women in Northern Ireland', in Ridd, R. and Calloway, H. (eds) *Caught up in Conflict: Women's Responses* (London: Macmillan).

EHSS (Eastern Health and Social Services Board) (1991) *Equal Opportunities Monitoring Report* (Belfast: Equal Opportunities Unit).

Eide, A. (1996) *A Review and Analysis of Constructive Approaches to Group Accomodation and Minority Protection in Divided or Multicultural Societies,* Consultancy Studies, no. 3 (Dublin: Forum for Peace and Reconciliation).

English, R. (1994) 'Cultural traditions and political ambiguity', *The Irish Review,* vol. 15.

English, R. (1995) 'Unionism and nationalism: the notion of symmetry', in Foster, J. (ed.) *The Idea of the Union; Statements and Critiques in Support of the Union of Great Britain and Northern Ireland* (Vancouver: Belcouver Press).

English, R. and Walker, G. (1996) *Unionism in Modern Ireland: New Perspectives on Politics and Culture* (Dublin: Gill and Macmillan).

EOCNI (Equal Opportunities Commission for Northern Ireland) (1993) *Where do Women Figure?* (Belfast: EOCNI).

EOCNI (Equal Opportunities Commission for Northern Ireland) (1995) *Men and Women in Northern Ireland* (Belfast: EOCNI).

Evason, E. (1982) *Hidden Violence* (Belfast: Fastnet).

Evason, E. (1991) *Against the Grain: The Contemporary Women's Movement in Northern Ireland* (Dublin: Attic Press).

Fairweather, E., McDonough, R. and McFadyean, M. (1984) *Only the Rivers Run Free: Northern Ireland: The Women's War* (London: Pluto Press).

Falk R. (1995) *On Humane Governance: Towards a New Global Politics – A Report of the World Order Models Project* (Cambridge: Polity Press).

Farrell, M. (1980) *The Orange State* (London: Pluto).

FEA (Fair Employment Agency) (1986) *Report on Employment in the Southern Health and Social Services Board* (Belfast: FEC).

FEC (Fair Employment Commission) (1995) *A Profile of the Northern Ireland Workforce: Summary of the Monitoring Returns, 1994,* Research Report 5 (Belfast: FEC).

Feldman, A. (1991) *Formations of Violence. The Narrative of the Body and Political Terror in Northern Ireland* (Chicago: University of Chicago Press).

Fisher, C. (ed.) (1995) *Policing in a New Society* (Belfast: Centre for Research and Documentation and the Belfast Community Forum on Policing).

Fisk, R. (1975) *The Point of No Return* (London: Andre Deutsch).

Foster, J. (ed.) (1995) *The Idea of the Union; Statements and Critiques in Support of the Union of Great Britain and Northern Ireland* (Vancouver: Belcouver Press).

Foster, R. (1993) 'Anglo–Irish relations and Northern Ireland: historical perspectives', in Keogh, D. and Haltgel, M. (eds) *Northern Ireland and the Politics of Reconciliation* (Cambridge: Cambridge University Press).

Foucault, M. (1979) *Discipline and Punish* (Harmondsworth: Penguin).

Foucault, M. (1985) *History of Sexuality* (Harmondsworth: Penguin).

FPR (Forum for Peace and Reconciliation) (1995) *Paths to a Political Settlement in Ireland,* policy papers submitted to the FPR (Belfast: Blackstaff).

Frank, Andre G. (1969) *Latin America: Underdevelopment or Revolution* (New York: Monthly Review).

Frobel, F., Heinrichs, J. and Kreye, O. (1980) *The New International Division of Labor* (New York: Cambridge University Press).

Furedi, F. (1994) *The New Imperialism* (London: Pluto Press).

Gill, S. and Law, D. (1989) 'Global hegemony and structural power of capital', *International Studies Quarterly*, vol. 33.

Gillespie, P. (1996) 'Britain in Europe: the politics of identification' in Gillespie, P. (ed.) *Britain's European Question: The Issues for Ireland* (Dublin: Institute of European Affairs).

Goldring, M. (1982) *Faith of Our Fathers: The Formation of Irish Nationalist Ideology* (Dublin: Repsol).

Goodman, J. (1996) *Nationalism and Transnationalism: The National Conflict in Ireland and European Union Integration* (Aldershot: Avebury).

Goodman, J. (1997) 'The EU: reconstituting democracy beyond the nation-state', in McGrew, A. (ed.) *The Transformation of Democracy? Democratic Politics in the New World Order* (Cambridge: Polity Press).

Gordon, H. (1990) 'Women, Protestantism and Unionism', in *Women in Ireland in the 1990s,* Report of conference organised by the Workers Educational Association Women Studies Branch, October 1991 (Belfast: WEA).

Gormally, B. and McEvoy, K. (1995) *The Early Release of Politically Motivated Prisoners: Learning from the International Experience* (Belfast: NIACRO).

Greenslade, R. (1996) 'True blue press turns orange', *Observer*, 19 May.

Gudgin, G. (1995) 'Northern Ireland after the ceasefire', *Irish Banking Review* (Autumn).

Hachey, T. (1989) 'Irish nationalism and the British connection', in Hachey, T. and McCaffrey, J. (eds) *Perspectives on Irish Nationalism* (Lexington: University Press of Kentucky).

Hackett, C. (1995) 'Self-determination: the republican feminist agenda', *Feminist Review*, vol. 50.

Hall, M. (1994) *Ulster's Protestant Working Class: A Community Exploration* (Belfast: Island Pamphlets).

Hall, M. (1995) *Beyond the Fife and Drum* (Belfast: Island Pamphlets).

Hamilton, D. (1992) *Inward Investment in Northern Ireland*, NIEC Report 99 (Belfast: NIEC).

Hazelkorn, E. and Patterson, H. (1994) 'The new politics of the Irish Republic', *New Left Review*, no. 207.

Heathorn, S. (1996) '(Re)discovering the national character: some recent work on the history of English nationalism and its influence on the construction of British national identity', *Canadian Review of Studies in Nationalism*, vol. 23, no. 1–2.

Hedetoft, U. (1996–7) 'Sovereignty and European integration: a Scandanavian perspective', *The Association for the Study of Ethnicity and Nationalism Bulletin*, no. 12.

Held, D. (1995) *Democracy and the Global Order: From the Modern State to Cosmopolitan Governance* (Cambridge: Polity Press).

Herz, F. (1986) 'The Republic of Ireland', in Girvin, B. and Sturm, R. (eds) *Politics and Society in Contemporary Ireland* (Aldershot: Gower).

Hickman, M. (1990) *Ireland in the European Community*, European Dossier Series (London: Polytechnic of North London Press).

Hirsch, J. (1995) 'Nation-state, international regulation and the question of democracy', *Review of International Political Economy*, vol. 2, no. 2.

HMSO (1972) *The Future of Northern Ireland: A Paper for Discussion* (Belfast: EOCNI).

HMSO (1995) *Frameworks for the Future*, A new framework for agreement: A shared understanding between the British and

Irish Governments to assist discussion and negotiation involving the Northern Ireland parties, February 1995 (Belfast: EOCNI).

Hobsbawm, E. (1996) 'Identity politics and the Left', *New Left Review*, no. 217.

Hogan, G. and Walker, C. (1989) *Political Violence and the Law in Ireland* (Manchester: Manchester University Press).

Holland, J. and McDonald, H. (1994) *INLA: Deadly Divisions* (Dublin: Torc).

Howe, L. (1990) *Being Unemployed in Northern Ireland* (London: Routledge).

Hyndman, M. (1996) *Further Afield: Journeys from a Protestant Past* (Belfast: Beyond the Pale).

Isles, K.S. and Cuthbert, N. (1957) *An Economic Survey of Northern Ireland* (Belfast: HMSO).

Jarman, N. (1997) *Material Conflicts: Parades and Visual Displays in Northern Ireland* (Oxford: Berg).

Kearney, R. (1988) *Across the Frontiers: Ireland in the 1990s* (Dublin: Wolfhound).

Kearney, R. (1997) *Postnationalist Ireland, Politics, Culture, Philosophy* (London: Routledge).

Kee, R. (1982) *The Green Flag: A Trilogy* (London: Quartet Books).

Kennedy, D. (1995) 'The realism of the union', in Foster J. (ed.) *The Idea of the Union; Statements and Critiques in Support of the Union of Great Britain and Northern Ireland* (Vancouver: Belcouver Press).

Kennedy, K. (1988) *The Economic Development of Ireland in the Twentieth Century* (London: Routledge).

Kennedy, L. (1996) *Colonialism, Religion and Nationalism in Ireland* (Belfast: Queen's University Press).

Keogh, D. and Haltzel, M. (1993) *Northern Ireland and the Politics of Reconciliation* (Washington: Woodrow Wilson Center Press and Cambridge University Press).

Kiberd, D. (1997) 'From nationalism to liberation', in Sailer, S. (ed.) *Representing Ireland: Gender, Class and Nationality* (Miami: University Press of Florida).

Kilmurray, A. and McWilliams, M. (1997) 'Athene on the loose: the origins of the Northern Ireland Women's Coalition', *Irish Journal of Feminist Studies*, vol. 2. no. 1.

Lechner, N. (1992) 'Some people die of fear: fear as a political problem', in Corradi, J., Fagan, P. and Garreton, M. (eds) *Fear at the Edge* (Berkley: University of California Press).

Lecky, W. (1892) *A History of Ireland in the Eighteenth Century* (London: Longmans, Green and Co.).

Lee, J. (1989) *Ireland, 1912–1985* (Cambridge: Cambridge University Press).

Lee, J. (1998) 'Why the English make the very worst kind of nationalists', *Sunday Tribune,* 12 April.

Lijphart, A. (1983) 'Consociation: the model and its applications in divided societies', in Rea, D. (ed.) *Political Co-operation in Divided Societies: Papers Relevant to the Conflict in Northern Ireland* (Dublin: Gill and Macmillan).

Livingstone, S. and Morison, J. (1996) *Re-shaping Public Power* (London: Sweet & Maxwell).

Lloyd, J. (1997) 'Adams has no business in No. 10', *The Times,* 12 December.

Longley, E. (1990) *From Cathleen to Anorexia* (Dublin: Attic Press).

Loughlin, J. (1995) *Ulster Unionism and British Identity since 1885* (London: Pinter).

Lourde, A. (1984) *Sister Outsider: Essays and Speeches* (California: The Crossing Press).

Lucey, G. (1994) *Northern Ireland Local Government Election Results 1993* (Belfast: Ulster Society).

Lyne, T. (1990) 'Ireland, Northern Ireland and 1992: the barriers to technocratic partitionism', *Administration,* no. 68.

Lyons, F. (1979) *Ireland since the Famine* (Fontana: London).

MacDonald, E. (1991) *Shoot the Women First* (London: Fourth Estate).

MacKinnon, C. (1987) *Feminism Unmodified: Discourses on Life and Law* (Boston: Harvard University Press).

McAuley, J. (1991) 'The Protestant working class and the state in Northern Ireland since 1930: a problematic relationship', in Hutton, S. and Stewart, P. (eds) *Ireland's Histories* (London: Routledge).

McAuley, J. (1994) *The Politics of Identity: A Loyalist Community in Belfast* (Aldershot: Avebury).

McAuley, J. (1995) '"Not a Game of Cowboys and Indians" – the Ulster Defence Association in the 1990s', in O'Day, A. (ed.) *Terrorism's Laboratory: The Case of Northern Ireland* (Aldershot: Dartmouth).

McAuley, J. (1996) 'From loyal soldiers to political spokespersons: a political history of a loyalist paramilitary group in Northern Ireland', *Études Irlandaises,* vol. 21, no. 1.

McBride, I. (1996) 'Ulster and the British problem', in English, R. and Walker, G. (eds) *Unionism in Modern Ireland: New Perspectives on Politics and Culture* (London: Macmillan).

McCafferty, N. (1981) *The Armagh Women* (Dublin: Co-op Books).

McCann, E. (1995) 'Managing sectarianism', *New Statesman and Society*, 25 August.

McClelland, M. and Dowd, C. (1992), 'British strategy in Ireland: imperialist plan or crisis management', *Starry Plough*, vol. 2, no. 1.

McDonnell, M. (1996) 'Women and peace in Northern Ireland 1990–1996', in Lentin, R. (ed.) *In From the Shadows: Vol. II. The UL Women's Studies Collection* (Limerick: University of Limerick).

McGarry, J. and O'Leary, B. (1990) *The Future of Northern Ireland* (London: Clarendon).

McGarry, J. and O'Leary, B. (1995) *Explaining Northern Ireland* (London: Blackwell).

McGrew A. (1995) 'World order and political space', in Anderson J. *et al.* (eds).

McIntyre, A. (1995), 'Modern Irish republicanism: the product of British state strategies', *Irish Political Studies*, no. 10.

McKittrick, D. (1994) *Endgame: The Search for Peace in Northern Ireland* (Belfast: Blackstaff Press).

McLaughlin, E. (1986) 'Maiden city blues', unpublished PhD thesis (Belfast: Queen's University of Belfast).

McLaughlin, E. and Ingram, K. (1991) *All Stitched Up: Sex Segregation in the Northern Ireland Clothing Industry* (Belfast: Equal Opportunities Commission of northern Ireland).

McNeill, M. (1988) *The Life and Times of Mary Ann McCracken 1770–1866* (Belfast: Blackstaff Press).

McThomas, H. (1992), 'What are the British doing in Ireland?', *Starry Plough*, vol. 2, no. 1.

McVeigh, R. (1994a) 'The politics of violence', *Peace Review*, vol. 6, no. 1.

McVeigh, R. (1994b) *Harassment: It's Part of Life Here* (Belfast: CAJ).

McVeigh, R. (1995) 'Cherishing the children of the nation unequally: sectarianism in Ireland', in Clancy, P., Drudy, S., Lynch, K. and O'Dowd, L. (eds) *Irish Society: Sociological Perspectives* (Dublin: IPA).

McVeigh, R. (1997) 'Symmetry and asymmetry in sectarian identity and division', *CRC Journal*, no. 16.

McWilliams, M. (1991) 'Women in Northern Ireland: an overview', in Hughes, E. (ed.) *Culture and Politics in Northern Ireland* (Milton Keynes: Open University Press).

McWilliams, M. (1993) 'The Church, the state and the women's movement in Northern Ireland', in Smyth, A. (ed.) *Irish Women's Studies Reader* (Dublin: Attic Press).

McWilliams, M. (1994) 'The woman "Other"', *Fortnight,* no. 328.

McWilliams, M. (1997) 'Violence against women and political conflict: the Northern Ireland experience', *Critical Criminology: An International Journal,* vol. 8, no. 1.

McWilliams, M. and McKiernan, J. (1993) *Bringing it Out in the Open: Domestic Violence in Northern Ireland* (Belfast: HMSO).

Madden, S. (1994) 'Self-determination, the joint declaration and women's participation', *An Camcheachta* (The Starry Plough).

Mallie, E. and Bishop, P. (1987) *The Provisional IRA* (London: Heinemann).

Mallie, E. and McKittrick, D. (1996) *The Fight for Peace. The Secret Story Behind the Peace Process* (London: Heinemann).

Mansergh, M. (1995) *No Selfish Strategic or Economic Interest?: The Path to an All-Island Economy* (Belfast: West Belfast Economic Forum).

Mansergh, M. (1996a) 'The future path of peace', *Irish Reporter,* no. 21.

Mansergh, M. (1996b) *Consent, veto and self-determination,* address to the Campaign for Democracy (Belfast: CfD).

Mansergh, N. (1981) 'The influence of the past', in Watts, D. (ed.) *The Constitution of Northern Ireland,* National Institute of Economic and Social Affairs, Studies in Public Policy, 4 (London: Heinemann).

Martin, F. and Moody, T. (1967) *The Course of Irish History* (London: Mercier Press).

Millar, D. (1978) *Queen's Rebels: Ulster Loyalism in Historical Perspective* (Dublin: Gill and Macmillan).

Millar, F. (1996) 'Tories get excited about "the Union" but without having the North in mind', *Irish Times,* 9 October.

Mjoset, L. (1993) *The Irish Economy in a Comparative Institutional Perspective* (Dublin: National Economic and Social Council).

Moore, C. (1995) 'How to be British?', *Spectator,* 21 October.

Moore, R. (1996) *Public Discussions on Aspects of Sectarian Division in Derry/Londonderry* (Derry/Londonderry: Templegrove Action Research).

Morgan, V. (1992) 'Bridging the divide: women and political and community issues', in Stringer, P. and Robinson, G. (eds) *Social Attitudes in Northern Ireland, 1991–2* (Belfast: Blackstaff).

Morgan, V. and Fraser, G. (1994) *The Company We Keep* (Belfast: University of Ulster).

Morgan, V. and Fraser, G. (1995) 'Women and the Northern Ireland conflict: experiences and responses', in Dunn, S. (ed.) *Facets of the Conflict in Northern Ireland* (London: St Martin's Press).

Morrow, D. (1995) 'The conflict as a set of problems', in Dunn S. (ed.) *Facets of the Conflict in Northern Ireland* (London: St Martin's Press).

Morrow, D., Birrell, D., Greer, J. and O'Keefe, T. (1994) *The Church and Inter Community Relations*, Centre for Study of Conflict (Belfast: University of Ulster).

Munck, R. (1993) *The Irish Economy: Results and Prospects* (London: Pluto).

Munck, R. and De Silva, P. (eds) (1998) *Postmodern Insurgencies: Political Violence, Identity Formation and Peace-making in Comparative Perspective* (London: Macmillan).

Murphy, R. (1997) *Ireland, Peacekeeping and Policing the New World Order* (Belfast: CRD).

Murray, D. (1985) *Worlds Apart: Segregated Schools in Northern Ireland* (Belfast: Appletree Press).

Murray, D. (1995) 'Culture, religion and violence in Northern Ireland', in Dunn, S. (ed.) *Facets of the Conflict in Northern Ireland* (London: St Martin's Press).

Murray, D. and O'Neill, J. (1991) *Peace Building in a Political Impasse: Cross Border Links in Ireland* (Coleraine: University of Ulster Centre for the Study of Conflict).

Murray, M. (1990) *The SAS in Ireland* (London: Mercier Press).

Nairn T. (1977) *The Break-up of Britain: Crisis and Neo-nationalism* (London: New Left Books).

Nairn, T. (1988) *The Enchanted Glass: Britain and its Monarchy* (London: Radius).

Nelson, S. (1984) *Ulster's Uncertain Defenders* (Belfast: Appletree).

NESF (National and Economic Social Forum) (1995) *First Periodic Report of the National Social and Economic Forum* (Dublin: DSO).

NIEC (Northern Ireland Economic Council) (1983) *The Duration of Industrial Development Assisted Employment*, Report no. 40 (Belfast: NIEC).

NIF (New Ireland Forum) (1984) *Final Report* (Dublin DSO).

Northern Ireland Council for Voluntary Action (1993) *Twenty Years of Deprivation: A Comparative Analysis of Deprivation in the Belfast Urban Area*, Briefing Paper 1, (Belfast: NICVA).

O'Brien, B. (1993) *The Long War. The IRA and Sinn Fein from Armed Struggle to Peace Talks* (Dublin: O'Brien Press).

O'Connor, F. (1993) *In Search of a State: Catholics in Northern Ireland* (Belfast: Blackstaff Press).

O'Dowd, L. (1981) 'Shaping and reshaping the Orange state', in *Northern Ireland, Between Civil Rights and Civil War* (London: CSE Books).

O'Dowd, L. (1990) 'The limits of decolonization', Introduction to Memmi, A., *The Colonizer and the Colonized* (London: Earthscan).

O'Dowd, L. (1994) *Whither the Irish Border? Sovereignty, Democracy and Economic Integration* (Belfast: CRD).

O'Dowd, L. (1998a) '"New Unionism", British nationalism and the prospects for a negotiated settlement in Northern Ireland', in D. Miller (ed.) *Rethinking Northern Ireland* (London: Longman).

O'Dowd, L. (1998b) *Negotiating State Borders: A New Sociology for a New Europe?* Inaugural Lecture at Queen's University, Belfast, March.

OECD (Organisation for Economic Cooperation and Development) (1985) *Ireland, Economic Survey* (Paris: OECD).

O'Hearn, D. (1989) 'The Irish case of dependency: an exception to the exceptions?', *American Sociological Review*, vol. 54, no. 4.

O'Hearn, D. (1990) 'The road from import-substitution to export-led industrialization in Ireland: who mixed the asphalt, who drove the machinery, and who kept making them change directions', *Politics and Society*, March.

O'Hearn, D. (1994) *Free Trade or Managed Trade: Trading Between Two Worlds* (Belfast: CRD).

O'Hearn, D. (1997) 'Irish linen in the changing world-system', in Cohen, M. (ed.), *The Warp of Ulster's Past: Interdisciplinary Perspectives on the Irish Linen Industry, 1700–1914* (New York: St Martin's Press).

O'Hearn, D. (1998) *Inside the Celtic Tiger: Reality and Illusion in the Irish Economy* (London: Pluto Press).

O'Leary, B., Lyne, T., Marshall, J. and Rowthorn, B. (1993) *Northern Ireland: Sharing Authority* (London: Institute for Public Policy Research).

O'Leary, B. and McGarry, J. (1993) *The Politics of Antagonism: Understanding Northern Ireland* (London: Athlone).

O'Malley, P. (1990) *Biting at the Grave: The Irish Hunger Strikes and the Politics of Despair* (Belfast: Blackstaff).

Paisley, R. (1992) 'Feminism, unionism and "the brotherhood"', *Irish Reporter*, no. 8.

Pat Finucane Centre (1995) *One Day in August* (Derry: PFC).

Patterson, H. (1989) *The Politics of Illusion. Republicanism and Socialism in Modern Ireland* (London: Hutchinson Radius).

Percival, R. (1996) 'Towards a grassroots peace process', *Irish Reporter*, no. 22.

Phoenix, E. (1994) *Northern Nationalism 1890–1940* (Belfast: Blackstaff).

Pollak, A. (1993) *A Citizens' Inquiry: The Opsahl Report on Northern Ireland* (Dublin: Initiative '92 and Lilliput Press).

Porter, N. (1996) *Rethinking Unionism: An Alternative Vision for Northern Ireland* (Belfast: Blackstaff Press).

Price, J. (1995) 'Political change and the Protestant working class', *Race and Class*, vol. 37, no. 1.

Quigley, G. (1992) 'Ireland – An Island Economy', Speech to the Confederation of Irish Industry, 11 February.

Radford, J. and Russell, D. (eds) (1992) *Femicide: The Politics of Women Killing* (Buckingham: Open University Press).

Ridd, R. (1986) 'Powers of the powerless', in Ridd, R. and Callanan, H. (eds) *Caught Up in Conflict: Women's Responses* (London: Macmillan).

Robinson, P. (1995) *The Union Under Fire: United Ireland Framework Revealed* (Belfast: published by the author).

Roche, P. and Birnie, E. (1995) *An Economics Lesson for Irish Nationalists and Republicans* (Belfast: Ulster Unionist Information Institute).

Roche, P. and Birnie, E. (1996) 'Irish nationalism: politics of the absurd', *Unionist Review*, no. 20.

Rooney, E. (1996) *Power, Politics, Positionings: Women in Northern Ireland* (Belfast: Democratic Dialogue).

Rooney, E. and Woods, M. (1995) *Women, Community and Politics in Northern Ireland: A Belfast Study* (Belfast: University of Ulster).

Rosenberg, J. (1994) *The Empire of Civil Society* (London: Verso).

Roulston, C. (1989) 'Women on the margin: the women's movement in Northern Ireland, 1973–1988', *Science & Society* vol. 53, no. 2.

Rowthorn, B. (1981) 'Northern Ireland: an economy in crisis', *Cambridge Journal of Economics*, vol. 5, no. 1.

Rowthorn, B. (1987) 'The Northern Ireland economy in crisis', in Teague, P. (ed.) *Beyond the Rhetoric* (London: Lawrence and Wishart).

Rowthorn, B. and Wayne, N. (1988) *Northern Ireland: The Political Economy of Conflict* (Cambridge: Polity).

RP (1996) 'Towards a grassroots peace process', *Common Ground,* vol. 3, no. 1.

Ruane, J. and Todd, J. (1996) *The Dynamics of Conflict in Northern Ireland: Power, Conflict and Emancipation,* (Cambridge: Cambridge University Press).

Ryan, M. (1994) *War and Peace in Ireland. Britain and the IRA in the New World Order* (London: Pluto).

Ryder, C. (1991) *The Ulster Defence Regiment: An Instrument of Peace?* (London: Methuen).

Said, E. (1985) *Orientalism* (Harmondsworth: Penguin).

Said, E. (1997) *Covering Islam: How the Media and the Experts Determine How We See the Rest of the World* (London: Vintage).

Sales, R. (1993) The Limits of Modernisation: Religious and Gender Inequality in Northern Ireland (London: Unpublished PhD thesis, Middlesex University).

Sales, R. (1997a) *Women Divided: Gender, Religion and Politics in Northern Ireland* (London: Routledge).

Sales, R. (1997b) 'Gender and Protestantism in Northern Ireland', in Shirlow, P. and McGovern, M. (eds) *Who are 'The People?':* Unionism, Protestantism and Loyalism in Northern Ireland (London: Pluto Press).

Shankill Think Tank (1995) *A New Beginning,* Island Pamphlet 13, (Belfast: Island Publications).

Shirlow, P. and McGovern, M. (1995) 'Counter-Insurgency, De-Industrialisation and the Political Economy of Ulster Loyalism', paper presented to conference on 'Protestantism and Identity', Queen's University Belfast, February.

Shirlow, P. and McGovern, M. (eds) (1997) *Who are 'The People'?: Unionism, Protestantism and Loyalism in Northern Ireland* (London: Pluto Press).

Sieghart, P. (1983) *The International Law of Human Rights* (Oxford: Clarendon Press).

Sinn Fein (1986) *The Politics of Revolution* (Dublin: Sinn Fein).

Sinn Fein (1987) *Scenario for Peace* (Dublin: Sinn Fein).

Sinn Fein (1992) *Towards a Lasting Peace in Ireland* (Dublin: Sinn Fein).

Sinn Fein Women's Department (1994) *Women in Struggle* (Dublin: Sinn Fein).

Smith, A. (1981) *The Ethnic Revival in the Modern World* (Cambridge: Cambridge University Press).

Smith, M. (1995) *Fighting for Ireland? The Military Strategy of the Irish Republican Movement* (London: Routledge).

Smout, T. (1980) 'Scotland and England: is dependency a symptom or a cause of underdevelopment?', *Review*, vol. 3, no. 4.

Stevenson, J. (1996) *We Wrecked the Place: Contemplating an End to the Northern Irish Troubles* (New York: The Free Press).

Sugden, J. and Baines, A. (1993) *Sport, Sectarianism and Society in a Divided Ireland* (Leicester: Leicester University Press).

Taillon, R, McKiernan, J. and Davies, C. (1992) *Who Cares? Childcare and Women's Lives in the Shankill Today* (Belfast: University of Ulster).

Taylor, P. (1991) 'The English and their Englishness: "a curiously mysterious, elusive and little understood people"', *Scottish Geographical Magazine*, vol. 107, no. 3.

Taylor, R. (1994) 'A consociational path to peace in Northern Ireland and South Africa?', in Guelke, A. (ed.) *New Perspectives on the Northern Ireland Problem* (Aldershot: Avebury).

The Times (1997) 'On democracy's steps: Blair welcomes Adams to Downing Street' (Editorial), 11 December.

Todd, J. (1995) 'Beyond the community conflict: historic compromise or emancipatory process?', *Irish Political Studies*, no. 10.

Tomlinson, M. (1994) *25 Years On: The Costs of War and the Dividends of Peace* (Belfast: West Belfast Economic Forum).

Tomlinson, M. (1995a) 'Can Britain leave Ireland? The political economy of war and peace', *Race and Class*, vol. 37, no. 1.

Tomlinson, M. (1995b) 'Fortress Northern Ireland: a model for the new Europe', in Clancy, P., Drudy, S., Lynch, K. and O'Dowd, L. (eds) *Irish Society: Sociological Perspectives* (Dublin: Institute of Public Administration).

Townshend, C. (1983) *Political Violence in Ireland* (Oxford: Oxford University Press).

Trimble, D. (1996) 'Address to Ulster Unionist Party Annual Conference, 1996', *Irish Times*, 21 October.

Walker, B. (1990) 'Ireland's historical position – "colonial" or "European"', *Irish Review*, no. 9.

Wallerstein, I. (1980) 'One man's meat: the Scottish great leap forward', *Review*, vol. 3, no. 4.

Wallerstein, I. (1988) *The Modern World-System III* (New York: Academic Press).

Ward, M. (1983) *Unmanageable Revolutionaries: Women and Irish Nationalism* (London: Pluto Press).

Ward, M. (1991) 'The women's movement in the North of Ireland: twenty years on', in Hutton, S. and Stewart, P. (eds) *Ireland's Histories* (London: Routledge).

Ward, M. (1993) 'Suffrage first – above all else! An account of the Irish suffrage movement', in Smyth, A. (ed.) *Irish Women's Studies Reader* (Dublin: Attic Press).

Ward, M. (1995a) 'Finding a place: women and the Irish peace process' in *Race and Class, No. 37 Ireland: New Beginnings*.

Ward, M. (1995b) 'Conflicting interests: the British and Irish suffrage movements', *Feminist Review*, vol. 50.

Ware, J., Seed, G. and Palmer, A. (1998) 'Assassination by proxy', *Sunday Telegraph*, 29 March.

Weaver, E. (1994) *Right of Silence Debate: The Northern Ireland Experience* (London: Justice).

White, R. (1994) *Provisional Irish Republicans. An Oral and Interpretative History* (Westport, Connetticut: Greenwood Press).

Whyte, I. (1990) *Interpreting Northern Ireland* (Oxford: Oxford University Press).

Whyte, J. (1983) The permeability of the United Kingdom–Irish border: a preliminary discussion, *Administration*, vol. 31, no. 3.

Wilford, R. (1992) 'Inverting consociationalism? Policy, pluralism and the post-modern', in Hadfield, B. (ed.) *Northern Ireland: Politics and the Constitution* (Buckingham: Open University Press).

Wilson, R. (1996) 'Ten steps to reconstituting politics', in Wilson, R. (ed.) *Reconstituting Politics,* Democratic Dialogue Report 3 (Belfast: Democratic Dialogue).

Womens Support Network (1996) *Development Plan 1996–2000* (Belfast: WSN).

Index

Labour Party (British), *continued*
process, 37, 132–4; record on
Ireland, 126–9, 138–9; and
weak variant of nationalism,
110–11
Left, The, role in Loyalist peace
moves, 204–7
Lemass, Séan, 91, 93, 96–7
Liberal Democrats (British), 116,
119
Liberty, civil rights group, 169,
171
Lloyd George, David, 127–8, 139
Lloyd, John, 125n
local government, 45, 151
London, 171; bombings in, 18,
34
Londonderry (Derry), Apprentice
Boys Parades, 162–3, 164
Loyalist organisations: strategies,
37, 39, 146, *see also* DUP;
PUP; UDP; Ulster unionism;
UVF
Loyalist Volunteer Force (LVF),
38, 189, 195, 210n

MacDonald, Ramsay, 127
Major, John, 17–18, 132, 255n
Mansergh, Martin, 104, 233
Mason, Roy, 129
Mayhew, Sir Patrick, 18, 256n
McAliskey (Devlin), Bernardette,
151, 156, 184
McCartan, Joyce, 141
McCartney, Robert, 117–18,
119, 125n, 193, 255n
McCracken, Mary Ann and
Henry Joy, 252
McGuinness, Martin, 189
McLaughlin, Mitchel, 185
McMichael, Gary, UDP, 195,
202
McNamara, Kevin, 129
media: and anti-terrorist legisla-
tion, 172; British, 12, 32;
cross-border, 87n; and nation-
alism, 110, 112
Metropolitan Police, Special
(Irish) Branch, 165, 173
Mitchell, Senator George, 13, 18

Molyneaux, James, 117
Moore, Charles, 120–1
Morrison, Herbert, 128
Mowlam, Dr Marjorie (Mo), 18,
129, 132, 216; and Orange
marches, 131–2; and principle
of consent, 135

nation state(s), 8, 12, 111, 232,
242
National Front, 120
nationalism(s), 2, 3–4, 7, 234;
flaws of, 8, 252–4; and
national identity, 19, 20–2,
112; official (state), 89, 90,
91–3, 108, 111; theories of,
19, 20–3, *see also* British
nationalism; Irish nationalism
neutrality: British claim to, 15,
28, 37–8, 97, 113–14, 131;
politics of avoidance, 143–4,
150
North American Free Trade
Agreement (NAFTA), 47
North–South institutions, 2–3, 5,
12, 73, 86; and economic integration, 48–9, 79–82; hopes
for, 18–19, 136, 233–4,
236–7, 254; Island Social
Forum proposed, 249; limitations on, 83–4, 123;
pre-existing, 74–5, 95, 256n;
resistance to, 24–5, 235–6, *see
also* cross-border integration
North-South Ministerial Council:
proposed, 137, 139, 237, 246,
248; risks to, 239–40
North–South Parliamentary
Forum, proposed, 248
Northern Ireland Assembly, 138,
139, 203, 239, 246; risks to,
239–40
Northern Ireland Development
Agency (1976), 59
Northern Ireland (Emergency
Provisions) Act (EPA), 166–7
Northern Ireland Finance
Corporation (1972), 59
Northern Ireland Labour Party,
210n, 251

Sunningdale Agreement (1973),
15, 16, 97–8, 101, 236, 255n
symbolism, and identity, 112,
144–5, 220–1

taxation, and cross-border integration, 83, 99
'technocratic anti-partitionism',
91, 93
territorial sovereignty, 7–8, 17,
73; and globalisation, 12; need
to rethink, 12–13, 19, 234,
244–6, 252–3; and self-determination, 104, see also state
sovereignty
terrorism, 28, 167–8; counter-
terrorist organisations, 173;
Prevention of Terrorism Act,
166, 167–8, 170–2
Thatcher, Margaret, 110, 177
tourist industry, 80–1
Towards a Lasting Peace (1992),
182–3
trade union movement, 132, 134,
150; cross-border links, 75,
81, 85, 249, 252; democratisation of, 229–30
transnational corporations, 24,
62–3, 62, 78
transnationalism, 5, 6, 90–1;
prospects for, 19, 23–5, see
also cross-border integration;
North–South institutions;
sovereignty
Trimble, David, 118, 121, 237
Troubles see war

UDR see Royal Irish Regiment
UK Unionist Party, 119
Ulster Defence Association
(UDA), 38, 147, 195
Ulster Democratic Party (UDP),
132, 195–6, 205, 207, 209; and
Forum elections, 201–2, 203
Ulster unionism, 4, 108–9, 119;
British support for, 116,
117–18, 125n; ideology of,
198–9, 203–4, 205–6, 208–9;
inevitable losses in peace
process, 40, 136, 253–4;

movement towards peace, 132,
203, 204–7, 236–7; new
unionism/new Loyalism,
118–19, 121, 125n, 207–8;
and North-South institutions,
236–7, 240–1, 242–4; opposition to economic integration,
66–8, 86, 99, 243; opposition
to peace process, 186, 194–6,
197–9, 206–7, 214; opposition
to Southern constitutional
revision, 98, 105–6; and
Partition, 10–11; relationship
with British nationalism, 12,
34, 108–9, 113, 115–22; rivalries within, 200–2, 206;
structural intransigence of,
15–17, 118–19, 122, 199, 225;
women's role in, 224–6;
women's view of ceasefires,
157–8, see also DUP; Northern
Ireland; Orange Order; PUP;
UDP; UUP
Ulster Unionist Party (UUP), 36,
98, 113, 123, 189; and Forum
elections, 202–3, 203; opposition to cross-border institutions,
235–6, 237, 242; and Sinn
Fein, 255n; and women, 152
Ulster Volunteer Force (UVF),
38, 195, 198, 210n, 225
Ulster Workers' Strike (1974),
16, 129, 236
UNISON trade union, 229–30
United Irishmen, Society of, 1–2,
9, 164–5, 252
United Nations, 6, 33; Committee
on Torture, 169; Human
Rights Committee, 34, 36
United States: industrial investment in Southern Ireland, 55,
57, 58, 62–3, 69; Irish influence in, 32, 91, 115, 184; role
in peace process, 37, 132, 191

violence, 36, 146–7; against
women, 159, 221; domestic,
147, 213; sectarian killings,
37, 146; by women, 216–18,
219–20

*Index compiled by
Auriol Griffith-Jones*